PHILIP LONGWORTH

THE Three Empresses

Three fascinating women ruled Russia in the forty years before Catherine the Great: Catherine I, the peasant girl who became Peter the Great's mistress, wife, and successor; Anne, Peter's unhappy niece, widowed within weeks of marriage, suffered years of humiliation, and, once in power, planned elaborate humiliations for others; and Elizabeth, the beautiful and promiscuous daughter of Peter and Catherine, who seized her throne by coup d'état.

In their lifetimes, during the first half of the eighteenth century, Russia emerged from tradition-laden backwardness to become a leading European power; the rough-mannered Russian aristocracy was transformed into the most brilliant, luxurious, and decadent social group in Europe. The empresses pioneered western fashions, sponsored opera and theatre, founded the Russian ballet, built opulent rococo palaces—and presided over a decline in morals and a deepening of social divisions which was to have terrible implications for future Romanovs.

Each of these women was corrupted by power, and each unwittingly helped to corrupt the society she ruled. Based on court diaries, correspondence, mem-

(Continued on back flap)

By the same author

The Art of Victory

The Cossacks

PHILIP LONGWORTH

The Three Empresses

Catherine I, Anne and Elizabeth of Russia

'This will be a history of both reigns and vices.'

Prince Shcherbatov,
an eighteenth-century cynic

HOLT, RINEHART AND WINSTON
NEW YORK   CHICAGO   SAN FRANCISCO

ISBN: 0-03-001411-5

Library of Congress Catalog Card
Number: 72-78124

First published in the United States
in 1973

Printed in the United States of America

Contents

16 pages of illustrations follow page 116

Acknowledgements

The author and publishers express their thanks to the following: the Curator of the Hermitage Museum, Leningrad, for permission to reproduce the portraits of Catherine I and of Biron, and the engraved views of the first Winter Palace and of St. Petersburg from the Moika Canal; the Curator of the Tretyakov Gallery, Moscow, for the portraits of Anne and Elizabeth; and the Trustees of the British Museum for permission to reproduce the remaining illustrations, photographed by John Freeman.

Prologue

When George II ruled over Britons and Americans and Louis XV reigned in France three women occupied the throne of Russia. They were Russia's first Empresses, and between them they ruled Europe's largest empire for more than thirty years. Yet little has been written about them, and the neglect is not deserved.

Catherine I, Anne and Elizabeth were not 'great' rulers. Had they not become empresses they might easily have been forgotten altogether, passed over by historians as three quite ordinary women. It was their situation which made them extraordinary. Three women brought up to be subservient in a man's world were suddenly confronted with the challenge of governing an empire. It was an ironic situation—tragic, comical, grotesque. And their personalities and their environment command interest as well.

Theirs was an elegant age and artists painted elegant portraits of them. Demure faces gaze out from above *décolleté* bodices and ample crinolines. Each one of them was made to look majestic, gracious, magisterial. Yet in reality they were intriguingly dissimilar.

Catherine was an orphaned serving-girl, a Slavic Cinderella who became Peter the Great's mistress (a curious liaison which came to dominate her life). She was a simple, meek and undemanding woman who yearned only for security and love—and suddenly found power thrust on her. Anne, by contrast, was proud, self-willed, and the daughter of a Tsar—but her character was soured by a domineering mother and perverted by years of penury and unrequited love. As for Elizabeth, she was both a princess and illegitimate—a love-child surrounded by love and luxury from the cradle to the grave.

All three gained power in different ways and each reacted differently to its possession. One despaired and took to drink; another used her absolute powers vindictively to humiliate others as she herself had been humiliated; and one emptied the exchequer through her extravagance, lavishing money on her palaces and lovers.

A sot, a sadist, and a nymphomaniac—so historians have dismissed them, and though the limelight tended to exaggerate their frailties, power corrupted all of them. Yet, however unintentionally, they themselves helped to corrupt the society they ruled over. Their more publicized, if no more edifying, successor Catherine II (who also figures in the story) only built on foundations they had helped to lay.

This story of their lives and loves—and of the manners and intrigues of the Russian court which is part of it—has been reconstructed from diaries, memoirs, letters and despatches of the time. But their story concerns more than politics and passions.

In their lifetimes, Russia emerged from oriental backwardness to become a leading European power; under them, the simple, rough-mannered Russian aristocracy was transformed into the most brilliant, luxurious, and decadent social group in Europe. Under them, social taboos lost their former hold and old values were discarded. The Empresses pioneered western fashions, sponsored opera and theatre, founded the Russian ballet, built opulent rococo palaces—and presided over a decline in morals and a deepening of social and cultural divisions among their subjects which was to have bloody consequences for future Romanovs.

Genealogical Table

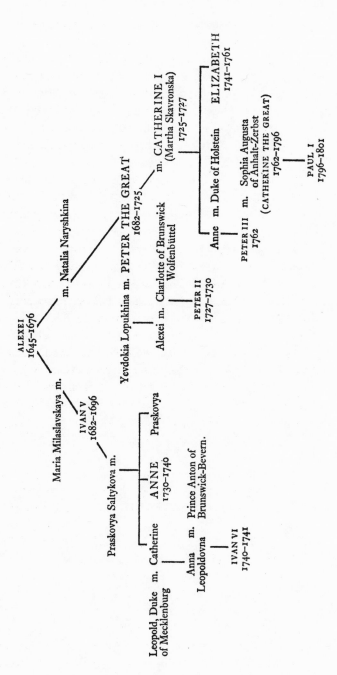

PART I
Catherine

Few families can ever have been more embarrassed than the Russian royal family was at having to count Martha Skavronska among its ancestors. It was not just that Martha, who ended her life as Catherine I Empress of all Russia, was a commoner and had been Peter the Great's mistress—she came from the very dregs of society, from the peasant class, and had been mistress to others before Peter.

Her memory was a skeleton of shame which had to be locked away in the safest of imperial cupboards, and for more than a century after her death the Tsarist secret police devoted their attentions to anyone who tried to pry too closely into her humble origins or the scandalous details of her early career. As a result an aura of mystery still clings to her; but the essential truths were to come out in the end.

Martha was the daughter of a Lithuanian slave called Samuel Skavronski, who had fled to the Swedish province of Livonia where he eked out a living as a gravedigger. The date of her birth, though still uncertain, was most probably 1683—a year when Charles II still ruled England and the 'Sun King' reigned in France.

Her father died when she was two and her mother a year later, whereupon the orphaned Martha was separated from her brother and sisters and adopted by an aunt. When she was twelve years old, however, she was sent into service. Though a Catholic by birth, Martha found herself in a strict Lutheran household—the household of Pastor Glück, Superintendent of the little town of Marienburg.

She became the skivvy there. She did the chores and helped look

3

after the younger of the Pastor's children. Much time was also spent in church, listening to the Pastor's long and learned sermons. But there was time for play as well—by the riverside where the local fishermen mended nets, around the ruined palaces on the west side of the city, and in the well-kept fields beyond. She received no formal education, however. Not for her the lessons that the Pastor gave his children. Martha learned to spin and sew; she never learned to read.

Yet these years of dependence and only partial security were lessons in themselves. Illiterate she might be, but Martha learned to keep a ready smile on tap, to hide her aspirations and her discontent—above all to please those round her. These lessons were to serve her better than any book-learning might have done.

By the spring of 1702 Martha had grown into an attractive girl of marriageable age. It is true that her features were by no means regular, but her nose had a pretty tilt, her eyes were velvety, and she had a lithe and sturdy figure. More than one head turned as she walked about the town, and on Sundays, when she sat respectably in church, there were young men who paid more heed to her than they did to the edifying words of Pastor Glück.

There was one man in particular—a tall young soldier, a trumpeter in the dragoons. Shy looks, then bolder ones, were exchanged across the pews, and the matter did not escape the notice of the vigilant Frau Glück.

The match-making process was accordingly begun. The young man was identified as Johann Raabe. The Major commanding the garrison spoke well of him and indicated that promotion to the rank of corporal was in the offing. Then Johann was approached, and agreed very readily to the idea of taking so beguiling a creature as his wife. Martha, of course, was the last to know, but when the offer was explained to her she accepted. It was as much as she could hope for, placed as she was on the very lowest rung of the social ladder.

The betrothal took place; the wedding day was fixed—and then suddenly brought forward. The peaceful life of Marienburg was about to be disturbed by the sound of marching armies.

Two years before a war had broken out between Russia and Sweden. So far it had hardly touched the people of Livonia but now, in the summer of 1702, refugees had begun to arrive in Marienburg with the news of the enemy's approach and hair-raising tales of Russian atrocities. Everyone knew that the small Swedish garrison could not hope to hold the town. Occupation was inevitable, and worse was feared. The outlook was gloomy when Martha married her dragoon.

Within days of the ceremony the Russians were sighted, and the Swedish Commandant promptly led his troops out in the opposite direction. Johann Raabe was among them, but for some reason Martha stayed on in Marienburg with the Glücks. And when the Pastor, accompanied by a crowd of his parishioners, walked out to the Russian camp to plead for the safety of the people of the town, she went with him.

It was not a pleasant experience. Groups of fearsome-looking Cossacks and evil-smelling tribesmen with bows and arrows on their backs watched them slit-eyed as they passed. Pastor Glück seemed not to notice them as he strode on, his winged collar fluttering in the breeze, a specially selected Slavic Bible clutched tight under his arm, desperately rehearsing his few words of pidgin Russian. But at the centre of the Russian camp the soldiers, dressed in frock-coats, gaiters and black tricorn hats, seemed to be more civilized, and the brigadier who received them turned out to be a German in the Russian service.

Glück choked back the Russian phrases he had carefully prepared, held his Russian Bible less prominently, behind his back, and made his plea. But Brigadier Bauer's hands were tied. He would do what he could for the Pastor and his family but, as he explained, his orders were strict—to ravage the province and cart one-third of its inhabitants off to Russia. For the moment Glück was free. But Martha was kept prisoner. Her destination was the baggage train.

Here, among the carts and tents and cooking pots, and the bustle of camp-followers we momentarily lose sight of her. Years later an old court servitor recalled seeing her there 'dressed in nothing but a shirt'. But the half-naked form caught the eye of Brigadier Bauer. On his orders a caftan was thrown over her, and she was led away to safer quarters.

Martha had found a protector. But the bright lips, the tumbling hair and the appealing black eyes of the prisoner from Marienburg soon attracted the attentions of an officer of even more exalted rank—the Commander-in-Chief of the Russian army in Livonia himself—Boris Sheremetev. At any rate she was soon transferred to the General's household.

Sheremetev was an imposing figure of a man. He dressed magnificently in the French fashion; his uniform was covered with gold and silver lace, and an immense and uncomfortable horse-hair wig tumbled down in ringlets over his shoulders. Everything around him was magnificent as well. He kept a large domestic staff with him even though he was on campaign—a battery of cooks, a host of washerwomen and a veritable harem of serving-maids, and it was these aristocrats among camp-followers whom Martha joined.

She served the General at his table; she made his bed, and presumably shared it too from time to time. But in the words of a British observer, Boris Sheremetev was 'the politest man' in Russia. Martha was fortunate in finding so mannerly a protector. Yet within a few months she was transferred—some say sold—to another master, this time to a young officer, a favourite of the Tsar himself—Alexander Menshikov.

Alexander was still in his twenties and very much a coming man. He had only recently been promoted Major-General and made Governor of a province, and there were many who thought that he would soon rise further still. There were even more who resented him and his inordinate ambitions. Rumour had it that Alexander had peddled pies in the streets of Moscow as a boy; but he was brave, energetic, able and witty. Indeed, it was his particular talent to amuse which first gained him a place in the Tsar's affections.

The contrasts between the calm, aristocratic Boris Sheremetev and Alexander, the fiery meteor from the Moscow slums, were considerable—yet Martha seems to have borne the change with equanimity. After all, she had been used since early childhood to being passed from one hand to another. And in many respects she and her new master were two of a kind. Both had started at the bottom of the social pile, and both were climbers. Alexander had come much further than she had so far, but the fear of returning to poverty was to remain an obsession with them both. It was the basis of a relationship which would last all their lives—a relationship, however, in which sentiment was to play only a secondary part.

From the beginning Alexander schemed to use Martha's charm and physical attractions in the furtherance of his own ambitions.

There was no routine in the Menshikov household. His Excellency worked long, irregular hours. No one knew when he would rise or when he would retire, nor, when he rode away on business, if he would be absent hours or weeks. Meals had to be ready at whatever time he chose to eat, accommodation prepared for whatever guests might suddenly descend. The household was used to sudden panics. But on one particular afternoon it was stirred to quite unusual activity. A dust-covered messenger had arrived with news that the Tsar himself was on the way.

Cooks bustled to prepare a banquet more opulent than usual; bottles of the Tsar's favourite wine, Hungarian Tokay, were rushed up from the cellars; the entire store of silver was brought out, and every corner searched for black beetles, which, it was known, the Tsar detested.

Yet the great man arrived in a small, fast carriage with only a couple of attendants, and when Alexander ran out to greet him, he treated him not as a monarch would a subject, but as a man would greet a friend—he embraced him, warmly. There was nothing ceremonious about Tsar Peter. Yet it was obvious that he was no ordinary man. At six foot eight inches Peter was a giant; his stride was gangling, his movements awkward, he wore no wig, and his huge, tanned hands were as calloused as a labourer's.

This, then, was the man reputed to be the most eccentric of all monarchs—the autocrat of the most servile state in Europe who took pride in having qualified as a shipwright; a Tsar who cared more for carpentry than hunting, and who had joined his own army as an ordinary bombardier. Here was a tyrant with all the worries of a great war on his mind who yet took the trouble to ensure that backwoods noblemen learned to read and use sines and logarithms. Here was God's anointed who had altered God's calendar (so that New Year's day 1703 was celebrated on the same day the godless foreigners celebrated it rather than on the true Russian date, 1 September 7212). Here was the visionary who built canals, the savage who had killed a man with a blow from his fist—and yet he seemed informal, awkward, human. His dark expressive eyes betrayed nothing of the grandeur, the madness, the cruelty or the genius with which men said he was endowed.

Tsar Peter was obviously in good humour, and the dinner went extremely well. Care had been taken to prepare his favourite dishes —sucking pig in sour cream, fish with a sharp sauce, fruit steamed in honey, hard black bread, and fresh and salted cucumbers. They had warmed up on vodka, and prodigious quantities of Tokay were served during the meal. The Tsar drank quarts of it, and since he expected his companions to keep pace with him, several of the diners were soon considerably the worse for wear. Alexander Menshikov, however, seemed to keep his head.

As the banquet progressed and the Tsar became more expansive and ever more relaxed, his eyes fixed more than once on Martha as she moved round the table refilling empty beakers. Words passed between the guest of honour and the host, and when the Tsar indicated that he wished to retire, Martha was told to lead him to his room.

When Peter left next morning he pressed a golden ducat into her palm. As for Alexander, his place in the Tsar's favour seemed to have been strengthened overnight—and he determined to strengthen it still further by the judicious deployment of the seductive Martha.

The field was open. The Tsar had sent his wife into a nunnery years before and he had just dismissed his mistress, the blonde and voluptuous Anna Mons, the daughter of a Moscow wine-shipper of foreign origins. The affair had lasted twelve years and might well have lasted longer. But Anna had been too demanding, and foolish enough to share her favours with another man. Peter had found out, and refused to have anything more to do with her. So now the Tsar was without a permanent companion and Alexander Menshikov meant Martha to fill that vacancy. If things were managed properly Peter would owe him a debt of gratitude; and so would Martha who could surely be prevailed on to influence the Tsar on his behalf when need arose in future.

Yet when the Tsar called again, Martha did not appear, and when, as Alexander hoped he would, he enquired after her, he was given an evasive answer. Only when the Tsar became insistent was Martha eventually produced. And this time she appeared, not as some peasant beauty in white stockings and embroidered shawl, but as a fully-groomed Venus in a low-cut satin gown, with her hair dressed and darkened in contrast to her pale, soft skin.

This second meeting lasted hardly longer than the first. The Tsar teased her to the point of tears; then handed her a consoling bumper of Tokay. But a few days after his departure a captain of the Guards arrived with orders to fetch her to Moscow. She left clutching a bag containing some jewels and trinkets supplied by Alexander, excited by the prospect of new places, and awed at the prospect of coping with her latest guardian, the great Tsar of all the Russias, the huge and unpredictable man called Peter.

The weather was hot and the journey uncomfortable. The carriage had cushions on the floor instead of proper seats and leather blinds instead of doors and windows. There were no springs and the vehicle jolted mercilessly over the rutted, dusty roads. The post-houses which gave accommodation on the way were miserably poor, usually a single smoke-blackened room which travellers had to share with the keeper's family. The food provided in these places usually consisted of some gruel slopped out of an earthenware pot with the addition of such tit-bits of meat or vegetables as her escort had been able to obtain by threats or overpayment. Martha had known discomforts worse than these, but she must have been glad enough to reach her destination.

Moscow, capital of Russia, Moscow the Great of the thousand churches, was the largest city in Europe, and a place of teeming contrasts. There were clusterings of golden domes and squalid alleyways, shanty tenements and immense, imposing squares. It was a bustling place with its own smells—of tanneries, pie-shops, incense, garbage; and it had a music of its own as well—clog-like rushings over timbered pavements, strident street cries and the boom and chimes of bells.

At the centre stood the Kremlin with its onion domes and towers enclosed by red brick fortress walls. But this was not Martha's destination. Tsar Peter hated the Kremlin. When he was ten he had stood there horrified, clutching his mother's hand, watching an unruly mob of Muscovite soldiers hunting down members of his family and their friends, killing and mutilating them. Ever since he had preferred to live away from Moscow, or in the suburb on the east side of the city, the so-called 'German' quarter, and it was here that Martha's carriage eventually halted.

The German suburb was more familiar to western eyes. It was a place of spacious residences, warehouses and gardens where not only Germans, but expatriates from several Western European countries built their homes. In a word it was a ghetto—a place of safety protected by deep ditches and a river from the inhabitants of Moscow proper, for central Moscow was the haunt of robber gangs and particularly dangerous for foreigners. Peter had had many friends in the suburb since his childhood days; he preferred its atmosphere and Martha would be safe there.

The house at which she arrived looked modest enough outside though its interior was quite sumptuously furnished. She was greeted by Alexander's sister, Anna, who was mistress of the household, and introduced to the other residents—Barbara Arsenyev, her sister Daria, whom Alexander was to marry, and her aunt, a genial woman called Anisia Tolstoi. They took Martha in hand.

Alexander was a frequent visitor between August 1703 and the end of the year, but Peter called more rarely. Besieged by problems in governing his vast and backward country and with all the worries of a great war on his mind, he was an incessant traveller about his kingdom, and did not find time to come to Moscow until the end of October. He stayed only for five weeks, and though he returned again towards the end of December, in the first week of March 1704 he resumed his frantic journeyings and she saw little of him.

Circumstances had altered radically for the twenty-one-year-old Martha, and this time the changes were extremely welcome. She wanted for nothing now except her lover's company, and it was wonderful to be treated as a lady—she who had been a servant all her life. True, her new environment was very strange, but she had become used to the unexpected, and she seems to have adjusted well. Thanks to the help of her almost constant companion, Anisia Tolstoi, her spoken Russian improved considerably, and she learned much about Russia and the Russians.

The household she lived in was quite untypical and untraditional, she discovered. Normally, Muscovite gentlewomen were secluded in a sort of harem called the *terem*, forbidden to be seen by strangers, still less speak to them. Most of them still wore curious gowns with ridiculously long sleeves and painted their teeth black, and only now were some of them beginning to emerge from this inferior position. Thanks to Tsar Peter some women dined with their menfolk nowadays and went about in open carriages; a few even wore stays as women did in civilized countries. But such innovations affected very few, and they were widely resented by the mass of Russians.

Peter's modernism had affected men as well, so Martha learned. A government decree, from which only priests were exempt, forced them to wear western-style clothing instead of clumsy Russian robes, and go about clean-shaven. But many Russians still defied the law, and many a peasant who observed it was superstitious enough to keep his shorn beard stuffed inside his shirt so that when he died, he should be able to face his Maker bewhiskered like a proper Christian. Despite the Tsar's zeal, his reforms had so far produced only a surface trimming, and Russian society as a whole remained as hidebound as ever. Outside the German suburb everybody knew his place. Peasants humbled themselves before their lords, the lords before the Tsar, and everyone spat on his inferiors.

Apart from the Tsar's power the only institution which united all Russians was the church. Russian Orthodoxy and Russian patriotism were inextricably bound up together, and even Tsar Peter, for all his innovations, paid lip service to God's own Russian church. So it was, then, that when Martha was found to be carrying his child, he thought it proper, indeed necessary, that she be instructed in the true religion.

One may imagine that the pregnant Martha did not find regular attendance at church too burdensome. The services, though longer, were more mysterious and entertaining than those of Pastor Glück. There were magnificent choirs to listen to, incense to smell, and icons glittering with silver, gold and precious stones to gaze upon. Nor was the instruction intellectually demanding. Most Russian priests were hardly more literate than she was, and few of them understood the passages of the Bible they read out so sonorously in church.

Towards the end of 1704 Martha gave birth to a boy. Mother and child were baptized almost simultaneously. The boy was christened Paul, and Martha was also given a new name—the name she was to carry down in history, the name of Catherine.

Her godfather on that occasion was none other than the Tsarevich Alexei, Peter's son by his cast-off wife, Yevdokia. Alexei was a tall, good-looking boy of thirteen, but he was very attached to his banished mother, and Catherine could sense his resentment of her as an interloper. Still, for the moment she seemed secure enough in his father's affections—at least she was soon pregnant again. Peter, who had left a trail of abandoned mistresses right across Europe had apparently tired of temporary relationships.

Yet he had had more permanent relationships which failed, and the warning examples set by his cast-off wife Yevdokia, who was now imprisoned in a nunnery, and of his cast-off mistress Anna Mons were not lost on Catherine. Fortunately she bore no resemblance to the proud, disdainful Tsarina, and she took good care to contrast herself to Anna, even to the extent of dying her hair black.

Catherine was endowed with a calm, affectionate and undemanding disposition, and she devoted all her energies now to studying Peter's moods and making herself agreeable to him. In brief she set out to be the perfect courtesan. But it was no easy task to build a lasting relationship with the Tsar of all the Russias.

Peter was besieged with difficulties and frustrations. His armies were in retreat before the powerful Swedes, and he was obstructed at almost every turn in his self-imposed task of dragging his backward country into the modern age. Everything seemed to depend on him. Only he seemed able to eradicate delays and bottlenecks, encourage his defeated troops, cajole the reluctant, bully the slack, stamp out opposition. No wonder he had moments of exhaustion and despair, and when they came he turned to Catherine.

Life with him was rarely easy, and at times it could be frightening. He was subject to terrible bouts of temper and sometimes even fits when his eyes would stand out from their sockets and his face would twitch uncontrollably. At such moments even so close a friend as Alexander Menshikov dared not come near him. Yet somehow Catherine learned to cope.

According to reliable witnesses she would take his head in her lap and caress him as a mother would a child, soothing the tensions and the pain away until he fell into a deep exhausted sleep. Indeed it was her ability to mother Peter which was one of the strongest points on which their relationship was founded. Peter himself recognized this when he began to call her 'mother' in the letters he sent her when he was away—letters which had to be read to her by her companion 'Auntie' Anisia Tolstoi, who would also write down her replies.

Their two babies strengthened the bonds between them too, and the notes he sent her usually included some reference to them, usually jocular in tone. 'Don't neglect my little Petrushka', ran one, referring to his new-born second son. 'Have some clothes made for him soon, and, whatever you do, see to it that he gets enough to eat and drink'. Yet however teasing the style, his letters became more important to her as he spent more time away from her and she found herself worrying about him more and more.

In January 1706 Peter was on the western front and the war was going badly. By the spring the situation seemed even worse. The enemy was moving closer to Moscow; the outcome of a revolt at Astrakhan was still in doubt; tribesmen east of the Volga were treading the warpath, the Don Cossacks were restless, and high taxation, recruitment, and the Tsar's adoption of 'godless foreign ways' were creating such discontent in the country as a whole that a general rising against him was expected at almost any moment.

It was at this point, according to the British envoy Whitworth, that Peter's ministers tried to divert him 'from the melancholy thoughts of his Countrys Ruin' by encouraging him to go north to the Finnish Gulf where he could amuse himself with his two favourite pastimes, shipbuilding and sailing. Catherine soon joined him there.

The point where the river Neva flows out into the Baltic Sea seemed a strange place to spend a holiday. It was an isolated, bleak, unhealthy spot, ice-bound in winter and not much more hospitable in summer. But here, among the marshy islands of the estuary Peter was building a new port, a new city—a city of noble buildings and beautiful canals, a sort of Russian Amsterdam. He called it St. Petersburg.

So far, however, the city only existed in his imagination. For the rest it consisted of a fort surrounded by a rambling, disordered log encampment. No one lived there except the labourers and soldiers who had been drafted in and apart from Peter no one would have wanted to.

He and Catherine lived in a small log cabin there, which still exists. It consisted of two rooms bisected by a narrow hall. One served as Peter's study and reception room; the other, which doubled as a dining room and bedroom, was Catherine's domain. The ceilings were low, the rooms were tiny, and yet the gigantic Peter loved it there; and Catherine was happy too. It was springtime and they planted sweet-scented flowers outside their cabin, and tried, unsuccessfully, to get peonies to grow. Peter spent hours working in the ship-yards, helped cut canals and sink foundations, discussed plans with his architect Domenico Trezzini, and visualized a city of broad avenues and dreaming spires, apparently oblivious of the fact that the Swedes might march in and snatch the dream away from him at almost any moment. For him the miserable place was already 'Paradise', and for the undemanding Catherine, intent on more immediate, domestic matters, it seemed a sort of paradise as well.

By now it was obvious that Catherine saw Peter as more than a protector, more even than her lover and the father of her children. He was her hero too, and she had become as emotionally dependent on him as he seemed to be, from time to time, on her. From now on her life was to revolve around him to the exclusion of almost all things else. Yet their relationship was illicit, unofficial, with no guarantee of security such as marriage might have given her, and that summer when they went to Kiev to celebrate the wedding of Alexander Menshikov to their friend Daria Arsenyeva the point must have struck home. Yet what chance could there be of Peter marrying her with his wife still living in her nunnery and her own husband Johann God knows where? It was a wistful Catherine who set out on the road back to St. Petersburg.

She arrived there with Peter early in September—in time for a great autumnal flood. Their own hut stood in two feet of water but Catherine, as equable as ever, did not complain, and Peter was highly amused. He thought it 'very funny to see people perched on roofs and trees, just as at the time of the Great Flood'. And he remained in good spirits which made him an easier companion.

They had recently acquired a dog which they called 'Lisette' and on which both of them lavished their attention, playing games with it and sending it scampering into each other's rooms with *billets-doux* pinned to its collar—a device Catherine found particularly useful when she wanted to attract Peter's attention away from business to herself, or to soften him when some petty altercation arose between them.

But this period of domesticity and contentment was very brief—another happy intermission in what was proving to be a long tense period of separation. That November, news came that Peter's ally, the King of Poland, had gone over to his enemies. Russia seemed virtually defenceless now, and Peter rushed off to organize his armies—leaving Catherine pregnant again.

She gave birth to her third child, a girl, on 27 December 1706, decided to call her Catherine, and sent Peter the news. 'Please remember us', she added plaintively. 'Come to us or else bring us to you.' But Peter was far away and weeks passed before a letter bearing the Tsar's red seal reached her. He was obviously pleased—relieved that 'mother is well' and delighted to have a daughter—'more so than to have two sons if that is possible'. But it was May before they met again, and then they had to face the grimmest months they had yet experienced.

To begin with, Paul, their first-born son, died; then, in September, they lost little Peter too. In October King Charles of Sweden resumed his advance; the Don Cossacks were in a state of open rebellion, the Bashkir tribesmen too. Catherine and Peter spent Christmas together in Moscow, celebrating in the traditional way 'singing ... carols and feasting from house to house', but the shadow of insecurity hung like a pall over their hectic feasting, and on 6 January, with the Swedes on the move again, Peter left her again to join the army.

Towards the end of February 1708 Catherine gave birth to a second daughter, Anne, and exactly four weeks later, the Swedes having halted, Peter took time off from the war and joined her in St. Petersburg. But seeing her was only part of his intention. He had also ordered the royal family to join him there from Moscow, so that they might see the ships he had been building and taste the joys of sailing. The Tsar wanted to create a nation of seafarers out of the land-lubber Russians, and the royals had to show an example.

The reluctant relatives arrived—the fat, red-faced Praskovya, widow of his half-brother Tsar Ivan, and her brood of quarrelsome daughters, his resentful son, the Tsarevich Alexei, and the rest. On 2 May Peter took them all out on the river. It was a new and extremely disagreeable experience for them, as Catherine observed. But she herself was spared the ordeal, having no public position— and she saw little of Peter otherwise. He was closeted with his advisers for hours each day, and was forever inspecting fortifications and going out to sea. True there were snatched meals taken together, moments to admire their two small daughters, to stroll in the gardens they were laying out, and to enjoy the twittering chaos of the aviary for which, in a munificent mood that April, he had ordered eight thousand singing birds. But the war was never far from either of their minds and in June, hearing that the Swedes had resumed their advance, Peter hurried off again.

Soon afterwards their elder daughter died and though in those days most children were not expected to survive into maturity, Catherine seems to have felt the blow more keenly than usual. Peter was writing to her much less frequently and she was miserable with worry—worry about him, and about what would become of her if a Swedish bullet should strike him down.

It was September before she heard from him again. 'Don't be surprised that I have not answered you for so long', he wrote. 'Our guests, the enemy, have been constantly before our eyes— and we got so bored watching them that yesterday morning . . . we attacked the Swedish King's right wing . . . and . . . with God's help beat them from the field. . . . Truly, I haven't seen such a little game since I began to serve. . . . Tell me about yourselves, Peter.' He made light of everything to her, like a jolly uncle talking to a child. But she heard from other sources that he had been suffering from repeated bouts of fever, and another note from Peter, dated 26 September, only served to increase her anxiety:

'Your two letters have been handed to me. Don't be surprised that I've taken so long to answer; there have been plenty of other things to see to here, and now we've caught sight of the enemy. God grant us his mercy—but for the moment all is well, thank God. Peter.'

He was prone to fever, and he was liable to be killed in battle at almost any moment. News took so long to reach her that, for all she knew, he might be dead already. Her companion 'Auntie' Anisia tried hard to raise her spirits, but in vain, and in desperation she wrote to Alexander begging him to tell her what was happening. Eventually she heard that Peter was still safe, but the situation was so dangerous that he refused to leave the front that winter, and only after Catherine had begged and begged again did he allow her to visit him.

The reunion was particularly happy, and now, for the first time Catherine felt confident enough to put a request to him that was tinged with politics. She had been Peter's mistress for almost five years now, and with almost everyone aware of their relationship it was inevitable that she should be asked to intervene on behalf of people out of favour. Normally, she tried to avoid involvement, but the latest came from Peter's own son Alexei. Alexei was heir to the throne. She would be at his mercy if Peter died. It was as well, she decided, not to alienate him now.

The Tsarevich and the Tsar had never cared for one another. Son feared father, father despised son, and relations between them had deteriorated of late. Alexei had been made responsible for fortifying Moscow and Peter was not pleased with the results—in fact he was furious with the boy for failing his country at so dangerous a time. In view of all the circumstances, Catherine was venturing where even angels might have feared to tread, but she went carefully, with charm. For her sake the Tsar relented, and favoured Alexei with another task—bringing reinforcements to the battlefront—and when the Tsarevich fell sick along the way, Peter was persuaded to go and see his son. The reconciliation was not to be a lasting one, but for the moment this problem at least was shelved.

In February 1709, torrential rains turned the hard ground of the battlefront into a sea of mud, and since campaigning had become impossible, Peter started on a tour of southern Russia. Catherine went with him. She watched him work like a navvy in the shipyards at Voronezh, and sailed with him down the river Don. They visited the quaint Cossack capital, Cherkassk, where loyal atamans came out to greet them holding horse-tail banners, and showed them the severed heads of rebels they had executed; they saw the famous

citadel of Azov, and then sailed out into the Black Sea before turning back to the Ukraine. The Swedes were on the march again,
and Catherine was sent back north to safety.

Peter sent a bottle of Tokay after her with a message begging her
'not to be sad, for God's sake', and then turned to business. The
battle of Poltava, the decisive moment in the war, took place on
27 June 1709. Catherine waited for news of the outcome in an agony
of fear, and it was mid-July before it came. Anisia tore open the
seal and read the letter out aloud. It was very brief:

'Greetings, little mother! I tell you that the All-gracious Lord
has given us an indescribable victory over the enemy. In a word,
their entire army has been knocked on the head. You'll hear more,
but you must come here yourself and congratulate me—Peter.' He
did not tell her he had got a bullet in his hat and another in his
saddle.

Catherine experienced an overwhelming sense of relief. Peter
was safe at last. The tension which had marred their happiness and
yet served to deepen their relationship had lifted at last; and the
years of separation, the long months of repeated pregnancy she
had had to bear alone, would also be over—or so it seemed. In fact
their reunion was disappointingly short. In August Peter was off
yet again, though this time only briefly and mercifully not to war.
And while he visited Poland and Prussia Catherine, pregnant for
the fifth time, at least had the comfort of regular letters from him.

'Life is dull without you, and I think that it's the same with you.'
She was not so much bored, however, as worried—this time for his
safety from the arms of other women. She sent him a present and a
warning to behave himself. 'Thanks for the gift,' he replied, 'I am
sending you some fresh lemons. As to your joke about diversions,'
he added, tongue in cheek, 'we don't have any. We are old men,
and not that sort.'

Catherine replied with a mixture of playfulness and respect,
addressing him by his naval rank: 'Lord, my little father, Mr.
Commodore, Greetings for a life of many years. Thanks for the
present. . . . Don't stop writing. . . . I long to hear from you with
every hour. I have received your Grace's three letters. It is a pleasure
to receive your writings.' She teased him about his drinking too,
but the keynote of her letter was longing. 'My dear little father,

come quickly. Oh, my little father, I have been so lonely without your Grace. . . . God grant me to see you quickly and in joy.'

Peter was soon back in Russia, celebrating his victory over the Swedes with a huge fireworks display in St. Petersburg before riding on to Moscow where Catherine, expecting her new baby, waited for him impatiently in the rambling old wooden palace of Kolomenskoye, just outside the city. But her baby arrived first.

On 19 December Peter made his triumphal entry into Moscow. He was attending a *Te Deum* in the Cathedral when the news was brought to him. At once, the priests were ordered to hurry the service to an end, whereupon he rushed off to see Catherine and his child. It was another girl. They called her Elizabeth.

Within days, Catherine was up enjoying a riotous New Year's carnival dressed as a charming Friesland milk-maid, while Peter joined the long procession of masqueraders in the guise of a Dutch sea captain complete with long clay pipe. The strain was truly over now. They were in happy and expansive mood.

The year that followed, 1710, was probably the happiest Catherine had yet experienced. She felt secure in Peter's affections and was openly acknowledged by him. She was introduced to foreign envoys, including the English Mr. Whitworth, addressed respectfully by important people, and recognized, more or less reluctantly, by members of the royal family. Peter himself was full of optimism and plans for great reforms, and though she could not fully understand them all she shared his pride in his creations—in the navy which he hoped would one day rival England's, in the victorious army, and in St. Petersburg where they returned that spring.

The place was an encampment still—a mess of shacks and logs and canvas. Deer and elk still grazed in the marshy meadows between the buildings and wolves still prowled the streets at night. Fires consumed over a hundred shops that year; dozens of the reluctant working population had drowned in the destructive autumn floods and thousands more had perished from exposure or disease. Peter, however, did not seem to notice the primitive realities. Poring over the plans drawn up by his chief architect, Trezzini, he already visualized the place as it would be. The grandees of the empire were already beginning to build there, and now Peter ordered Trezzini to design a summer palace for himself and Catherine to be built in the gardens by the river.

The gardens themselves were beginning to thrive after six hard years. The poplars, yews and chestnuts they had planted were prospering at last; the briar hedges that lined the alleyways were ready to be clipped, and the trellises were covered now with hardy climbing plants. But until their twenty-roomed palace was finished they continued to live in their modest log cabin—a residence more appropriate to a peasant than to the great all-Russian Tsar. Yet Catherine was still enough of a peasant to feel more at ease with the intimate, domestic scale of living it enforced—and when Peter had to entertain she was content for him to do so in someone else's residence, on board a ship, or at an inn called *The Four Frigates*.

In all, Peter was much easier to live with now his throne and his country no longer seemed to be in danger. At thirty-seven he seemed to be in splendid health and the English envoy, Mr. Whitworth, noted that he seemed to be much more controlled these days. Much of the credit for this was due to Catherine. So energetic, determined and temperamental a man could never be easy to live with, but she had learned to ride along with his enthusiasms and his passions, and though he still had occasional moods of violence or suspicion, she could generally be relied upon to soothe him into a cooler mood.

She had gained his trust over the years, and she was now in a position to exploit it. Alexander Menshikov seems to have been the main beneficiary. She put the more delicate of his requests before the Tsar and more than once when it seemed that, favourite though he was, he was heading for an inevitable fall because of his corruption she interceded for him. Peter would rant and threaten to chop off Alexander's head, but recognizing the man's value as well as his faults, he invariably gave way to her in the end. So she was able to pay her debt of gratitude to Alexander—and she was to continue paying it.

That year, Peter's chief enthusiasm was for the navy. As soon as it was possible, he donned his Commodore's uniform and led his fleet to sea. He returned at the end of July to take Catherine for a cruise on his new yacht which he had named after her, then left again until October. He reckoned it to be a successful summer.

Swedish Karelia had been occupied, Riga captured, and the Russian occupation of the Baltic lands where Catherine had been born was now complete.

Shortly after his return Catherine joined him for the first great public occasion ever to be held in St. Petersburg—the wedding of his niece Anne to the young Duke of Courland. The banquet, given at Alexander Menshikov's house, was attended by the great men of Russia and the diplomatic corps—and for the first time at an official function, Catherine was seated in a place of honour.

But by Christmas another cloud was looming nearer. War with Turkey was expected: and afraid that Peter would desert her to fight another endless series of campaigns, Catherine embarked on a campaign of her own. She had two objectives—to go with him when he left for the front, and to make sure her two daughters were provided for in case Peter should not return. On the first point Peter baulked; on the second he gave way. On 3 February he publicly recognized their daughter Anne as a princess, giving a court dinner in her honour. Then he went even further and prepared to acknowledge Catherine herself.

Despite his grossness and his ruthlessness, Peter was a vulnerable human being and needed a stable, intimate relationship, a haven from the cares of life, which only Catherine, of all the many women he had known, could provide. She was simple, she was meek, but for him these qualities were lovable. So was her low birth and her ignorance which made her so dependent on him. His relationship with her had stood the test of seven stormy years. In Peter's view it merited public recognition on this count alone. But there was another count as well. Catherine was an excellent bearer of children. By giving her official status their offspring could be legitimized and the future of the dynasty doubly insured.

So, on 7 March 1711 he called the members of the royal family together and coolly informed them that Catherine was his 'Consort'. Henceforth they must all pay her the respects due to a Tsarina, and if any misfortune should befall him on campaign, she should be accorded the rank, privileges and revenues of an imperial dowager. He countered all objections in advance. It was true that his first wife was still alive, but Catherine was his wife to all intents and purposes, and though he had not yet 'had the time', as he put it, to go through a ceremony of marriage with her, this he would do 'at the first opportunity'.

Peter's relatives took the news rather better than might have been expected. His sister the Princess Natalia accepted Catherine graciously, for her brother's sake; the old Dowager Praskovya was shrewd enough to bend to any wind of change; the others followed suit. When the announcement was made public, no one dared to protest. Peter was autocrat; his power was now unchallengeable; he could do exactly what he wished.

But though Catherine was acknowledged as Tsarina in Russia, it remained to be seen if she would be received as such abroad. The matter was soon put to the test. Immediately after the announcement Peter took her to Poland with him.

Things began well. Prince Radziwill gave a ball in her honour, and the King himself greeted her with every courtesy—but then he was virtually a Russian puppet. The Ambassador of the little German state of Wolfenbüttel for one had grave doubts about the propriety of making an official call on a woman of such ill repute.

However, since he had business to transact with the Tsar—negotiating a marriage between Princess Charlotte of Wolfenbüttel and the Tsarevich Alexei—he reckoned it would only be politic to do so. When the Ambassador called, Peter was in her room pretending to be absorbed with various mathematical instruments and maps, but he listened anxiously to every word that passed between the Ambassador and his mistress.

The Ambassador 'congratulated her . . . on the announcement of her marriage'—the marriage which had not yet taken place—and Catherine, having been carefully coached in her part, thanked the Ambassador, and said how much she wanted to see and embrace the Princess Charlotte. She managed to behave with propriety and yet with a certain unaffected charm. It was a minor triumph for her —and who cared if these aristocratic foreigners sneered at her behind her back?

Peter could refuse her nothing now. Even his former insistence that she should return home once he left to join the army went by the board, and when he set out for the Turkish border on 1 June she went with him.

Catherine turned out to be a Jonah for the expedition. Once it was known she was going, various officers brought their wives along as well. As a result the baggage train was larger, and progress slower, than it would otherwise have been. The weather was hot, water was short and, beyond the town of Jassy a cloud of locusts descended on the camp, devouring all the fodder round about. The troops bore it all as patiently as they endured the vicious discipline. But worse yet was in store. By 7 July they had reached the river Pruth, and that evening a scout galloped into camp with awful news. The enemy army, five times as strong, was heading towards them. The attack came two days later.

For hours Catherine sat in her coach in the safest part of the camp while the din of cannonade and the cries of men intensified outside. When she emerged at last she was almost overwhelmed by a stench of blood and dust and gunpowder. The wounded lay sprawled between the corralled wagons, tormented by flies and, beyond them, lines of green-coated soldiers manned the improvised defences. There was a confusion of guns and horsemen, glinting sabres, terrifying flashes; and amid the smoke, on the distant hills, she could make out a sea of tents that formed the Turkish camp.

At last the shrieks of pain, the cries for water, drew her back to practicalities, and together with such of her companions as were not hysterical or paralysed with fright, she began to tend the wounded, bringing them flasks of precious water and strong wine.

Meanwhile the battle went from bad to worse. Food was running short and the casualties were mounting. A last sortie failed. The army seemed doomed, Peter and Catherine along with it, and on 10 July a grim-faced council-of-war decided to request a truce. But the slaughter continued until the 12th when the Turks at last agreed on terms. Peter and his surviving troops were to be allowed to march home—but he must surrender the fort of Azov to the Sultan. Peter complied, and the firing ceased at last.

Popular myth gave Catherine the credit of saving the whole army. It told of her approaching a gloomy Peter in his tent and exhorting him to send a large bribe to the Grand Vizier, of her surrendering all her jewellery for this purpose and of going round the camp collecting rings and valuables from all the other women. One account goes even further. 'The Czarina', it runs, 'had all the glory of this delicate Negotiation; and it may be said that she

preserved the Life or at least the Liberty of the Czar her Husband.'
It is doubtful, however, if she played any part in it at all; but Peter
deliberately fostered the legend in order to make Catherine more
acceptable to his people.

So the Russian army began its inglorious march home, and on
24 August Catherine and Peter arrived in Warsaw. From there
they went to Thorn but Peter was in poor health and very depressed,
and at last he accepted his doctors' suggestion that he take a cure at
Carlsbad. He arrived there on 13 September and next day wrote to
Catherine:

'Katerinushka, my love, how are you? ... This place is about as
merry as a dungeon ... hemmed in between such high mountains
that I can hardly see the sun. Worst of all there's no decent beer.
But we hope, God willing, that the waters will do us some good.'
For once, Catherine was anxious that he should not rush back, and
she was soon gratified to hear that the waters were having some
effect. 'Our stomachs are all swelled up,' his next letter ran, 'since
we have nothing else to do but drink like horses.' He was obviously
in better spirits. He even teased her for telling him not to hurry
back. This must mean 'that you've found someone healthier than
me,' he wrote. 'That's the way you daughters of Eve treat us old
men.'

In October, when Peter went to Torgau to attend Alexei's wedding
to the Wolfenbüttel princess, Catherine did not accompany him.
She was not quite acceptable even to that most minor of the German
princely courts. But afterwards she accompanied him to Mitau, the
home of Peter's niece, the widowed Anne of Courland, who was
forever grumbling that her allowance was too small and then to
Riga and Reval. Here they were welcomed by the sound of guns and
crowds of cheering people. This was the district where Catherine
had been born, and its people saw her as a heroine. It seemed
unlikely that the Russians would be so enthusiastic.

Arriving back in St. Petersburg, Peter kept his promise, and on
9 February 1712 he went through a formal ceremony of marriage
with her—though in order to suggest that they had really been
married secretly some time before, the invitations were issued for
'His Majesty's *Old Wedding*'.

The couple arrived at Menshikov's chapel before nine in the

morning. Peter was wearing a Rear-Admiral's uniform and the plump Catherine looked radiant in a brocade gown glittering with gems. The bridesmaids were their own daughters aged five and two, though they soon became fractious, and had to be replaced.

Towards ten o'clock the happy couple left for the reception. There was a whole procession of sledges, Alexander Menshikov bearing his Marshal's staff, military bands—and all St. Petersburg turned out to see them as they rode across the river ice. But before his sledge drew up outside the newly-built Winter Palace an impatient Peter suddenly jumped out and ran inside ahead of everyone else, clutching a bulky object in his hand.

It was his wedding present for his wife—a fine candelabrum in ebony and ivory, carved with his own hands. He had it hanging in its place by the time Catherine came in. They smiled at each other from beneath their respective canopies on either side of a huge round table, while the guests—ambassadors and ministers, generals and governors, aristocrats, bearded clergymen, merchants and their wives—took their places at segregated tables in the great hall and in various adjoining rooms.

'The dinner', wrote Whitworth, was 'magnificent, the wine good, from Hungary, and what was the greatest pleasure not forced on the Guests in too large quantities.' Still, many toasts were drunk, each announced by Alexander stamping his Marshal's wand upon the floor and accompanied by the roar of guns outside. Peter was in high spirits. He approached Whitworth with a twinkle in his eye and assured him confidentially that the marriage was 'guaranteed to be fruitful' since he 'already had five children' by his new wife!

The banquet lasted until six in the afternoon. Then the tables were cleared away to make room for dancing, and the party ended at eleven with a grand display of pyrotechnics. Rockets screamed into the air, and an elaborate firework on the far side of the river spluttered incandescently to life. Five huge letters forming the word 'Vivat' appeared hanging in the air, and as the apparition faded candles were placed, by prearranged order, in every window of St. Petersburg. The city twinkled like a fairyland. Catherine, the Cinderella from Livonia, had captured her Prince; the camp-follower at nineteen was now Tsarina at the age of twenty-nine.

The day after the wedding the guests were assembled again to eat fruit and cake and dance till midnight. Next day Alexander Menshikov, the man who, nine years before, had brought them both together, provided a lavish entertainment, and on the Saturday the Dowager Praskovya was persuaded to give a party in honour of the bride's belated nuptials. Throughout the proceedings people took good care never to let slip a mention of the Tsar's first wife.

Catherine was now Tsarina. Yet as their friend the Scottish mercenary Patrick Gordon wrote, she was 'never forgetful of her former condition'. Indeed, sometimes she seemed to invite remembrance of it. Once at a ball she saw Whitworth who had known her when she was only Peter's mistress, and immediately rushed over to squeeze his hand and whisper 'Have you forgot little Kate?' Her openness seemed to do her little harm, however, and her lack of airs and her flirtatious brand of charm induced many men at least to forgive her for her past.

Even so, people gossiped. Rumours spread that her first husband, Johann, officially assumed to have been killed ten years before, had been taken prisoner at Poltava and sent off to Siberia to die. Others, more favourably disposed, said that Peter had tracked Johann down and compensated him for the loss of Catherine. There is no evidence to support either story, however. Johann had simply disappeared. He was no more than a spectre now.

Becoming a Tsarina brought few changes to Catherine's daily life. Peter disliked magnificent living and they kept few servants even now. Two pages and an orderly served them when ministers and generals came to dine; otherwise they ate alone or with the children, served only by a page and maid. Peter still spent most of his time at the Senate, in the shipyards, at the local taverns chatting with his English craftsmen as he had done at Deptford years before, or in his workshop practising one of the fourteen trades to which he laid claim. He seemed almost constantly preoccupied—planning new industries, pondering the next move in the now quiescent Swedish war, fuming about dilatory officials and about tax-collectors who were pocketing the proceeds. Even at dinner or in bed his attention was always liable to stray to business, and he would turn away to scribble in the notebook he kept by him.

And once spring came he was away playing his 'games of Neptune' again. He did return to take her to spend a few days at their little summer house at Catherinenhof—a charming place with terraces running down to the water's edge—and again to attend various functions in St. Petersburg, but he seemed to have very little time for her, and Catherine, who was expecting another baby, felt neglected. Even when they were together he would go off sailing with Dutch and English merchant friends promising to return within the hour, and then not turn up till midnight, and soon he was off to Germany again leaving her behind.

Catherine sent piteous letters after him, but he replied rather irritably. 'I yearn for you as well', he wrote once, 'but you must understand that . . . one mustn't postpone business.' He even spent Christmas away from her visiting Russian army units stationed in Mecklenburg, and though he sent her presents from time to time— some clothes, and 'as many oysters as I could find'—he would not let her join him. 'We must postpone that for a while', he wrote, 'The time has come for you to pray and for us to work. Yesterday the Swedes attacked the Danes. . . .' A disconsolate Catherine faced another winter without Peter.

He paid her a flying visit in February and another late in March when she gave birth to her sixth child—another daughter. But the war kept him away for most of that summer, and the next, and she had to be satisfied with such fleeting moments as he felt able to spare her. The best of these were spent at their little house at Peterhof where they discussed plans for embellishing the gardens there with labyrinths and groves, fished in the pools and went walking together in the woods. But these happy, halcyon days seemed all too brief when set against the long months of separation, and whenever Peter was away, moods of restlessness and inexpressible *ennui* descended on the household.

'The Tsarina', reported Princess Golitsyn who was now attached to Catherine's suite along with several other ladies, 'is never ready to sleep before three in the morning, and I have to sit constantly by her side while Kirilovna [another lady-in-waiting] dozes standing by the bed. . . . Mary [Hamilton] wanders about the room with a mattress which she spreads in the middle of the floor. . . . Matrena [Balk] walks through the apartments scolding everybody, and little

Christine stands behind a chair and just stares vacantly at the Tsarina.' Catherine drove her ladies to distraction.

Sometimes she relieved the tedium by having gentlemen to dine, though taking care to assure Peter that these 'cavaliers' were all 'gentlemen of great age'. Sometimes she would travel out to a Baltic port in hopes of seeing him, and she was always writing to her 'heart's friend', giving news of the family or of foreign ships arriving at St. Petersburg, which she knew would please him.

At last in July 1714 Peter won a handsome naval victory over the Swedes at Hangö, promoted himself Vice-Admiral, and came home. That autumn, Catherine presented him with yet another daughter, Margaret, and on 24 November, her name day according to the Russian custom, he rewarded her by making her the first recipient of a new Order of chivalry instituted in her honour, the Order of St. Catherine the Martyr. Its motto—'Through Love and Fidelity' —was meant to recognize her devotion, but traditionalists still found it difficult to stomach this honouring of a foreign interloper.

Catherine did not seem to care. Her chief worry now was Peter's health, which had been poor of late. He was getting frequent stomach cramps, had a swollen leg and suffered rushes of blood to the head. His doctors' prescriptions, consisting chiefly of pounded worms and wood lice, gave him little relief, and poor health meant a bad temper. There were days when no one but Catherine dared approach him, and even she had to go carefully.

Peter, as usual, was worried about corruption. Fingers had been pointed to a Vice-Governor of a province and at a Senator. One of them was a protégé of Alexander Menshikov's so he, too, came under suspicion. That November there was an ugly scene between a raging Peter and his favourite. Catherine calmed him down, but Peter soon boiled over again, accusing Alexander publicly of being a villain and a protector of villains. In four years, Peter stormed, Alexander had embezzled a million roubles in one province alone. The luxury in which Alexander lived—and whose hospitality Peter himself so much enjoyed—was obvious proof of his dishonesty. The investigations went wider; the arrests and interrogations multiplied. Even old Boris Sheremetev, one of Catherine's first protectors, fell under suspicion, and though Alexander remained at liberty, he trembled for his life.

Thanks largely to Catherine he was saved—allowed to purge himself of his sins by surrendering a part of his ill-gotten gains. Others, less fortunate, suffered knouting, tongue-burning, confiscation and exile. Peter was a harsh man—he had to be if he was to realize his vision of bringing Russia up to date. But he would have been harsher still without Catherine to remind him of his debts of friendship and to beg him to have some compassion.

Yet though he was the terrible Tsar at times, he had his lighter moments. He would take Catherine tobogganing, and he rarely let slip an opportunity to indulge his taste for the bizarre. When his ancient tutor Zotov remarried he had the ceremony conducted by a ninety-year-old priest, and by way of celebration ordered a grotesque masquerade. There were 'footmen' so fat that they could hardly walk, old men dressed as wizards riding on sledges drawn by bears, and over four hundred revellers dressed as burgomasters and archbishops, Chinamen and 'Americans'. He and Catherine joined in as sailorman and peasant girl.

But if there were high notes that winter, sadness overtook them in the spring. Their daughter Natalya died, and some weeks later the infant Margaret. Then in October, the Tsarevich Alexei's wife, Charlotte, gave birth to a boy, named after his grandfather. Peter ordered a general salute, but he himself was less than joyful. He would have preferred to see the succession pass to a son that Catherine might bear, rather than stay with the descendants of his first wife, and of the wretched Alexei. And, ironically, within a few days Catherine did bear him a son.

This time Peter was overjoyed. He announced the new arrival as 'a little seaman', 'a new recruit to be called after his father. God grant that I may one day see him holding a musket'. Firecrackers were let off in the streets, vodka was supplied for the inhabitants, and grandees came like Magi bringing gifts to Catherine and her child. Despite the death of Alexei's wife a few days later, a huge, gay, christening feast was held, and a great display of fireworks with the motto 'HOPE WITH PATIENCE'.

Hope and patience were just what Catherine was to need in the months that followed—hope for the future of her new-born son, patience to endure the trials that she was soon to undergo for, that winter, Peter fell seriously ill. The doctors despaired, the last rites were administered, and a succession of grim-faced notables arrived to pay their last respects.

Catherine went through torments—fearing for Peter, and frightened for herself and for her children if he should die. Alexei was the heir apparent and though he was always respectful to her she knew he hated her as well as Peter. Most observers thought that once he came to power he would set out to destroy everything that Peter had created, and that Catherine and her children might not be safe.

Then suddenly, the crisis passed. On Christmas Eve Peter was able to attend a thanksgiving service with Catherine and he soon returned to normal health. But the problem of Alexei remained. Early in 1716 Peter, who always saw him as 'an unworthy son', gave him an ultimatum—'become worthy to succeed me or else become a monk'. Yet when the Tsarevich chose the cowl Peter gave him a year in which to reconsider. Catherine continued to fret about the whole affair. She wanted her new son groomed for Tsardom, but there were dangers implicit in any course of action. Meanwhile she redoubled her care of Peter. So long as he lived the evil day of reckoning would be postponed.

Towards the end of January, Catherine entrusted her baby boy to the care of nurses and left Petersburg with her husband for a grand tour of Europe. They visited Riga and Königsberg, met the Polish King at Danzig, and moved on west travelling separately since Peter had a full and tiring schedule of engagements while Catherine had found herself to be pregnant once again. In May the King of Prussia entertained them at Stettin and they met up again at Schwerin, but Peter seemed tired and Catherine was relieved to see him go on to Pyrmont Spa to take another cure.

He had been complaining of eye strain recently, and she sent a pair of spectacles after him. 'Katerinushka, my heart's friend,' he replied. 'Many thanks for the present. . . . You send me something to help my old age; I am sending you something to adorn your youth.'

At thirty-three Catherine had left the prime of youth behind, but the forty-four-year-old Peter was ageing fast. She continued to try, without success, to persuade him to reduce his rate of work, and, tactfully as ever, to reduce his drinking too. Early in June he wrote again from Pyrmont, acknowledging her 'progressive spirit' in sending him only one bottle of his favourite wine when his doctors were restricting him to a single glass a day, but despite Catherine's attempts to reassure him he was feeling the advance of age, and those spectacles were an unwelcome reminder of it. 'You say you won't admit I'm old', he wrote, 'and try to cover up for the present you sent me. . . . But it's very easy to see that young people don't wear spectacles.' Neither of them mentioned the problem that haunted both of them—the Tsarevich Alexei.

Later that month they were invited to dinner by the King of Denmark, and, throwing precedence to the winds, the Queen made a personal call on Catherine. Despite their worries it was a summer of wonders and delights—masquerades at the Danish court at Rostock, visits to the allied fleets, walks in the palace gardens, a guided tour through the old quarter of the city.

All the time, they waited anxiously for news of their infant son, Peter—'Petrushka' as they called him—and savoured every snippet of information about him when it came. When Alexander reported that 'the master of St. Petersburg' had cut his fourth tooth, Peter was overjoyed. 'God grant', he wrote to Catherine, 'that he may cut all his teeth so easily and that we may see him grow up—which will reward us for our former grief over his brothers.' But while their child was a constant source of conversation, Alexei's son was never mentioned.

There was soon news of Alexei himself however. He had fled from Russia and persuaded the Emperor of Austria to give him sanctuary. His defection was a scandal of international proportions, and had dangerous implications too. Rumour was already rife that a plot had been hatched to assassinate Peter and put Alexei on the throne, and there was no knowing what mischief Alexei might do in exile, beyond the reach of the Russian secret police. An infuriated Peter ordered his agents to track him down, and Catherine, as concerned as her husband, wrote repeatedly to Alexander asking for news of Alexei. For the moment there was none. All seemed quiet in Russia. Concern subsided a little.

Peter had left for Amsterdam and Catherine, nearing the time of her confinement, followed on at a slower pace. She felt none too well and treatment received in Hanover had done her little good. The weather was bad, the journey was tiring. Peter, himself confined to bed in Amsterdam where he was waiting for her, wrote to her warning her to avoid certain bad roads—and not to bring too large a suite with her since the cost of living in Holland was so expensive.

Catherine had only reached Wessel when on 2 January 1717 she gave birth to another son. The child died within twenty-four hours, but Peter's letter reacting to the birth reached her some time afterwards. The news, he wrote, 'has delighted me doubly—firstly because of the new-born child, and also because God has freed you from your pains, at which I, too, feel better. I've not been able to sit up so long since Christmas, and as soon as possible I shall hurry to you both'. An exhausted Catherine could not hold back the tears.

Another note soon followed acknowledging the news of 'the unexpected event' which had changed joy to grief. 'What can I say?' he wrote, 'except to quote long-suffering Job: "The Lord has given; the Lord has taken away; blessed be the Name of the Lord." I beg you to think of it in these terms. I do, in so far as I can'. He was still not well enough to travel, and it was Catherine who recovered first. On 2 February she arrived in Amsterdam.

They were both in low spirits, Catherine particularly, since she had heard that Peter had taken a prostitute when he was in Germany. Peter attached little importance to what had become for him a comparatively rare indulgence. He spent less on other women, he boasted once, than any other monarch in Europe. Anyway, there was only one woman whom he loved, and she need have no fears about any transitory affair of his. So the quarrel was made up, though Peter took pains to track down the tale-bearer and have him soundly beaten.

By the end of February Peter was well enough to show her Holland. She toured Amsterdam, sailed the canals, and saw the little house at Zaardam where Peter had lived when, years before, he had worked as an apprentice in the shipyards. She went to Utrecht, to Rotterdam, and to the Hague, where 'all imaginable Honours were paid her', met the merchant Christopher Brandt and others of Peter's old friends, looked at buildings, admired van Dycks, Rubens , Brueghels, Rembrandts, but above all the seascapes of Adam Silo, of which they bought several to decorate their house at Peterhof.

But when Peter left for Paris, Catherine stayed behind in Holland, the French having made it clear that she would not be welcome at their court. As for the English, they refused to receive even Peter now, apparently on her account. He did his best to console her, sending her presents by every post. Lace arrived from Brussels, then a parrot, some canaries, a monkey, a selection of plants, a French dwarf, and, towards the end of April, a giant, seven foot five inches tall named Nicholas Bourgeois whom Peter had found in Calais and sent on with a note enjoining Catherine to have him well fed and cared for.

Catherine wrote frequently too, expressing fears that he might 'soon be looking for a lady'. But Peter dismissed the idea airily. That sort of thing 'would not be at all becoming at my advanced age', he assured her. But Catherine was also anxious about his success in broaching the subject of a possible marriage arrangement between their second daughter Elizabeth, now seven years of age, and the infant King Louis. In this she was to be disappointed; the proposal was turned down. Peter seemed as depressed about it as she was, but he made the most of his visit—toured the Invalides, the Gobelin factory, the botanical gardens and the Mint, inspected anatomical models made of wax, called on the Duchess de Berry and the Académie Française, saw Fontainebleau, the Tuileries and Versailles. By 17 June when he arrived in Spa to take another cure he was quite exhausted.

Meanwhile their daughters in Petersburg had fallen ill. Smallpox was suspected. So far, their son was unaffected, and young Elizabeth soon began to recover, but Catherine could not hide her concern about Anne. 'Your changed style', Peter wrote, 'has greatly saddened me. . . . God grant we'll hear the same good news about little Anne as about Lizzie. I believe you when you tell me . . . that you're very lonely. The bearer of this will tell you how lonely I am without you.' Then came a happy postscript: 'I have received good news . . . little Anne is better, and so I have begun to drink the waters with more joy.'

A more cheerful Catherine sent him a camisole and some vodka—

which Peter acknowledged in his usual bantering style—'the water is acting well. I wore the ... camisole for the first time today, and drank your health, but only a very little because it's forbidden'— and then some strawberries, herrings and another warning to steer clear of women, which Peter dismissed saying that 'since the doctors have forbidden domestic games while I take the waters, I have given my mistress a holiday'.

He rejoined her in Amsterdam later in July and before long they were homeward bound, though again by separate roads, largely because of difficulty in finding enough post-horses along the same route to pull both their sizeable suites. They spent four days together at the Prussian court where, after the snubs administered by London and Paris, Catherine was grateful for the reception the Queen gave in her honour and to be able to sit beside Peter at official banquets. Even so, she sensed that the Prussian courtiers were not all impressed by her. 'A small, thickset, very tanned' woman without 'dignity or gracefulness', wrote one of them, and she was upset by a rumour to the effect that some of her own ladies-in-waiting were pregnant by Peter. In all, she was glad when in October 1717 they arrived back in St. Petersburg.

Yet she was hardly popular here either. Many Russians had never forgiven Peter for marrying a Livonian whore, and blamed her for his reforms which they so much resented. She might be popular with Peter's devotees but to members of the royal family she was still an outsider, and especially to Praskovya, the Empress Dowager, who despite her displays of fawning respect, was known to sympathize with the oppositionists and with the runaway Tsarevich Alexei.

It was Alexei whom Catherine feared most of all, so she was intensely relieved when, that autumn, Peter's agents tracked him down in Italy and brought him home. Early in 1718 the Tsarevich was tried for disobedience, traitorous flight, drunkenness and ill-treating his late wife. He pleaded for mercy, which Peter granted—provided that he denounce his associates, renounce his title to the throne, and recognize Catherine's son as the future Tsar. Alexei did all three.

His friends were arrested, forced to confess to treason, and sentenced to death or other punishment. Priests admitted to offering absolution to anyone who murdered Peter; the Metropolitan of Rostov who had called Peter Antichrist was broken on the wheel. And although this purge of the disaffected and seditious produced no evidence to show that Alexei was more than a passive focus for the opposition he was re-arrested, interrogated, tortured. His confessions were vague and unsubstantial, but in Russia governments deal with potential opposition without waiting for evidence to become conclusive. Alexei was found guilty of wishing Peter's death, and condemned to execution. On 26 June, however, he died mysteriously in prison before sentence could be officially carried out.

Rumour had it that Catherine had had him poisoned. There is no reason to suppose she did, but the charge was plausible: Alexei's death had cleared the way for her son to succeed and had finally dispelled her terrible fear that Alexei might one day become Tsar. The day after Alexei's death she and Peter took part in a noisy celebration to commemorate the victory of Poltava; three days later they gave the late Tsarevich a royal funeral.

If Peter had a troubled conscience there was one sure cure for it— to be with his beloved ships again. Their correspondence when he was at sea that summer was full of references to the new Tsarevich— their little Petrushka. In fact, the child was obviously backward in walking and talking, but neither of his doting parents was disposed to recognize the fact. How proudly his mother reported that although he 'has been a little weak . . . with God's help he is now quite well and has cut three back teeth.' 'I beg your protection from little Peter', she wrote again, 'for I have great arguments with him when I tell him that Papa is away travelling. He can't bear such talk. If, on the other hand, I say Papa is here he likes it better and is very happy.'

The exchange of presents flowed as usual. Peter had his hair cut and sent her the locks; she sent him vodka, herbs, Tokay, figs, cucumbers and apples. Then, suddenly, she began to write less frequently and Peter, knowing she was expecting another child and worried about his son, became impatient. 'This is my fifth letter yet I've only received three from you. . . . For God's sake write more often.' And again: 'It's eight days now since I had a letter from you.' In August Catherine gave birth to another daughter,

Natalia, and Peter, having ordered a great feast of celebration, hastened to St. Petersburg.

In the months that followed Peter threw himself with new vigour into the task of turning Russian 'beasts' as he described his subjects, 'into human beings', and he was not easier to live with on that account. Reorganizing the administration, founding new industries, tightening the tax system, he ran up against inevitable frustrations, and Catherine had to exercise all her resources of tact and patience to keep the peace between him and various of his aides who from day to day fell out of favour. 'I lose my temper easily', Peter admitted once, but added that he did not 'take offence when people on familiar terms with me tell me of it and remonstrate with me, as does my Catherine.'

She understood little about his reforms and projects, but there was one which, having seen Amsterdam, she sympathized with utterly—the development of St. Petersburg. Peter had just appointed a Master of Police for the city with orders to see that new buildings were erected according to plan and regulation, that the river banks and fire-fighting services were maintained, and that the streets and canals were kept clean and safe. He further insisted that the canals be used, issuing the inhabitants with boats and ordering them to gather on the river every Sunday so that 'anyone may travel without fear on sea and river waters at times of great winds and storms.' But above all, Peter was ensuring that St. Petersburg should be a beautiful city.

His chief architect was now Leblond, a pupil of the great Lenôtre. His initial designs proved to be impractically expensive and had to be severely modified, but as Peter said, the man was 'a wizard' and already the shanty town was beginning to take on the shape, if not yet the sky-line of a great city. The tide of mud was slowly receding and the Nevski Prospect was already in existence— a long straight thoroughfare paved by Swedish prisoners.

Catherine took rather more interest in Leblond's plans for individual palaces and gardens however, and particularly in his plans for Peterhof which was to be transformed into a lavish Italianate palace with wings curving out from the central block, domes and galleries, and a spectacular terrace of fountains stretching down to the sea. Fine pavilions were already being built in the gardens there, inspired by the follies they had seen abroad—the 'Marly' pavilion surrounded by a pond, and at the water's edge a pavilion of red brick which they called 'Monplaisir'.

And, again inspired by their recent travels, Peter and Catherine set about breathing a new social life into their city. True, dinners and balls were already quite common occurrences, but the social graces of the West were lacking. So with typical directness Peter, encouraged by his wife, ordered that soirées, or 'assemblies' be given regularly throughout the winter season. He designated the hosts and gave them meticulous instructions as to who was to be invited, what refreshments to provide, the times at which guests were to arrive and leave. Cards and chess would be played and there would be mixed dancing in the western style. Manners were to be informal, but refined, guests were to cultivate the art of small-talk and though men might smoke they were not to get drunk. Women must appear in satin and damask, not shapeless old furs, and wear muslin head-dresses, not old Russian 'roof hats'.

Since there were all too few Russians of taste and refinement, foreign merchants and officers were to attend in order to set an example and raise the tone. But Russian aristocrats could not be transformed into westerners simply by royal decree, and Peter himself set an example of bad behaviour in his more bear-like moods.

Catherine could not bring herself to share Peter's scientific bent seen in his growing collection of 'very ancient or unusual things'—bones and fossils, iron weapons, a 'flying dragon', snakes and serpents, the organs of a hermaphrodite, the pickled corpses of Siamese twins and 'the hand of a man who died by excessive drinking, with all its blood stagnated in the veins.' Still, his chief interests always centred on the living, and above all, on his little 'Petrushka'.

They petted and coddled him, fretted over him, doted on him, refusing to admit that he was sickly or backward. When an artist was commissioned to paint his portrait, they wanted their hopes portrayed rather than the child itself. So he depicted Petrushka as a pink and sturdy cherub with dimpled knee, brandishing a bow and arrow. The light fell on his red curls like a halo. This was the son they wanted to succeed. Even the Autocrat of all the Russians needed his illusions.

Early in 1719 they spent a month at Olonets where, to Peter's joy, mineral springs had been discovered. But the venture was not a success. Peter caught a violent cold, the place was bleak and uncomfortable, and Praskovya's morose daughter, the Duchess of Courland, who was one of their party, proved a constant source of irritation to them both. As if this were not enough, a surgeon severed one of Peter's nerves when trying to bleed him, and then when they left Olonets an unsavoury incident came to light which threatened a serious breach between them.

News reached Peter that Mary Hamilton, one of Catherine's favourite attendants, had killed her new-born child. Upon enquiry it transpired that she had had abortions twice before. Catherine had known and said nothing. She knew infanticide to be common enough in Russia and she knew the reasons for it. But Peter was outraged. Death was the penalty he had proclaimed for the killing of an infant and he was adamant that Mary was not to be exempt. Catherine pleaded for her friend in vain; Mary was duly led off to execution.

But with the spring came reconciliation, and a resumption of their indulgence in the cruder sort of pleasures. Once they went to see a tight-rope dancer recently arrived in Russia, and were greatly amused to notice some elderly boyars in the audience looking at them nervously, obviously afraid that with his enthusiasm for new skills Peter might take it into his head to make them learn tight-rope dancing too. Then there was their prank on April Fool's Day when everyone of importance was summoned to the play-house for a command performance (for which, however, they were made to pay). The distinguished audience duly assembled and waited for the play to start, but nothing happened, and afraid to disobey a royal command, they waited a full two hours before the curtains parted—at which a jester appeared, bowed to the audience and informed them that they were a pack of fools. According to an English observer people looked uneasily at each other and began to sneak out, 'some ashamed of having been imposed on, and others grumbling for the loss of their money.' And Catherine and Peter laughed till they cried.

But if April began on a high note, it ended with disaster. On the afternoon of the 25th they were celebrating the wedding of the giant Nicholas Bourgeois to a giantess Peter had found for him when a messenger interrupted them. Suddenly, without warning, their little idol Petrushka had died.

At five the next morning, to the mournful boom of minute guns, the little coffin was taken on board a barge and borne downstream past floating icebergs to the Monastery of Alexander Nevski. When Peter returned from the funeral he went immediately to his room and locked the door behind him. Outside, Catherine could hear his cries, and sometimes a series of grim, despairing thuds as he beat his head against the wall.

Even when this first storm of grief subsided the door remained locked and Catherine's own sorrow gave way to anxiety about her husband. Time and again she begged him to come out or let her in. But there was no response. For three days Peter took no food and spoke to no one. Yet, when he emerged at last and Catherine ran up to him, he took her in his arms and said: 'We've afflicted ourselves enough. . . . We'll mourn no longer against God's will.' Next day they sailed to Catherinenhof.

In the weeks that followed Peter had several convulsive seizures but though he needed quiet he was as restless as ever, rarely spending more than two nights under one roof. They moved incessantly between St. Petersburg and their various country houses. One of them, Tsarskoye Selo, brought particular consolation. Catherine had found the site two years before and had a lodge built there as a surprise for Peter. The larger house in the Dutch style which he had commissioned was hardly begun yet, so they stayed in the lodge, prayed in the little wooden church close by and took quiet walks together in the surrounding woods. They emerged from mourning to celebrate Peter's forty-seventh birthday at the end of May, and soon afterwards he left to join the fleet.

By now the full significance of the loss of Petrushka was clear to Catherine. When she had lost other sons there had always been hope that she might bear more. But the prospect now seemed utterly remote. She had to take consolation in her three surviving daughters and be content to accept Alexei's son as heir apparent. In Peter's absence she kept up appearances as bravely as she could, but now more than ever she waited for news of him, fretted over reports that he was ill, and then, when he was better, worried about his sudden surge of hope that she might yet give birth to another boy, which she knew was impossible.

He seemed in a softer mood than usual. He reported on the progress of their gardens at Reval and sent her 'some flowers and . . . mint which you planted.' The dried flowers and sprigs of mint pressed between the pages of his letter touched her. So did his concluding words. 'Everything is merry enough here thank God, except that when I go into the summer house and you're not there, I feel so sad and lonely.'

She mirrored his sentiments. The summer gardens in Petersburg, she replied, looked 'better than last year . . . but whenever I go out I'm sorry I'm not walking with you. Thanks for the present, my darling. It's dear to me not because I planted it but because it comes from your fair hands.' He wrote back joking about his age again and enclosing a newspaper cutting about a Welsh couple who had been married 110 years. 'God grant', she replied, 'that in due time I shall truly be able to call you a dear old man, but for the moment I cannot admit that you are. . . . Pray God this is the last summer we shall have to spend apart, and that in future we shall always be together.'

She welcomed Peter home again towards the end of August 1719, and after visiting their country houses, they settled down to a comforting routine in St. Petersburg. He would rise at four and leave the house at six, returning for dinner at about mid-day. Sometimes he would bring guests back but usually they ate alone together. After dinner he would take a nap, his head resting in her lap, and then return to work. Supper he usually took alone since Catherine ate with her daughters in the evening, and they were almost always in bed by ten.

It was a pleasant, informal, almost frugal, existence. Peter seemed to like going about in scuffed shoes and in stockings Catherine had darned for him. Sometimes he was positively mean—he even measured the cheeses to make sure the servants were not pilfering. But Catherine was given everything she wanted, including a social life. In December 1719 Peter threw a splendid party to celebrate Elizabeth's tenth birthday, and besides the general run of weddings, christenings, funerals and launching parties, there was the second season of 'assemblies' to attend.

St. Petersburg assemblies were still a very rough school of manners. Peter stood by ready to thrash anyone who danced wearing a sword, who spat on the floor, picked his nose, or talked with his mouth full. Conversation positively creaked. Men and women tended to form separate groups—and even Peter joined the men-folk after a dance or two with Catherine. But she, who had felt nervous at the courts of Poland and of Prussia, enjoyed them greatly —probably because most people at them felt even less certain and socially assured than she did.

In March 1720 they went again to Peter's 'spa' near Olonets, where he found time for carpentry and introduced Catherine to spillikins and a sort of billiard game called 'Drucktafel'. But April in St. Petersburg, with the ice on the river breaking up, brought back memories of that awful time the previous spring when little Petrushka had died. Peter seemed unusually subdued; he was taking more medicine than usual, and taking Catherine to church more often, sometimes every day. Still, their parks and gardens were a joy to them, and with the shrubs and trees peeping into life again, and with the arrival of the long northern days, they took leisurely evening strolls down the oak and maple alleyways of the Summer Gardens. They visited Catherinenhof and Strelna too, and Alexander invited them to his handsome new palace at Oranien-baum which was a good deal larger and more sumptuous than any of their own. But their favourite resort was Peterhof.

From the windows of the Monplaisir pavilion there they could gaze right out to sea, or inland up the slope where workmen were finishing a series of cascades. Sometimes Peter would go out fishing and once, in August, they went hunting, though neither of them cared much for it. But the park there had a sylvan charm which was particularly agreeable. They arranged evening trysts and rustic picnics there. It was an ideal place to rediscover the romance of youth.

When autumn came they withdrew indoors again and winter fireworks and a new season of assemblies replaced the pleasures of the gardens. Time was passing quietly, but with Catherine ap-proaching forty and Peter nearing fifty they realized it was time to make provision for the future.

Alexei's son Peter was now the only surviving male Romanov heir, but though Peter chose tutors for him and saw that he was put on show on public occasions, he did not seem to want the child to reign. Indeed, by February 1721 he was already thinking of nominating his own successor—which would otherwise have been unnecessary. As for Catherine, she realized it would be foolish to alienate the boy who might yet be Tsar, but she resented the new Tsarevich almost as much as she had disliked his father. The boy was a living reminder of Petrushka who would have been the same age had he lived. Most probably she wanted the next Tsar to be the husband of one of her daughters, both of them as yet unmarried. But in any case it was time to think of suitable consorts for them, and in the spring she joined Peter in Riga in order to meet a suitor for their eldest daughter Anne.

His name was Karl Friedrich, Duke of Holstein-Gottorp, a nephew of Peter's enemy Charles XII of Sweden. He was twenty-one, short, immature and, as dukes went, very poor. If Peter had doubts about this thick-lipped, lisping princeling however, Catherine was charmed by him, and encouraged him to stay on in Russia. After all, a Duke was no mean catch for the daughter of a peasant girl born out of wedlock, even if her father was the Tsar. And Catherine was more sensitive about her humble origins just now than she had been for a long time. There had been discomforting reminders of it recently.

Not long before Peter had confronted her with a rough-looking stranger. She had taken one look at him and fainted. There was no doubt about it even after all these years. It was her brother Karl.

While she had been climbing to the top of the social ladder Karl Skavronski had been earning a living as a stable hand. Rumour of Catherine's success had reached him and he had reacted by attracting attention to himself, making apparently ridiculous claims to royal connections, and being insolent to important travellers. This had led to his arrest, and ultimately to the confrontation. Now his claims had been substantiated, but it was impossible to put such a shabby fellow on public display, so for the moment he was kept in discreet confinement while it was decided what to do with him. Then, one stormy day in Riga, Catherine came face to face with another memory from childhood.

A duty officer reported that a ragged peasant woman was at the gate demanding to see her. Catherine agreed to receive her—and within moments was convinced that the bedraggled figure that fell to her knees before her was her long-lost sister Christina. Becoming Tsarina and hob-nobbing with foreign kings and queens had not robbed Catherine of spontaneity or family feeling. Her immediate reaction was one of joy. But it was soon matched by embarrassment. It would be impossible, she realized, to keep a crowd of uncouth peasants round her. Not only would they damage her own vulnerable image and make life more difficult for Peter, but they could ruin her daughters' chances of marriage. So, for the moment, sister Christina was given money and entrusted to the care of the local Governor.

Catherine mentioned nothing of her rediscovered relatives, nor of the prospective suitor, the Duke of Holstein, when she wrote to her daughter, the thirteen-year-old Anne. She sent her a diamond ring, another for Elizabeth 'with a kiss from me', and a crate of oranges and lemons, telling Anne to give some of them to Alexander 'as if they came from yourself'.

Illiterate herself, Catherine followed her daughters' educational progress with constant wonder and mounting pride. Anne was learning French and German, dancing and etiquette, and could already read and write. She even wrote to Catherine in German. Yet her mother could only dictate her reply. 'My heart,' it ran, 'I can see that you have taken great pains in writing. . . . Continue to write as well in future so that your dear papa may praise you for your letters.'

When she and Peter returned to St. Petersburg they brought the Duke of Holstein with them. Little Anne's first impressions of him are not recorded, but one of the Duke's entourage described his impressions of the scene. It was a reception in the Summer Gardens. A buffet had been laid out in the gallery where Peter's favourite statue, a gilded Venus, stood. A group of men, Peter among them, were smoking and drinking nearby, while Catherine stood a little way off, near a fountain, attended by liveried pages, four gentlemen-in-waiting, a pair of turbanned blackamoors—and her daughters, the plump little Elizabeth and the taller, dark-haired Anne. They looked as 'lovely as angels' and the Duke promptly asked Catherine if he might walk with them. She graciously agreed, but the girls were shy and found almost nothing to say to him. After the reception came dinner and dancing and the whole affair impressed the visitors as being as 'fine and brilliant as at almost any court in Germany'.

Quite a different impression was gained at a royal ship-launching party given that summer. On that occasion heavy drinking drove all remembrance of the hard-learned rules of etiquette from the befuddled minds of those attending. Violent quarrels broke out in some parts of the room, while in others maudlin guests made sudden discoveries of eternal friendship and drank to it with tear-filled eyes. Grand Admiral Apraxin finished the evening 'weeping like a baby' while that veteran imbiber Alexander Menshikov 'fell to the floor dead drunk' and had to be carried home and revived with smelling salts.

And just as these orgies contrasted with the attempts to introduce a semblance of propriety to the newly-built mansions of St. Petersburg, the graceful perspectives and tumbling cascades at Peterhof which Peter and Catherine visited that summer provided an incongruously civilized setting for their coarse practical jokes. They had jets of water hidden under sunshades and garden seats, and derived much amusement as unsuspecting guests activated them and got soaked as a result. But September gave occasion for amusement of a more wholesome kind.

Peace with Sweden was concluded at last. The war which had brought Catherine to Russia nineteeen years before, and which had so long dominated Peter's life, was over—and on the most favourable of terms. Everything that Peter had hoped for was won, and more. And the celebrations were on an appropriately heroic scale. Trumpets blared and church-bells pealed; the entire court met on the river and sailed, to the accompaniment of music, to a great banquet at the Post House. There followed a riotous masquerade where guardsmen appeared as Roman soldiers, and notables as 'Turks' and 'Indians'; the giant Bourgeois and an immense companion both dressed as little children were led on reins by dwarfs made up to look like old men while Alexander's dancing-master showed off his prowess by prancing about disguised as a satyr.

The Duke of Holstein was also there, looking rather effete in the guise of a French vine-dresser, while Catherine in peasant costume looked serene among her blackamoors, and Peter, in velvet sailor suit and Dutch skipper's hat, urged the revellers on, beating a drum. The procession led by 'cardinals' riding in coaches drawn by bears, dogs and pigs, crossed the river on carnival floats, and when the riotous concourse reached its destination, everyone threw off his mask and danced round a specially erected pyramid.

And this was only one frantic climax in a week of celebrations. Day after day the exhausted revellers turned out for some party, masquerade or glittering display of fireworks. They had to. Absentees were fined for disobedience. And when the peace was ratified three weeks later, the celebrations began all over again. This was Peter's great moment of release, and everyone had to share it with him. He addressed crowds in the streets, had wine distributed among the people, proclaimed an amnesty, a remission of tax arrears, and promoted himself full admiral.

For once everybody seemed delighted, and when Chancellor Golovkin addressed him publicly as 'the Emperor Peter the Great' and praised him for his 'tireless labours' in bringing his people 'out of the darkness of ignorance' into the light, Catherine stood by looking radiant. Her black eyes glinted, her cheeks flushed with excitement and she joined enthusiastically in the cries of 'Vivat'. Peter's years of struggle had been magnificently justified, and she was happy for his sake.

But the junketings were to prove too much even for her strong constitution and early in October she took to her bed exhausted, footsore, overwhelmed. Peter returned to work and she spent a quieter winter during which she became better acquainted with the Duke of Holstein. It seemed to her that he had all the social graces. He was unfailingly solicitous, a gracious flatterer and an accomplished dancer. She felt that they looked particularly well together on the floor, especially since most of the other couples seemed to have so little sense of rhythm.

The Duke even brought his private band of twenty musicians to serenade her. The beguiling sounds of woodwind, viols and waldhorns brought Anne and Lizzie to their window too, and even Peter came out for a moment waving his arms about, trying to beat time. Sometimes Holstein was over-zealous, however. Once when

Peter proposed Catherine's health, he attempted to drain an immense bumper of wine in order to prove his esteem for her. It was fortunate that Peter, a shrewd judge of drinking men, should realize that the feat was quite beyond him, and interpose—though tactfully for once. Catherine liked young Holstein, and even Peter was warming to him. So when the Court went to Moscow that December, Holstein went as well.

Peter's purpose in visiting Moscow was only partly to celebrate the Swedish peace with the inhabitants of Russia's largest city. He also meant them to feel his power. Moscow had favoured Alexei, and now it favoured Alexei's son. The Emperor had come to force all Muscovites to swear loyalty to his successor—a successor he had not yet named who would displace the young Tsarevich. And since Moscow represented all the old Russian traditions that he hated, Peter was determined to transform it with the talismans of western culture he had introduced to St. Petersburg.

The Muscovites liked none of it. They resented the Tsar calling himself Emperor, his tampering with the succession, his insistence that 'assemblies' be held there, and his appointment of a 'Master of Police' to supervise the city's planning and keep order in the streets. Nor did they like Peter's decision that Moscow must celebrate the peace as St. Petersburg had done with allegorical parades and fireworks complete with Latin mottos which hardly anyone could understand.

Peter's triumphal entry into the city started from a village seven miles away. The party travelled on immense sledges, each bearing a float modelled as a ship and drawn by vast teams of sweating horses. A carved and gilded 'galley' came first, its oarsmen plying their blades into the snow; Peter followed in a 'frigate' complete with miniature cannon and three masts fully rigged with sails. Then came Catherine in a gilded gondola, a 'Neptune' on a giant sea shell, and thirty other 'wherries', 'pinnaces' and 'barges', their crews dressed in the styles of different nations.

The astonished Muscovites were sure such curious machines must be the inventions of the devil. But Peter and Catherine were oblivious of their opinions, and however resentful of Peter's demands and his breaks with tradition, Moscow was obedient to him in everything.

Catherine passed the winter there happily enough with a round of church services, dinners, dances and receptions. Peter found time to play billiards and spillikins with her and to take her sledging too. But a much greater adventure was soon in prospect—an expedition into Asia. The Shah of Persia had been deposed; his Caucasian subjects had attacked a caravan of Russian merchants; Peter had an excuse to step in and snatch control of the trade routes to the Orient. He pounced on the chance, and, dismissing the memory of the disastrous Pruth campaign from his mind, promised to take Catherine on the expedition.

They left Moscow in mid-May, and at first at least the journey had more in common with a pleasure tour than a military undertaking. They travelled by river at the head of a huge convoy on a magnificent, purpose-built galley. After eight days they arrived at Nijni-Novgorod on the Volga where they were sumptuously entertained by Stroganov, the wealthiest merchant in all Russia, and sailed on south between wooded banks to the city of Kazan, where Peter took her to see the ruins of an ancient Bulgar city. These fascinated her rather less, however, than the local Cheremis and Chuvash peoples. The women, she noted, plaited their hair and decorated it with red silk and little brass bells. They seemed charming, ignorant and easy-going—pagans who cared little even for their religion. They once admitted to a British visitor 'that in former times they had a book of religion; but as nobody could read it, a cow came and swallowed it.' It was curious that Catherine should have been so charmed by qualities that mirrored her own.

They cruised downstream to Simbirsk and then to Saratov where Ayuka, Khan of the fierce, nomadic Kalmyks, had pitched his tents. Catherine was there when the wrinkled oriental came aboard to promise his services to Peter. The old Khan was a cheerful man, the atmosphere was pleasant, and when Catherine became curious to see his wife an indulgent Peter at once arranged it. The Khan departed and duly returned with a retinue of mounted warriors, followed by his consort and their children in a curious 'wheel-machine'.

The lady, Catherine noted, was about twenty years younger than her husband; she wore fine Persian brocades and a sable-edged bonnet, and though conversation was limited, Catherine was intrigued to see the Khan's wife so curious about the repeating watch, set in diamonds, which she gave her as a present.

On they sailed towards the southern warmth, Catherine lounging under an awning under the poop like some latter-day Cleopatra. They drifted past banks of wild asparagus, past islands which once had been the haunt of Cossack river pirates, and at last they came to Astrakhan, Russia's centre for the eastern trade, and beyond it, the great blue Caspian Sea. With Peter busy with last-minute arrangements for the expedition Catherine continued her ethnographical investigations by visiting the local vineyards and the market, the Armenian quarter and the *ghat* where members of the local Indian community burned their dead. These were experiences she had not dreamt of as an innocent serving girl twenty years before. And there were more in store for her.

On 18 July 1722 the fleet put out to sea. They anchored near the fort of Terka, the troops disembarked, and the long march south began. It was August now, and stiflingly hot—so hot that Catherine was advised to cut off all her hair and wear a tight fur cap to protect her from the sun. But while she had the protection of a carriage, the soldiers outside suffered torments.

Fifteen miles a day was heroic progress for them. Clouds of dust were churned up from the hardened tracks, and the sun was terrible. One night a sudden storm hit the camp, tearing tents down with its force, and then the expedition lost many of its horses after they had grazed on toxic weeds. Peter drove himself as hard as he drove his men, but at last Catherine persuaded him to call a halt at noon each day and take a short rest in her coach, while his soldiers also sought some rest and shade. Nevertheless, everyone was tired out when on 12 August they camped near the flat-roofed village at the gateway into Daghestan.

Daghestan was the mountainous home of fierce and hostile Muslim warriors. Groups of them had already been sighted perched high up on the mountain-sides, and many more were sharpening their sabres in expectation of the Russians. Peter tried negotiating with the local lowland chieftains. Diplomatic courtesies were observed and reciprocated, and Catherine also became involved when members of the village chief's harem called upon her.

The grapes they brought were quickly put aside in case they had

been poisoned but the ladies themselves were made extremely welcome. The local women were known to be 'incomparably beautiful
both in feature and shape' and they aroused great interest in the
Russian camp, the more so since their husbands took such pains to
keep them out of sight of intruding infidels. So Catherine earned a
good deal of popularity by ordering officers who wished to see these
beauties to be admitted to her tent. Immediately a long queue
formed, and night had fallen before every applicant had had his
glimpse and the ladies had departed, having satisfied Catherine
that they really were impressed with the freedoms enjoyed by
western women.

The army marched on, and soon saw action. Twelve thousand
shaggy warriors had grouped menacingly on the mountain flank.
But in a sharp engagement the Russians drove them off, and when
the expedition reached Derbent the governor offered up the keys of
the citadel without a fight. But the mountain tribesmen were still
watching the invaders.

Next day Catherine inspected the town and climbed up to the
battlements of its lofty citadel. From here she had a splendid view
out to sea, and inland to the mountains. Snow-capped Shah-dag,
tallest peak in all the eastern Caucasus, was only thirty miles away,
and Catherine, a child of the northern plains, could only marvel at
the sight—the more so since she was erroneously informed that she
was looking at Mount Ararat itself.

Peter had intended to march south beyond Baku, but the supply
convoy which was due did not appear, and early in September, he
decided to turn back, having achieved only a very moderate success,
albeit with some ease. The retreat went harder than the outward
march. Food was short now and so was drinking water, and though
the days were still hot the nights were turning frosty. More men were
falling sick and the tribesmen followed them all the way, swooping
down like vultures from the mountainsides to carry off the stragglers
and the weak. Peter himself suffered several sharp attacks of illness,
and was drinking more than was good for him, so Catherine was
intensely relieved when, early in October, they arrived in Astrakhan.

Back in Moscow Peter was forced to take to his bed. Trouble in the
urinary tract was diagnosed, and though the doctors' palliatives
soon had him on his feet again, the affliction was to return and with

increasing intensity. The pain made his temper worse, but he still worked like a demon—almost as if racing against time, desperately trying to complete his work before death should overtake him.

His renewed campaign against corruption brought fresh troubles on the head of Alexander Menshikov who was constitutionally incapable of financial honesty. As Peter's right-hand man he had more opportunity than most, and when he dipped his hands into state coffers, he dug them deep. Peter gave him a thrashing with a knout, and threatened him with death. Somehow Catherine managed to save her erstwhile protector, but others were less fortunate. The diplomatist Shafirov was banished in disgrace; the chief fiscal, Nesterov, went to the gallows.

Peter's furious rate of work and recurring bouts of pain emphasized his melancholic streak. His temper became more choleric, his black moods blacker. Only Catherine seemed to be spared the full force of his rages and, as his dependence on her became more widely recognized, she was drawn unwillingly into the political arena. Relatives of threatened men came begging her to intercede; petitioners of all kinds came knocking at her door, and since in Russia personalities were politics she came to exercise influence and therefore a certain power—though she always used it in what she imagined to be Peter's interests.

Even when his illness subsided she found him difficult to manage. Sometime his enthusiasms broke all bounds. On New Year's Day 1723, he called on the Dowager Praskovya who was confined to bed with gout, confident of his skills in 'doctoring' and determined to 'cure' her. Catherine remembered how he had hastened the death of a Dutch merchant's wife once by tapping her for dropsy (though he had insisted that it was a hopeless case anyway). Somehow she managed to stop him this time, but only with the greatest difficulty.

Peter was still in an ebullient mood at the Butter Week Carnival that year, at which Catherine appeared in the guise of an Amazon. On the last day she and Peter led a crowd of revellers out on sledges to see a wooden palace, built when he was a boy, burned down in a great display of fireworks. Peter rushed about setting light to fuses, and since it was bitterly cold insisted that everyone drink a bumper of Hungarian wine, which proved altogether too much for many of the ladies present. Before long, drunken masqueraders were staggering and falling about in the snow, acrid smoke billowing around them, while hissing Catherine wheels and flaring rockets lit up the night sky as brightly as a summer's day. It was all too hectic and exhausting. Catherine was glad when, next day, they left for St. Petersburg.

She had been twenty years in Russia and had seen many cities in Europe and the east. But she felt happiest in St. Petersburg, Peter's own city, which she had seen growing out of the desolate marshes over the years. The shanties were still there in plenty, but there were handsome buildings too now, their orange-yellow stucco brightly reflecting the spring light; there were their miraculous gardens, and a delightful new orangery at the new Winter Palace.

Catherine had passed her fortieth birthday and was content with quieter pleasures such as Petersburg—and food—afforded. She was growing stout. Since she had known hunger as a child, food had always played an important part in her life—and now more than ever. Her figure now betrayed the fact; so did her food bill. In the spring and early summer of that year alone her kitchens disposed of a whole ton of beef besides quantities of mutton, lamb and veal, salmon, sturgeon, carp and herrings, and chickens and game-birds by the score. The month of August alone saw the consumption of forty chickens, a hundred eggs and twenty pounds of butter; cabbages, cucumbers and water-melons, leeks and radishes for the sour sauces Peter liked, and a hundred other items —all meticulously noted down and costed by her principal gentleman-in-waiting William Mons and their chef Hans-Jurgan Patkan.

There were healthier, outdoor occupations as well. That year at Peterhof she and Peter fished for carp in the ponds by the Marly pavilion and picnicked with the children. That summer, too, he threw a splendid party to mark the arrival from Moscow of his first boat—a derelict old English yacht, newly refurbished and repaired. Almost the entire Russian fleet was present to receive it as, steered by Peter and rowed by half-a-dozen Admirals, it moved down-stream to the flagship where Catherine 'and all her court, very finely dressed' stood waiting.

There followed a feast lasting ten hours. Everyone was there:

the gouty Praskovya, all sly smiles as ever, Anne and Lizzie who soon lost all decorum and began rushing about draining the wine from abandoned glasses—and the young Holstein, recently created a Rear Admiral, who was obviously being groomed for greater things.

That autumn when the Dowager Praskovya died experienced Kremlinologists of the day took special note of the fact that no orb or sceptre had been placed beside the coffin as was usual when a Tsar's wife died. From this they concluded that Peter did not intend Praskovya's daughters to succeed. Indeed, opinion was growing that he was thinking of marrying his eldest daughter Anne to the Duke of Holstein and giving power to him.

So the proclamation read out in the streets of St. Petersburg on 15 November 1723 took most observers by surprise. It listed Catherine's virtues, praised 'her valour and heroism' and emphasized her 'great self-sacrifice' when she 'shared all the trials and discomforts of a soldier's life', notably on the Pruth campaign. The Emperor's 'beloved Wife', it continued, was such 'a great support' to him that 'by the authority given to Us by God, We have decided to reward these services of Our Consort, by crowning her with the Imperial Crown.'

People sucked their breath in at the news. A woman, a foreigner, a peasant, a common courtesan, was to be made Empress in her own right, to rule at Peter's side! It was unheard of.

Peter might try to justify his decision by listing precedents going back to ancient times, but there was hardly a Russian who had ever heard of Justinian and Heracles. And though shrill propaganda to the effect that Catherine had saved the army and the Tsar's life in the Turkish war gained some credence in the West where it was trumpeted by Fontenelle in Paris and by various English hacks in London, in Russia it cut very little ice, and only Peter's threats of death and ruin for anyone who uttered 'foolish and drunken rumours' about Catherine, her origins or her uncouth relatives, who were still kept in comfortable confinement out of sight, seemed to be of much effect.

Catherine's coronation was scheduled for the spring and Alexander

Menshikov and Count Peter Tolstoi were sent to Moscow to take charge of the arrangements. The preparations were on an extravagant scale. A purple mantle sewn with golden eagles costing four thousand roubles was ordered from France, and four pounds of precious stones were built into a special crown. Experts in protocol drafted orders of service, seating and procession plans, and a new, exclusive company of Life Guards, captained by the Emperor himself, was raised to honour Catherine on the day.

Meanwhile the great trek from St. Petersburg began. Long trains of sleds bearing courtiers and diplomatists followed the road south, and Moscow bustled as noblemen and merchants, tradesmen and servants poured in from all quarters of the empire. Accommodation became almost impossible to find and prices rocketed sky high. Excitement and anticipation grew; and as was to be expected it was the womenfolk who were the most excited, for this was to be above all a feminist occasion, an unprecedented opportunity, as a contemporary wrote, for 'the female sex . . . to adorn themselves in fashionable clothes and toilettes, enhancing the beauty of their faces and displaying their good figures.'

Unfortunately the services available in Moscow were not equal to this new demand. There was only one specialist hairdresser, for instance, and those ladies who did not have a competent coiffeuse among their attendants had to compete for this man's services. As a result many of them had to have their hair arranged days before the ceremony and sit up night after night for fear their crowning glory might be disarranged in bed. Dressmakers did an unprecedented amount of business. Everybody suddenly wanted to cut a dash, to outdo one another with richer clothes, with more gold braid, more embroidery, and more jewels sewn on them.

Peter himself spared no cost to make this a most glittering occasion, though he did try—and fail—to burden the foreign merchant colony with the cost of mounting the new Life Guards. Money was freely disbursed on food, clothes, jewels and coaches, on new regalia and the renovation of palaces. Peter even consented to wear a fine blue coat for the occasion—a coat heavily embroidered with silver braid by Catherine herself.

She arrived in Moscow on 27 March six weeks before the ceremony—in good time for her clothes to be fitted and to rehearse and memorize her part in the proceedings—for she knew that many in the audience would be waiting eagerly for any mistake or lapse in bearing.

Days before the ordeal was due unit after army unit marched into Moscow, and by the time a signal gun announced the dawning of the long-awaited day, eight infantry battalions and four companies of grenadiers were already in place along the streets. Ushers took up their places in the Uspenski Cathedral, its usually gloomy interior suddenly ablaze with light; at nine the clergy assembled, and within half an hour the guests were in their places.

The procession was magnificent—the new Horse Guards resplendent in coats of green, Catherine's pages, the Deputy Marshal carrying a mace, and, two by two, the provincial deputies and the generals. A pair of solemn heralds in gold and crimson proclaimed the climax of the grand parade—the Grand Marshal, two Ministers bearing the gold and ermine mantle, Prince Dolgoruki with the glittering orb, Count Pushkin with the sceptre, Count Bruce with the crown. Peter followed, his train held up by Alexander Menshikov and behind them followed Catherine leaning heavily on Holstein's arm, her train borne by the Grand Admiral and the Chancellor, and followed by the most prominent ladies of the land.

As church bells pealed and drums and trumpets sounded, Catherine was guided into the Cathedral and led up the steps of a great proscenium where, under a lofty gold and velvet canopy, stood two ancient, jewel-encrusted thrones.

Her small, clear voice with its slightly foreign accent rang out over the hush of the assembled audience, reciting the Creed. Then she knelt while the Archbishop intoned the benediction. 'Grant her long life; put the sceptre of salvation into her hands, seat her upon the throne of justice; defend her with the armour of the Holy Ghost; make her arm strong. . . .' They helped her to rise, and Peter arranged the imperial mantle round her shoulders. Then they both knelt down, and Peter placed the crown upon her head.

Tears poured down her cheeks and suddenly overwhelmed by the thought of how much she owed to Peter, she lost all sense of decorum, grasped his hands and tried to smother them in kisses. Embarrassed by her sudden loss of dignity at the very climax of this of all occasions, Peter restrained her, irritably, even roughly, and the ceremony proceeded.

Mass was sung and a bare-headed Catherine was led into the sanctuary to be anointed with holy oil. Then came the lesson and a seemingly endless sermon from the Archbishop. Oppressed by the heat and the heavy weight of her regalia, Catherine had more than once to remove her crown and pass it to Cabinet Secretary Makarov who was standing by her. But at last the ordeal was over and the Empress walked slowly to the north door and out into the warm spring air.

A tumult of shouts and bells and gunfire rose up around her as she moved in procession to the Cathedral of Michael the Archangel, then to the Monastery of the Ascension. And as she went attendants scattered handfuls of coins into the crowds on either side. At last she arrived at the foot of the Red Staircase again, where Holstein was waiting to lead her up into the Hall of the Facets for the banquet.

She took her place on the dais next to Peter. Below her, the grandees and their ladies took their places at separate tables glittering with gold and silverware. The strains of music drifted down from a gallery as the dishes that made up the first course were handed up along a line of kneeling dignitaries to Grand Admiral Apraxin who waited on them.

Only the thickness of a wall separated this dignified assembly from the common people on the square outside. Yet the mob was also given cause to celebrate. Two huge oxen stuffed with game and poultry were roasted for them, and from time to time more propitiary coins were scattered over them from the safety of the palace windows.

Long lines of notables queued up to kiss the Empress's hand; fireworks lit up the Moscow night; there were balls, receptions, masquerades. 'Universal joy', wrote one observer, 'displayed itself in every form.' And yet the joy was not entirely unconfined. Merchants grumbled at the extra taxes levied on them to pay for the show; the expected general amnesty did not materialize; people muttered darkly about the absence of the little Prince Peter Alexeyevich.

The hacks employed by Peter churned out their praises of

Catherine's piety, her 'Endowments of Mind', her 'transcendent Virtues', her 'consummate Understanding'. They compared her to Judith and to Deborah, to Semiramis and the Amazons, to Anne of Austria, Queen Christina of Sweden and Elizabeth of England. According to them she was not merely an Empress but 'an Angel in human Form'. Yet behind the glittering regalia, Catherine still looked for all the world like Peter's mistress—a short, corpulent woman with large feet and blackened hair.

And though she was Empress now she was so in name only. She exercised no more power than she had done before, and she could do nothing to lessen the strain on Peter. He looked a sick man and often seemed to be in pain, and she was not well either. Soon after her coronation she collapsed suddenly from exhaustion. The doctors bled her as usual, but this only made her weaker, and her condition was soon thought to be serious enough for official prayers to be said for her recovery. She rallied, but at the end of May had a relapse, and Peter, who had gone away on business, returned straightway to Moscow. By the time he reached her, however, she seemed a little better and he went away again. But he sent regular letters to his 'Little Catherine' reporting the progress of their gardens. 'I found everything growing in beauty like a child', he wrote, 'but when I go into the palace I want to run right out again. Everything's so empty without you. . . .' He got Anne and Elizabeth to sign his letters too. 'God grant you in joy to meet us in Petersburg and quickly too', he wrote, and at last, in June, she was well enough to travel. Peter sent a boat to meet her loaded with sustaining Hungarian wine, oranges and lemons, beer and salted cucumbers, and greeted her with a deafening salute of guns.

The summer air of St. Petersburg seemed to revive her, and she was soon enjoying the round of launching parties, weddings and visits to their country homes nearby. But Peter's condition still gave cause for concern. He had recently undergone a bladder operation performed by Dr. Bidlo and the English surgeon Mr. Horn. But though the operation relieved the pain, it was only partially successful. Perhaps this is why their life took on a more hectic pace now. It was as if they shared some grim presentiment, that they must be as merry as possible before the inevitable night drew in.

Yet when darkness came, it was due to a quite unexpected storm that blew up, threatening to send Catherine's world crashing about her ears in ruins. The cause was not Peter's health, but a scandal in her own entourage.

Her court had become larger and ever more luxurious, especially since her coronation. Gone were the days when she had one or two attendants, and a larger suite only to impress some foreigners or to keep her company when Peter was away. She had dozens of pages, grooms and lackeys in attendance now, befeathered negro boys, handsome gentlemen-in-waiting—and to supervise them all her fair-haired chamberlain, William Mons, the brother of Peter's erstwhile mistress Anna Mons who had died some time before.

In plumed cap, velvet suit and silver cummerbund, William cut the most elegant of figures. He was also an accomplished writer of sentimental verse, a charming hand-kisser, and extremely discreet. Since he controlled access to Catherine and since she had the ear of the Emperor, it was inevitable that a great many presents should come William's way. Most of them were small—a crate of tea or coffee, a fine coat, a dog, a bag of coins, a golden snuff-box. But some paid rather more for William's friendship. Prince Alexei Dolgoruki gave him a coach with two teams of horses, and no less a personage than the Princess Praskovya, the Dowager's youngest daughter, gave him an entire estate with the peasants to go with it.

As William became richer, he had become even more charming and even better dressed. His wardrobe was filled with grey, gold and coffee-coloured suits, elegant gloves and dozens of silk shirts. And since his name no longer seemed appropriate to his life-style, he had begun to sign himself not simply as 'Mons', but as 'de Monse' or, even better, 'de la Mons'.

It was natural that a man in his position should attract jealousy and gossip, but the gossip was not confined to his unofficial exercise of patronage. Evil tongues went so far as to suggest that Catherine had taken him as her lover.

An unsigned letter came to light which seemed to support this speculation. 'I am Your Grace's slave', it ran, 'and true only to you in this world—only to you, ruler of my heart. And I give you my heart for as long as I remain alive. Accept my unworthy heart with your white hands. . . .' But though the repetitious sentimentality of the style indicated William, the document proved no connection with Catherine. Indeed, since he always had access to her he had no need to write to her at all. Nevertheless the gossip continued and Villebois, one of Peter's *aides-de-camp*, went so far as to assert that Catherine's 'passion' for William was so 'violent that everyone perceived it'. Some such report presumably reached Peter.

One Sunday evening early in November, Peter came across Catherine and William in the gardens and bade him withdraw. William had barely had time to reach his apartment, undress and light a pipe, when the secret police knocked on his door.

William's arrest marked the beginning of a full-scale palace purge. His sister, Matrena Balk, her sons, and Peter's favourite jester, Balakirev, were also arrested. The interrogations and seizures established evidence of peculation, and as the news leaked out Petersburg buzzed with rumours that Catherine was also involved, and heading for a fall.

Peter's justice was quick. Matrena was sentenced to be knouted and exiled; her sons were ordered to the Persian front and her husband permitted to remarry. William was condemned to death.

When Catherine interceded for them, Peter told her coldly not to interfere, and he remained grim and unapproachable, even to his daughters. Whenever Catherine caught his eye it seemed to glare with anger and with pain. He would play irritably with a hunting knife and pace up and down like a tiger in a cage. Once, Catherine found him alone staring morosely out of the window and tried to intercede for Mons again. But Peter only began to beat his fists against the window panes, and when she persisted, he strode out, slamming the door so hard behind him that the whole room shook for several moments afterwards.

At ten the next morning William Mons was taken from the fortress of Saints Peter and Paul to the scaffold on Trinity Square. He said his farewells, and having left his gold watch and the portrait of herself that Catherine had given him to his friends, he took off his coat and placed his elegant head upon the block.

He had spent his last hours composing verse in German:

'It is love which brings about my downfall
'There is a fire burns in my breast

'From which I know that I must die.
'I know the reason for my downfall:
'That I have loved
'Where I should only honour.'

Even though someone other than Catherine—probably one of her daughters—seems to have been the object of his affections, there were plenty of intriguers about the court anxious to discredit the Empress, and Peter appears to have suspected the worst. He certainly set out to test her. The day after the execution he took her in a closed carriage to show her William's remains, but though she came through the ordeal without betraying great emotion, Peter was not satisfied. Soon after their return, he brandished a Venetian vase at her. 'Do you see this?' he asked. 'It's made from the simplest materials. Artistry has made it fit to decorate a palace, but I can return it to its former valueless condition'—and he smashed the vase onto the floor.

It was an oblique way of telling her that he had taken her from the gutter and could quite easily return her to it. 'Of course you can', she answered calmly, 'but do you think that you made the palace any more beautiful by breaking that vase?'

Their children finally brought about a reconciliation. Anne was sixteen years old now and had reached marriageable age. Her suitor, the Duke of Holstein, had been patient for three years now and he could not be delayed much longer. Catherine had always liked him, and since Anne also seemed to be fond of him Peter overcame his reservations and consented to the match.

The betrothal took place at the Winter Palace on Catherine's name day, 23 November. Peter exchanged their rings, kissed them both and wished them a long life; the Archbishop of Novgorod then pronounced the blessing.

At the ball which followed Catherine partnered Holstein in a polonaise, and though Peter refused to dance he seemed to be in better humour—he even teased his prospective son-in-law about his preferring Moselle to good strong Hungarian. The fireworks that night threw up a picture of Venus in a chariot drawn by a swan. The motto, 'Happy Concord', seemed doubly appropriate.

Catherine's satisfaction was obvious to everyone. But it was equally obvious that Peter, though cheerful enough, was very seriously ill. Some weeks before he had dived into an icy sea in the course of rescuing the crew of a grounded ship, since when all his old symptoms had returned. Yet he insisted on dragging himself out to the ceremony of the Blessing of the Waters on 6 January and during the next ten days he was seen at a wedding and at 'assemblies' given by Count Tolstoi and Admiral Cruys. Then, on the night of the 16th, he suffered a fierce attack of strangury.

Cries of pain echoed through the palace and when a distraught Catherine quizzed the doctors about his condition, they only sighed and shrugged their shoulders. The apothecary Lazariti had concocted a new medicine, but it did no good, and on the night of the 20th there came another attack and on the next night an even worse one, accompanied by convulsions. At this the doctors decided to operate again. They managed to draw off a quantity of fluid and the pain and the fever seemed to decrease. By the 24th Peter seemed to be out of danger and on the Tuesday morning he asked for something to eat. Catherine sighed with relief. . . . But it was a false dawn. Two days later the pain, the fever and the convulsions all returned. Gangrene had set in.

By now, Catherine, who hardly left his bedside, realized that he was dying. So did Peter. He ordered an amnesty and then, though she begged him to rest, he sent for Anne and asked her to take down his will. 'Give everything', he began—but then his words became incomprehensible. That afternoon he fell into a coma and priests came to administer the last rites.

Suddenly, Catherine understood the vulnerability of her position. Peter had made no will, and the supporters of the young Prince Alexeyevich must already be preparing to take over. If they succeeded, she and her daughters would be in danger. They might even be lynched. In desperation she turned to Alexander Menshikov. He promised to do all he could; and she returned to Peter's bedside. For a day and a half she maintained her vigil. Then, at 5.15 on the morning of 28 January 1725 the end came. She closed his eyes and sobbed her last farewell: 'O Lord, open thy Paradise to this blessed soul.'

Meanwhile the grandees had assembled in the palace and the ante-
rooms buzzed with talk of the succession. Some argued for Catherine
on the grounds that she had been crowned Empress; others argued
against her on the grounds that she was not a Romanov. A few
spoke for her eldest daughter Anne—others said no, that she was
illegitimate; and many supported the eight-year-old Prince Peter
even though that would involve a regency.

But private rather than the public interest dictated the position
each man took. Menshikov, Tolstoi and the other 'new men' who
had been involved in the trial and death of the Tsarevich Alexei
did not fancy their chances of survival if the Tsarevich's son were to
become Emperor. Those against Catherine wanted the scalps, and
the jobs, of upstarts like Tolstoi, Menshikov or for that matter
Bishop Theophanes of Pskov. In all, a majority of Senators as well
as the old aristocrats were for Prince Peter. So was Prince Repnin,
Head of the College of War. As the Prussian Minister reported,
Catherine seemed to have 'no chance at all'.

Such was the feeling when, shortly before dawn, an orderly came
up to General Buturlin who was standing by a window in the Winter
Palace and whispered something into his ear. The General promptly
opened the window and shouted a command. A sudden roll of
drums was heard, and an uneasy hush descended on the room.
Startled grandees rushed to the windows and peered out into the
gloom. They could make out long ranks of Guardsmen drawn up
outside.

'Who dared to arrange this without my knowledge?' Prince
Repnin demanded. 'I did, your Excellency', replied General Buturlin
stiffly, 'on the orders of Her Imperial Majesty, the Sovereign
Empress Catherine, to whom we both owe absolute obedience.'

Hours before, some of Catherine's supporters mobilized by
Alexander Menshikov had visited the barracks. They had warned
the officers of the dangers of civil war if the question of the succession was not resolved quickly, and reminded the men of Catherine's
many kindnesses to them. But their promises of increased pay
backed up with some hard cash on account was the decisive factor,
and having been whipped up to the required degree of enthusiasm
for Catherine the troops were marched out to surround the Winter
Palace.

Inside, Prince Dmitri Golitsyn, one of Prince Peter's supporters, was making a last-ditch plea for a formal conference to decide the issue. But a now confident Alexander Menshikov countered him immediately. Secretary Makarov, he said, could confirm that the late Emperor had made his intentions perfectly clear in having Catherine crowned; the Bishop of Pskov had actually heard the late Emperor say that he wanted Catherine to succeed. But the troops outside were the strongest argument of all.

Suddenly, the doors were flung open and Catherine entered, red-eyed, and leaning heavily on Holstein's arm. Apparently unaware of what had passed, she began to plead with the grandees to protect her and her children, but Grand Admiral Apraxin interrupted her by falling on his knees and begging her to assume power. 'Long live our beloved Empress!'—the cry was taken up by Catherine's supporters in the hall and by the troops outside. Recognizing the inevitable, Prince Golitsyn joined in, so did the cautious Chancellor Golovkin—and finally even Prince Repnin himself.

Within hours, everyone of importance had sworn allegiance, and couriers were galloping out to Moscow and the provincial capitals with copies of the proclamation declaring 'the most Magnanimous and August Lady Catherine Alexeyevna Sovereign of all the Russian Empire'.

Her first public act was to address the Guards. Her tone was conciliatory. She promised to take good care of Prince Peter, and hinted that he would succeed her; she said she would be 'a mother to her country' and the troops took up the theme, breaking ranks and crowding round her. 'Our father is dead', they shouted, 'but our mother still lives.'

Back in the palace, Peter's body had been embalmed and placed upon a catafalque in the great hall. In the days that followed Catherine sat long hours there as her subjects filed by to pay their last respects. At other times she would wander distractedly about the Palace gazing at the portraits of her husband, visiting rooms she used to share with him, and the workshop with all the tools laid out which he would never use again.

She seemed vague and confused when Ministers called, and when documents had to be issued, she sat passively while Secretary

Makarov guided her limp hand over them to form the necessary signatures. The only interest she displayed concerned the funeral arrangements and Peter's memorial. She had the catafalque hung with Gobelin tapestries which he had brought back from his visit to France, and engaged Italian sculptors to design a mausoleum.

She was just beginning to control her grief when her youngest daughter, Natalia, fell ill and died. So a smaller coffin joined Peter's under the golden canopy, and Catherine was cast back into despondency. Then on 8 March she followed both coffins to the Cathedral of Saints Peter and Paul for the funeral, and listened, obviously moved, to Bishop Theophanes of Pskov who delivered the funeral oration. His text was Genesis xli, his theme Joseph, the provident governor of Egypt. Peter, he said, had also 'increased his country's stores'; he had been 'a Joseph who had brought you out of darkness into light, out of ignorance into knowledge, out of contempt into glory. . . .' Earth was sprinkled on the body, the lid fixed on the coffin and the imperial mantle draped over it. Then the congregation departed.

Returning to the palace, Catherine found herself overwhelmed with problems of government. Suddenly, everything seemed to depend on her. Her anterooms were crowded with petitioners; her counsellors pressed contradictory advice upon her; decisions were constantly demanded of her. And she had no idea what to do. She was totally bewildered, quite lost without Peter.

In her confusion she clung to the one strong man she trusted absolutely, the man who had managed her introduction to Peter so many years before, the man who had procured her accession to the throne—Alexander Menshikov. And Alexander did not fail her. After all, in protecting her he was protecting himself.

Having seen Catherine installed in power his first concern was to keep her there. He knew very well that the country as a whole would not readily accept her. No woman had ruled Russia as Empress before. Moscow was thought to want Prince Peter, and so was Prince Michael Golitsyn who had command of 60,000 troops in the Ukraine. But Alexander handled matters deftly. He sent a reliable general to root out oppositionists in Moscow and recalled Golitsyn without informing him of Peter's death. Even so, the regime was still vulnerable, and various conciliatory measures were taken to conjure up support among the people. Petitioners were favourably received; amnesties were offered to political prisoners on promises of loyalty; and though real power was now exercised by Alexander Menshikov and to a lesser extent by Tolstoi and Paul Yagujinski, another of the 'new men', the cautious Golovkin, was retained as Chancellor, the elderly Apraxin as the naval chief, and even Prince Repnin as Minister for War so as to give the regime an impression of continuity.

Despite this, foreign observers remained unconvinced of Russia's stability under Catherine, and some countries were quick to try and exploit the situation. John Deane, the British consul-general, was discovered hatching plots on behalf of the British secret service and was promptly expelled; and the King of Sweden was only restrained by internal difficulties from invading Russia.

Russia under Catherine seemed isolated. Frederick William of Prussia was the only foreign sovereign to order his court into mourning on Peter's death, and the usual diplomatic notes congratulating a new monarch on accession were very slow to arrive.

Meanwhile, Catherine had continued in mourning, refusing to interrupt it even for the wedding of her daughter, Anne, to the Duke of Holstein which took place that May. While four hundred guests roistered in the great hall, the Empress dined alone, and when she finally emerged that evening, she went out to the meadow to review the Guards. Only after a solitary supper did she call on the wedding party to drink a cup of wine with the bride and groom. Next day she went to the meadow again to present a bull with gilded horns to each of the four regiments drawn up there and to hand each man a drink.

The priority she gave to entertaining her soldiers reflected no sudden dissatisfaction with young Holstein; indeed she was observed to 'love him with all the passion of a mother wanting her family's happiness'. But she knew how essential it was to keep the army loyal to her, and to show that her family's celebrations were theirs too. It was for similar, political, reasons that she showed herself to be a devout Christian by her frequent attendances at church; the devoted follower of the late Emperor by attending launchings, and as the loving guardian of Prince Peter, the last male Romanov, by taking him with her to public functions, and smiling benevolently as he rode his little pony round the Summer Gardens attended by his dwarf.

Now that summer had come, Catherine found new consolation in her gardens and in the aviary newly stocked with exotic songbirds by its keeper Simon Staal. She began to take an interest in her new Summer Palace too, ordering extra balconies to be constructed outside the upper windows. She found it much more difficult to take political decisions though.

Ministers called frequently, the Senate reported every Friday, and there were audiences to give to foreign visitors. But though she tried to be a figurehead only, leaving administration to others, she was drawn more and more into politics—simply because her Ministers were always quarrelling among themselves.

Already, Paul Yagujinski had had a blazing row with Alexander. They told her he had gone to the Cathedral afterwards, mounted Peter's catafalque, raised his arms histrionically towards the heavens, and prayed that the Emperor might 'rise from his coffin and see how his servants were insulted.' Somehow Catherine had managed to patch their quarrel up. But she was to need all her resources of tact to keep her Ministers from each others' throats in the months to come.

On 29 June a memorial service was held at which Theophanes, now promoted to the Archbishopric of Novgorod, delivered another eulogy of Peter. 'Your unbearable affliction is known to us all'— the stentorian voice echoed down from the wooden rafters of the church as if it came from God Himself—'Sons of Russia, console your Mother in truth and in obedience. Console yourselves—for in your Sovereign you can see certain proof of Peter's spirit.' The preacher was trying to be encouraging, but, alas, she felt that she had none of Peter's spirit. 'Console her Majesty, the Autocrat, and her most dear offspring', the Archbishop ranted on. 'Wipe away their ceaseless tears. Sweeten their heart's grief . . . give consolation to us all.' Yet the long sermon seemed to purge her of her grief. That afternoon she feasted in the garden with the princesses and went to see an elephant the Shah of Persia had sent her as a present.

In the following weeks she turned more to business, but Peter's vision—his abstract sense of duty to the state—was quite beyond her understanding. She found it impossible to distinguish between the individual and the public good; nor was she an autocrat confident of judgement. She needed guidance—but whose guidance? the fiery Paul Yagujinski's whom Peter had called an honest man, or Alexander's, their friend for twenty years and more? Almost every act became an issue in which it was impossible to separate the merits of the arguments put before her from the obvious eagerness of their proponents to discredit one another. She tried to hold a balance between the contending Ministers, following one voice, then another. Yet gradually a guiding policy did emerge—a policy of reducing the burdens on the people.

A memorandum Catherine received in 1726 gave the situation in a nutshell. Commerce was in decline, the money system was disorganized, the administration of justice was breaking down. Above all, the poll-tax which provided over half the income of the exchequer was hated by the people. 'Not only are the peasants ... in great poverty', the report read, but 'they are being driven close to final ruin by the high level of taxation.' The rate had been reduced, but many peasants were still too poor to pay it. More time was given, part payment was allowed in fodder or in food: but the tax still sat too heavily upon the people. So government expenditure was slashed. Recruitment for the army was reduced by nearly a quarter, the ship-building programme was cut back, and much of the existing fleet was allowed to fall into a state of disrepair.

Even so, many of Peter's projects were continued with her blessing. Captain Bering sailed out to plot the north-east passage between Asia and America, and the new Academy of Sciences went forward as Peter had planned. One rainy August afternoon that year, Catherine received its members—German scholars for the most part—and heard one of them declaim a learned oration of which she understood barely a word.

She allowed herself to be put on public display, and she enjoyed being surrounded with all the pomp and panoply of power, but she left more and more decisions to her Ministers, above all to Alexander Menshikov, and concentrated on private rather than on state affairs.

Her particular concern was for her family. She was anxious to gather her relatives to her and in February 1726 a Sergeant of the

Guards was sent to Riga to fetch her three sisters, their husbands and nine children. At first they were lodged, like her brother Karl, a few miles outside Petersburg to give them time to adjust to their new situation, and to undergo a crash course in Russian and in etiquette. But they were soon given splendid mansions in the capital, places at court, and noble rank. In due course the children were to be married into suitably noble families, so that at last the beggar family from Livonia was welded into the Russian aristocracy.

But above all, Catherine worked to promote the interests of her daughters. Russian diplomacy supported Holstein's claims to territory in central Europe, and revived the idea of marrying Elizabeth to King Louis. And all the while she showered them both with gifts. When Anne reached her nineteenth birthday, she gave her a hand mirror, a table mirror, an inkwell, a small chest, a set of golden dishes, a lacquered cabinet, a hand-washer with a glass top, a precious goblet on a tray, and 'other gallanteries set with diamonds and brilliants', besides a golden beaker for her husband Holstein.

And Catherine continued to seek the affection of her soldiers. Once, when a Guards Captain fell on his sword rushing down the stairs of the Winter Palace to salute Elizabeth, she had him carried off to her own apartment and sent her own physician to attend him. She visited the military hospital and brought the inmates extra food and comforts. She dined frequently with her officers, watched parades from her palace window, ordered them to stop when she thought the men were getting cold, and appeared regularly in soldier's coat and tricorn hat to ladle drinks out to the men.

As yet she rarely appeared at social gatherings, though the rules of etiquette laid down for them were still enforced. Gentlemen were never allowed to be drunk before nine o'clock, the ladies not at all; no one was to strike, or kiss, a lady, and no lady was to be either noisy or riotous. New rules were soon added. The ladies were not to wear ermine with tails, nor to dress both sides of their head with diamonds. Such adornments were reserved now solely for the Empress. Catherine had become sensitive about her appearance in middle age.

More cloth and more dresses were imported from abroad for her; more retainers were engaged. Gilt barges and golden coaches were ordered, and though she had cause enough to delight in her palaces as they were, lavish additions were built onto them. Peterhof in particular with its woodland setting and its antique statues smuggled out from France and Italy was already beautiful, but it was given splendid new fountains and a new pavilion called the 'Hermitage' equipped with a wonderful machine which raised and lowered chairs and tables from the kitchen to the first-floor dining room, so that Catherine could entertain her guests in privacy.

In a society that was beginning to appreciate luxury, only Alexander, it seemed, was allowed to compete. That summer he welcomed her to his newly finished palace at Oranienbaum. It was of a magnificence never seen before in Russia. Catherine seemed delighted, though she took good care to make a conciliatory call on Yagujinski on her way back to St. Petersburg.

However hard she tried she found it impossible to escape from politics. But on 8 February 1726 she inaugurated an important new governmental institution which was to save her the fatigue of much decision-taking—the 'Supreme Privy Council'. The innovation, however, was not her idea. Alexander had long been urging her to form a small, exclusive group of Ministers to stand between her and the governing Senate, and to supervise the more important ministries. The Council consisted of six people—Alexander who sat as Minister for War, Apraxin the naval chief, Chancellor Golovkin, Tolstoi head of the secret police, and the Vice-Chancellor, Andrei Ostermann, a German diplomatist who had worked his way up the hierarchy by dint of hard work and by keeping important papers to himself—a device which gained him the reputation of being 'indispensable'. The inauguration of the Council was a triumph for Alexander. His old enemy Paul Yagujinski had been carefully excluded from it, and his was clearly the most powerful voice in its deliberations.

The Council met twice a week—dealing with home affairs on Wednesdays and foreign policy on Fridays. Catherine was present at its first few sessions and even took part in the discussions, but her attendance became ever less frequent, and she eventually contented herself with signing its decisions into law.

Old Apraxin rarely bothered to attend either. 'All the foundations the late Emperor laid', he complained bitterly, 'have dis-

appeared without a trace.' The navy, one of Peter's primary achievements, was certainly being allowed to rot away, and the old Admiral
had been able to do nothing about it. Alexander seemed to be the
ultimate arbiter of public affairs these days; Catherine, titular
Autocrat of Russia, was no more than a puppet now.

She signed the papers put before her; she entertained ambassadors
and showed the more favoured of them over Peter's workshop, his
talent as a handy-man being a quality she could fully comprehend.
Yet though, by her own choice, she exercised virtually no power,
she was becoming increasingly susceptible to its trappings.

She was becoming more vain, more self-indulgent, and ever more
luxurious. That April when she reviewed her Guards she was
attended by a suite of magnificent cavaliers and a host of lackeys,
running footmen, moors and pages, all dressed in liveries and lace.
She herself wore a three cornered hat with a feather in it, a white
peruke, and a green velvet décolleté dress underneath a uniform
great-coat—a combination of styles intended to be both regal and
martial, but which only succeeded in making her look something
of a slut. She began to appear more frequently in public, and
revelled in the royal salutes, the flags, the honours and respects, and,
not least, the splendid balls and banquets given in her honour, at
which she often stayed until the early hours. She was enjoying
acting the role of Empress.

No crisis of state or international affairs was now allowed to
interrupt her dedicated round of pleasure. In April 1726 when
George I of England announced that he was going to blockade the
Russian fleet, the news produced something close to consternation
in St. Petersburg. But though Catherine is reported to have expressed
the intention of leading her fleet and army out to battle personally,
the court records display no sign of any change in her routine.

Fortunately the crisis passed, but it triggered off another furor
which threatened to involve her. Alexander had gone to the Baltic
territories ostensibly to organize defences against the English fleet.
In the event, however, he had devoted the greater part of his energies
there to promoting his own claim to the Duchy of Courland. His
strong-arm methods in Mitau, Courland's capital, gave his enemies
their opportunity. Holstein, who hoped to gain the Duchy for a
member of his own family, Tolstoi and others leapt at the chance

to discredit Alexander, and together they persuaded Catherine to recall him in disgrace. The disgrace, however, turned out to be only temporary, and despite the storm which blew up round her Catherine continued to lead a life of luxurious indiscipline which, as the court diaries indicate, took no account of night or day.

Arriving at the Summer Palace on 1 July she went to bed at seven in the evening. She dined at three the following morning, retired at seven, and rose at five in the afternoon. She did not go to bed until three the next morning, rising at two the following afternoon when, having been 'pleased to hear mass in the palace chapel' and eaten dinner, she attended a christening. Returning home 'at the fourth hour in the morning' of the 4th, she was 'pleased to stroll in the garden' instead of going to bed, and retired, at last, at nine in the morning, rising again at eight the same evening. Next day she was up at five in the afternoon, and retired at the mercifully early hour, so far as her retinue was concerned, of 3 a.m.

On 6 July she slept the clock round, dined at seven, made a rare appearance at a Supreme Privy Council session, then left by barge for 'her new Italian House', returning to bed at mid-morning on the seventh. On 8 July she rose at the sprightly hour of 10 a.m., dined at three to the accompaniment of music, and spent some time in the gardens before returning to her apartments to examine eight boxes of rich sables just arrived from Siberia.

In St. Petersburg in July it is never quite dark even at four in the morning, and the long hours of light seem to have unsettled Catherine. But there is little doubt too that she was drinking much more heavily than usual. In the two years following Peter's death she is said to have spent 700,000 roubles on Hungarian wine alone, and another 16,000 on Danzig Schnapps.

Much as she liked being surrounded by wealth and by attention, she felt basically inadequate and insecure. Her whole life had revolved so exclusively round Peter that now he was gone she could find no focus for her existence. The illusions produced by luxury, and even drink, were not adequate as substitutes.

Yet she had other reasons to feel insecure. Pasquinades, even anonymous threats to murder her, were dropped about the streets; and powerful men were said to be plotting on behalf of young Prince Peter. So far the Guards remained loyal to her, and there were important people who owed their very safety to her remaining on the throne. But though drink fuddled her senses and her entourage strove hard to protect her from realities, she could not have been totally unaware of her unpopularity.

Once, when she was reviewing a Guards regiment, a bullet flew past and struck a bystander dead. She appeared to be quite unaffected. Her reactions were slow now and it is possible that she barely realized what had happened at the time. But on 10 July a new *ukaz* was read out in every church: people guilty of 'malicious and unseemly' talk about the Empress would not escape with hard labour sentences in future. They would be executed. And the edict had to be reissued shortly in even stronger terms.

Her fears, her sense of inadequacy, her heavy drinking, and her unhealthy round of pleasure-seeking were beginning to quicken into a vortex of self-destruction. She would rise at any time between seven in the morning and five in the afternoon, go to bed in the early hours, often after dawn. Military tattoos sometimes had to be held at night in order to accommodate her and cooks, musicians and prospective guests had to be prepared for any unearthly hour at which she might decide to entertain.

She would drive out to christenings and weddings, to parties thrown by some potentate, or, on a sudden whim, to enjoy the excitements of a fire which had broken out in some quarter of the town. Fifes and trumpets, gun salutes and gaudy banners still greeted her wherever she went; she was flattered and indulged. But her life was becoming little more than a desperate struggle to escape into forgetfulness.

She ate and drank, listened to her musicians playing in the galleries, drove through her parks in a little calash, and roamed for hours about her gardens, watching the fountains play and staring long and vacantly into reflecting pools. Sometimes she drank enough Tokay wine to get a good night's sleep, but often she would lie awake in bed for hours and fall into reveries contemplating the decorated walls and ceilings where artists had painted such subjects as 'The Triumph of Catherine'. But all her triumphs were in the past. She was no Minerva, goddess of wisdom, as her propagandists claimed, but still a spiritual peasant, trapped in a situation with which she could not cope.

That summer, while her gentlemen-in-waiting made meticulous note of every hurrah and cannon shot she reviewed the fleet at Kronstadt, taking little Peter and Elizabeth in tow. She also visited Tsarskoye and gave a great dinner at Peterhof. But official engagements were fast losing their appeal for her, and as she continued to drag herself out to function after function she began to acquire a strained impassive look. Such was her appearance at the official opening of the Academy of Sciences that summer. Optics meant nothing to her; the anatomical drawings she was shown seemed quite incomprehensible, while Professor Bulfinger's paper on advances in the application of lode-stone and needle in establishing longitude aroused only her indifference.

On 6 August she made a rare appearance at the Council and approved an alliance with the Prussians. But she had lost all real interest in foreign affairs ever since the French had finally rejected Elizabeth as a bride for King Louis. Elizabeth had no brilliant match in prospect now, and as if that was not sorrow enough there was trouble with her son-in-law Holstein who had begun to involve himself in politics and was now at daggers drawn with Alexander.

'Reichsmarschall Field Marshal, his Serene Highness Prince Alexander Menshikov', to quote his title, had ridden out the storm that had blown up over his activities in Courland. There had been a moment when everyone had been ranged against him—Tolstoi, Holstein, Yagujinski, Generals Buturlin and Ushakov, old Apraxin. But Catherine could not bear to let him go, and now he was in proud and arrogant form again.

She claimed that she had only protected him out of compassion since she knew how much he was hated, but few believed her. After all, Alexander had made her what she was—he had procured her as Peter's mistress, assured her accession as Empress, and manufactured her official image. And how she rewarded him! That year alone she gave him a whole town in the Ukraine and estates comprising two thousand households. His patronage, already immense, became unrivalled, and he exploited Russia as if it were his own private milch cow. He was almost universally detested, but he did not care. Others might fall out of favour, but except that once over Courland, he was never denied anything. He knew how to handle Catherine.

She felt at ease in the company of this strong, lean, tanned man, and the roots of her trust in him ran deep. She remembered the time when they used to eat off wooden platters. Now they both ate off golden dishes. But the luxury in which he had encouraged her bore her down. She had no energy to fight any more. Her first idea of ruling by reconciling the great men of the realm had been abandoned. She was no more than Alexander's creature now.

She was content to be so. That winter she hardly ever attended Council meetings and though she went regularly to church, received ambassadors and salutes, her domestic routine followed the same unhealthy course as it had done in the summer. Sometimes she rose at three in the morning, sometimes at four in the afternoon; she dined at any time from two till ten and never went to bed before midnight. Her delightful residences and gardens, her royal yachts ('almost as beautiful and fine as those of England'), her splendid entourage and stables—the sheer voluptuousness of her life, gave her no contentment any more, and her incessant drinking and her undisciplined midnight wanderings had begun to undermine her constitution. She had put on weight and let her hair grow long. She looked like a woman in decline—listless and old for her forty-three years.

Indeed, to a western visitor who had not seen her for fifteen years she seemed 'quite altered'. She had lost her florid complexion and 'become pale and tawny', and her increased bulk seemed to him 'to threaten a Dropsy'.

On the morning of 1 November 1726—it was a Tuesday—the Neva rose in flood again. As the water swept into the city the streets of St. Petersburg became clogged with flotsam. The carcasses of drowned men and of cattle floated on the surface. People struggled out onto the roofs, and boats were paddled through the streets on rescue missions. The Summer Gardens were soon under three feet of water; Peter's physic garden was submerged; water swirled about the great Neptune fountain, and on into the Palace.

While lackies bustled to remove the valuables, Catherine was bundled away to safety. As she was rowed along the river she could see graceful spires and coloured façades distorted in the reflection of the turbulent waters. And the illusion of a city dissolving in the swirling, eddying whirlpools of the flood reflected her own confusions and her state of shock.

The flood soon subsided, but it had given Catherine a severe chill. Soon afterwards she began to suffer violent bleeding from the nose, and her legs began to swell—a condition the gossips immediately attributed to venereal disease.

By the New Year, however, she seemed to have recovered. That day, the Cavalry Guard escorted her to the Trinity Church; there was a great assembly, and afterwards a dinner. Six days later she attended the ceremony of the Blessing of the Waters, dressing for the occasion with some of her old uncouth panache in a tight silver jacket and a florid petticoat.

But Alexander Menshikov was taking no chances. He had seen the warning light and, reckoning that the Empress would not last long, made haste to join the supporters of Prince Peter. Tolstoi and Buturlin opposed the move in vain. Even when they suggested that young Elizabeth should succeed, Catherine would hear nothing of it. Elizabeth was enjoying life; the Empress had no wish to burden her with all the risks of ruling Russia.

Catherine's health grew steadily worse. She suffered fainting fits, and by the middle of April she was dangerously ill. Once before at a time of crisis over the Mons affair, she had dreamt that serpents were slithering over her bed, trying to throttle her. Now, she told her ladies of another dream: she was sitting at a table surrounded by her court when the ghost of Peter suddenly appeared, dressed as an ancient Roman. She waved and walked towards him—and he took her in his arms and carried her away into the clouds. She regarded the dream as a premonition of death, but seemed to have no fear.

The doctors diagnosed an abscess on the lung but could do nothing for her. As soon as he heard, Alexander came hurrying to her bedside brandishing a will for her to sign. It left the crown to Prince Peter and then to her daughters, but only if Peter should die without issue. It was also designed to secure Alexander's own position. But Catherine was too ill to sign anything.

Then Tolstoi arrived to make a last attempt to gain the succession for Elizabeth. But the Empress seemed indifferent to his arguments. Shortly afterwards Tolstoi was arrested on Alexander's orders.

So was Buturlin. And with his most dangerous enemies out of the way, Alexander made his final bid to procure Catherine's signature to that will.

This time she signed obediently enough. She seemed content with the arrangement. Her only concern now was for her unmarried daughter. She expressed the wish that Elizabeth should marry Holstein's brother, the Prince-Bishop of Lübeck, who had arrived in Russia some months before. And having provided for her children Catherine was ready to depart this world. While her Guards stood vigil outside the Palace and the grandees waited impatiently inside, Catherine at last obliged them. She died shortly before nine on the evening of 6 May 1727, in the third year of her reign.

According to one of her biographers, she possessed such 'female Sagacity, Penetration and Abilities as cannot be paralleled either in the Histories of ancient or modern Times'. It was not true; but Catherine was generous and a generous spirit deserves a generous epitaph.

Interlude

The night Catherine died the eleven-year-old Peter Alexeyevich succeeded to the throne. But Russia continued to be ruled by Alexander Menshikov. He expelled the Duke of Holstein and the Princess Anne, sent Tolstoi and Buturlin into exile, and tried to marry his daughter to the Emperor. But the marriage did not take place and, thanks to the skilful manipulations of Vice-Chancellor Ostermann, Alexander was eventually packed off to Siberia a ruined man.

The aristocratic Dolgorukis and Golitsyns took over the Regency, but in January 1730 Peter II died suddenly of smallpox and the grandees met to choose another sovereign. According to Catherine's will one of her daughters should have succeeded. But the grandees passed them over in favour of Peter the Great's half-niece Anne, the almost forgotten Dowager Duchess of Courland. They thought she would make a quiet, tractable Empress who would be eternally grateful to them and obey their every order. They made a terrible mistake.

PART II
Anne

Aₙₙₑ was born on 29 January 1693 into a Russia of the old values—a Russia of almost oriental protocol where men wore beards and heavy robes, where women were secluded, and where contact with the 'godless' western world was totally abhorred. Her father was Tsar Ivan V, her mother Praskovya Saltykova, a proud woman of impeccably aristocratic descent.

Tsar Ivan ruled in name only. He was retarded and retiring—what Russians call 'a sad-head'. But his influence on Anne was slight. He died when she was only three, and her recollection of the family and its retainers wailing round his open coffin, of being lifted up to kiss his stiff, cold hand, remained always a dim one. The dominating influence on her younger years was her mother's.

The Tsarina Praskovya was a formidable woman. She had once been beautiful—with an oval face, auburn hair, and bright blue eyes. But having borne five children, of whom three survived, her features had become coarse, her body flabby, and high blood-pressure gave her a florid look.

Praskovya was also a wealthy woman. She had inherited estates in three different provinces, and in addition drew a comfortable state pension as royal dowager. She was energetic too, but as a woman she could not hawk and hunt or work in government. Instead she played the tyrant with her household and found an outlet for her considerable prejudices and rare capacity for bearing malice by engaging in petty intrigue.

Anne grew up with her elder sister Catherine and her younger sister, also called Praskovya, in the old wooden palace of Ismailovo, a dark and labyrinthine structure outside Moscow. They lived in

79

the secluded, luxurious style of old Muscovy, served by a host of servile lackeys, stewards, grooms and watchmen supervised by Praskovya's brother Vasili. It was a little claustrophobic kingdom of its own with its own entertainments, schemes and hatreds; an isolated nest dominated by a fierce mother-eagle.

The centre of the household was the hall, its floor straw-covered, its wooden walls carved with lions and hung with carpets, tapestries, and icons. The hub round which the day revolved was dinner, at which the huge wooden table would be laid out with loaves of bread plaited into a variety of artful shapes, with sturgeon, caviare and salt salmon, meats and sweetmeats, peas and mushrooms, and flagons of fruit-flavoured mead to wash it down. The hours not spent eating and sleeping were passed with embroidery and gossip, chapel services and watching the antics of tumblers and buffoons.

The incongruous played a bigger and certainly a more serious part in her life than it ever did in Tsar Peter's. Besides filling the place with singing-birds in cages, Praskovya made the palace into a sort of human zoo with dwarfs and jesters, the monstrously deformed, the weak of mind. Any soothsayer, religious fanatic or supposed worker of miracles could be sure of a welcome, for she was a superstitious woman and a good touch for every teller of tall stories.

Among Praskovya's favourites was a fool called Timothy who prophesied that Anne would end her days as a nun. There was nothing remarkable about such a prognostication. The nunnery seemed a likely prospect for royal princesses at that time, and Anne had had good training for it. She knew her catechism, observed all the frequent fast days and had been well schooled in obedience—for her mother was quick to anger and her anger was terrible. Her tongue was as rough as her eyes were sharp. The Dowager Praskovya was not a woman to be crossed, and only one man ever dared to—young Tsar Peter.

As part of his programme for bringing Russia up to date, Peter decided to transform the quality of Praskovya's life and of her children's upbringing. He installed one of his own men as steward of her household, commanded her to attend functions in Moscow's foreign suburb, and to bring her daughters with her. Worse still, he instructed her to receive visitors, including foreigners and their wives.

Praskovya shuddered at each new step the Tsar took to force western ways upon her. But she was a shrewd woman, and having no wish to end up in a nunnery as the Tsar's first wife had done, she complied with as good a grace as she could muster.

As a result of the Tsar's orders, a new element was introduced into the princesses' upbringing. Until she was ten Anne had been confined to a life of royal domesticity which dulled the wits and suppressed the personality. Now tutors were appointed to teach her and her sisters French and German and to instruct them in dancing and deportment. Johann-Christoph-Dietrich Ostermann and Stephen Ramburg were third rate standard-bearers of the new culture. The first managed to teach her the rudiments of German, but precious little else; the second instructed her in dancing and deportment well enough, but succeeded in teaching her practically no French since his own command of that language, like that of his colleague Ostermann, was very poor.

Anne already knew her catechism, her Bible, and a good deal of Russian folk-lore, but after five years' tuition by these paragons of western learning she could, in addition, dance reasonably well, make a tolerable curtsey, sit convincingly for a portrait in western dress, and express herself with reasonable effect in broken German. Some windows at Ismailovo had been opened onto the western world, but Praskovya's influence was still strong, and the clash of cultures within the household was not conducive to family harmony. There was constant bickering interspersed with flaming rows, in which Anne seems to have played a prominent part. She developed a stubborn, spiteful streak, taking after her mother to a sufficient extent to justify the nickname she was given—'Ivan the Terrible'.

In all, she had grown up a fairly predictable product of her mother's rather barbaric household—maimed by its severity, coarsened by its pleasures, inculcated with its superstitions, puffed up with its pride, and with a tongue sharpened by a good deal of domestic in-fighting.

From the age of thirteen, Anne was a minor figure at Peter's court. She went to the weddings of the Tsar's friends in Moscow dressed in the German fashion and attended royal banquets. In November 1707 she sat with her mother and sisters among the four hundred guests Alexander Menshikov had invited to celebrate his name day—an occasion which doubtless inspired her mother to utter some caustic remarks about the jumped-up commoners they were expected to honour nowadays. She met Peter's mistress Catherine, too, and in the spring of 1708 by royal command she accompanied the family to St. Petersburg.

This move was a highly complex operation. Only accommodation was to be provided. Everything else that they would need, including furniture, had to be taken with them. So it was a long train of creaking carts and unsprung carriages that took the rough road north. And if this discomfort was not enough, a few miles from their destination they were met by Tsar Peter who insisted that they complete the final stage by water—an unfamiliar means of transport which they regarded with much misgiving. Their first dismal sight of St. Petersburg did not encourage them either, and then to cap it all as soon as they arrived the great wooden house in which they lodged caught fire.

Praskovya hated the inconvenience of St. Petersburg, the wretched functions she had to attend, and the contemptible commoners she was expected to consort with. But for Anne it was a great adventure. She enjoyed her status and the respect society paid her. And she was already trying to attract the admiration of young men.

Not that she was good-looking. She had blue eyes, a luxuriant head of hair, and a good and upright bearing, but her features were large and her complexion sallow. Nevertheless within a year or two her uncle Peter found a match for her—Frederick-William Kettler, Duke of Courland, a nephew of the King of Prussia.

Anne was almost the last to hear about the arrangement, but the news must have pleased her well enough. The Duke's realm of Courland and Semigallia adjoined the Baltic territories Russia had taken recently from Sweden. It produced a revenue of 300,000 crowns a year for the Duke, who had a fine palace in its capital, Mitau, and a coat of arms featuring a red lion and a white goat. Anne would be the first Russian princess to marry a foreigner for two hundred years. Her dowry was to be worth 200,000 roubles and Tsar Peter himself would act as Marshal at the wedding.

That summer, under supervision, she composed a letter to her fiancee: 'I have learned with especial satisfaction of our forthcoming marriage. . . . I cannot refrain from assuring your Highness that nothing could have been more agreeable to me than to hear your declaration of love for me. For my part, I do assure your Highness that I completely reciprocate those sentiments, which I shall permit myself to express to you personally when, with God's help, we meet, which happy occasion I look forward to with all my heart. Meanwhile, Illustrious Duke, I remain your Highness's most humble servant, Anne.'

They met the following August in St. Petersburg. Anne was seventeen and Frederick only a few months older. He was as fair as she was dark, still unformed in personality and character, and very anxious to please. It might be reckoned that he had met rather more than his match in Anne.

The marriage took place on 31 October 1710. The bride wore a white velvet gown trimmed with gold, and a long red velvet mantle edged with ermine. Her hair had been beautifully dressed and she wore a splendid crown. Tsar Peter came to fetch her at nine in the morning, and her mother, her two sisters, and a bevy of royal aunts, all dressed in western fashion, followed them onto the royal barge. The ceremony took place in the grounds of Alexander Menshikov's residence, as yet the grandest in St. Petersburg.

It was a splendid affair. Gaily decorated boats stood in the river, there were lines of guardsmen, and a band. The Metropolitan of Novgorod officiated, and when the ceremony was over everyone moved on into the house for the wedding breakfast.

Anne and her husband sat beneath laurel wreaths at the end of the great hall. Opposite them, swathed in ermine and brocade, sat Praskovya, her auburn hair tied up with ropes of pearls, her face heavily rouged and decorated with black cosmetic patches. Next to her sat the royal princesses and beyond them, in order of rank, the rest of the distinguished company. The guzzling went on for hours, the Tsar in a very merry mood punctuating the proceedings with innumerable toasts, each accompanied by a salute of guns. There followed a fireworks display and a splendid ball which ended at three in the morning, whereupon, with almost everyone exhausted and more than half of them the worse for drink, Praskovya conducted Anne to the bridal chamber. After an interval the Tsar led in the groom and so, in true Russian style, the couple were brought to bed.

Next day in the banqueting hall, the Tsar tore down the wreath, the symbol of virginity, which hung above the groom's place while Frederick struggled clumsily to remove the one over the bride's. A second banquet then commenced—for which the Tsar had arranged a very special climax. As the revelry approached its height, two immense pies were carried in and placed before the newly-weds. Knives were about to be plunged into them, when, suddenly, the crusts burst open and out jumped two dwarfs—one male, one female, drank a toast to the bridal pair, and proceeded to dance a minuet upon the table. Everyone burst into peals of laughter and applause. Even the half befuddled groom managed an uneasy smile.

The following Sunday Anne and Frederick entertained the Tsar and all their relatives; and to round off the festivities, the Tsar presided over the wedding of his favourite dwarf. Seventy-two other little people, all decked out with blue and pink ribbons, attended the reception which Anne and Frederick were invited to watch along with the rest of the royal family. Frederick might have harboured an uneasy suspicion that this ridiculous wedding was intended as some parody of his own, but his goblet was so regularly filled, and he was so dutiful in emptying it, that, in the end, he could not have cared. As for Anne, the celebrations had been a delightful farewell to the old existence and she looked forward to the new.

They stayed on in St. Petersburg until after the New Year, then took the road to Mitau. But they had covered barely twenty miles when the Duke was taken ill, and died. The cause of death is not exactly known. Some said that he had caught a chill; others alcoholic poisoning. Neither theory gave any consolation to poor Anne, a bride of less than six weeks' standing, who had become a widow before her eighteenth birthday. She returned disconsolately to St. Petersburg, to her mother's stifling embrace.

The marriage contract provided for this unhappy contingency. Anne was to receive a residence in Mitau and a pension of 40,000 roubles a year. But the new Duke, Ferdinand, was not inclined to pay. The Russians, he claimed, had not paid the dowry in full, his predecessor had not been confirmed in his position by Courland's overlords, the Poles, and anyway, Dowager Duchesses of Courland were customarily entitled to only 8,000 a year. The upshot was that in 1712 Russian troops arrived in Mitau and the Duke retired to Danzig. It was not done for Anne's sake. Courland was strategically placed on Russia's border; the present Duke was the last of his line and unlikely to have children. Tsar Peter reckoned that if Anne moved into Mitau, and a competent agent were attached to her suite, a pro-Russian party might be formed among the Courland gentry, and advantage taken of the situation. Anne was merely a pawn in Peter's game of foreign policy. And if old Praskovya and her other daughters could be persuaded to go with her, so much the better.

Meanwhile Anne had returned to Ismailovo, visiting St. Petersburg only occasionally. She was there in February 1712, however, for Peter's wedding to his mistress, Catherine, when her mother suffered the indignity of sponsoring the bride and her sisters that of acting as stand-in bridesmaids when Catherine's own daughters were too tired to do so. From now on the *parvenu* Catherine took precedence over all of them. She had become a person of great importance; a person they must curry favour with if they hoped for concessions from Tsar Peter.

Praskovya had no desire to move to Courland. On the other hand she had no wish to relinquish motherly control of Anne either. She had managed to delay their departure for some time, but it could not be put off indefinitely and in the spring of 1712 she took Anne and her sisters to Riga, the last staging post on the road to Mitau.

Anne still hoped to find another husband, and Peter had been encouraging, even if he did tease her about it whenever they met. Her name was hawked around the European marriage market and Prince Christian of Prussia, the Duke of Saxe-Weisenfels and a son of the Swedish King were all thought to be in the running at various times. But there was no immediate result.

Meanwhile Anne and her mother remained at Riga while Peter's agent in Mitau, Peter Bestuzhev, nominally Anne's Chamberlain, pressed her claims with the recalcitrant Courlanders. In 1713 he succeeded in arranging for the revenues of certain villages there to be allotted for her upkeep, but by now Anne who had been allowed back to Moscow for the winter seemed none too anxious to enter on her inheritance. Even though she was always quarrelling with her mother, their relationship represented something certain in a world that had become very uncertain. So, she went to Ismailovo or St. Petersburg whenever she could and otherwise stayed in Riga, pleading illness and other excuses to delay the move, while her mother took up the cudgels on her behalf, taxing the Tsar about the provisions made for Anne in Mitau. Peter gave off-hand assurances that everything had been arranged, but Praskovya was not satisfied. 'What will she have to live on there?' she demanded. Would she be able to live in 'a decent style suitable to her rank as a princess'? Was her income to come from Peter's Treasury or from the Duchy itself? At last 12,000 ducats were promised for her maintenance, though she was never to be sure how much she would actually receive from month to month. So Anne had no choice now but to leave at last for Courland.

Her elder sister had just been married to the Duke of Mecklenburg, but she was twenty-three and had experienced five years of widowhood when in March 1716, in sour and apprehensive mood, she arrived at last, in Mitau.

It was all that she had feared it would be—an ill-built little town of dilapidated wooden houses. The countryside outside was desolate and in places quite deserted. It was nearly five years since the Russian troops had arrived, and the fighting had been followed by plague and famine. True, Courland was already beginning to recover something of its former modest prosperity, but the total impression was still one of barrenness. There was an appropriate irony in the emotionally impoverished Anne being forced to make her life in such an impoverished little country.

The palace in which she took up residence was reasonably large with tolerably well-furnished apartments, decorated with pictures representing her uncle Peter's victories. The only other surviving building of any merit was the castle where the embalmed bodies of the former Dukes lay in glass coffins dressed in gold brocade and coronets. But the grandeur they represented had departed. After the happy prospects when she had married Frederick, this seemed a pretty poor inheritance.

Life in Mitau was inexpressibly dull. There was almost no social intercourse—nothing to do except to eat and embroider. Her freedom there was only nominal and she felt her condition to be quite demeaning. She was a pawn in Peter's game and made to feel so. She had to turn to his man, her chamberlain, Bestuzhev, for the payment of every little debt, apply to him before she purchased any luxury. The Tsar vetted every item of her accounts, even counted the barrels of beer in her cellar.

Isolation bred suspicion. She became convinced that her staff was riddled with spies and informers, ready to report her every move to her mother or the Tsar. Of all of them only Bestuzhev seemed genuinely concerned to improve her material welfare. She came to depend on him, to trust him, to see him as a father figure— and this confirmed her mother's dislike of the man.

Anne was allowed back to St. Petersburg for the winter of 1717–1718 and tried desperately to avoid returning to Mitau, embarking on an intense campaign to ingratiate herself with the Tsarina and enlist her aid towards this end. She did everything to win Catherine's sympathy and took particular care to exaggerate the charms and abilities of the little son she doted on. But it was to no avail. In March she was sent back to Courland.

Still she did not give up. She was used now to swallowing her pride, and since her uncle Peter never took her seriously she again tried to draw his attention to her plight through Catherine. She was ready, she emphasized, to marry absolutely anyone the Tsar might care to name. But second-hand princesses were not so easily disposed of, and she waited in vain for hopeful news about her future.

To add to her troubles, her mother began to suspect that she was having an affair with her Chamberlain, Bestuzhev. As it turned out later, Praskovya's suspicions seem to have been founded on malicious rumour rather than on fact. But with her life in ruins and her prospects dim, a despairing Anne did form a liaison and with a man of even lower rank than Bestuzhev—Ernest Biren.

Ernest Johann Biren, a Courlander by birth, had been educated at the University of Königsberg where he had distinguished himself rather more by his brawling and wenching than by his academic attainments. He had served nine months' imprisonment for killing a watchman in an affray, and had been thrown out of Prussia, at which point he had set about building a career on the basis of such assets as he possessed—a handsome figure, a measure of Germanic charm, and sheer determination. He found employment as a tutor in Lithuania, then, in 1714, he had gone to Russia where the skills of foreigners were so much in demand. Not his however. So he came back to Courland where Bestuzhev gave him an appointment on his staff.

Anne first noticed him when he brought her some papers to sign. The sight of a new face was an event for Anne these days, and his was not a displeasing one. At twenty-seven, Ernest Biren was a good deal younger and more personable than Bestuzhev. From then on he attended on her every day.

In the months that followed, Ernest's polished manners (which seemed to her almost the last word in refinement) and his rather coarse good looks, were not the only qualities she discovered in him. He was charming and an excellent companion. She could not share his interest in cards, but she was persuaded to share his passion for horses, and she allowed him to teach her how to ride. Above all, perhaps, she was delighted by his obvious dependence on her. Here at last was a man who sought her patronage. No one else of any quality had ever done so, and his very commitment to her seemed to revive forces in her which had lain dormant since she first became a widow. Her interest in life began to increase and in time her friendship for Ernest began to blossom into love.

Yet even Ernest could not reconcile her to her position. In March 1719 she returned from another winter in Russia discontented with the latest provisions Peter had made for her, and distressed by a serious altercation with her mother, who now refused to have anything more to do with her on account of her supposed affair with Alexei Bestuzhev. Some time before Praskovya had sent her brother Vasili to Mitau to keep an eye on her. Vasili beat his wife and Anne had taken up her cause to the extent of helping her to escape to her family in Warsaw. Vasili was furious with his niece. Noticing the esteem in which she held Bestuzhev, and putting two and two together, he had reported back to Praskovya, feeding her with tales about her daughter, and she believed them. At once she demanded that Peter dismiss Bestuzhev, claiming that his presence in Mitau was 'quite insufferable'. Peter, however, refused to do anything of the sort. The man, he explained, had other responsibilities there besides Anne's household. That July Anne wrote to Catherine:

'Your Majesty, my aunt. God keep you in your unchanging graciousness. Apart from you, my light, I have no hope.' Her mother's displeasure and the scandal—which could not improve her declining chances of marriage—had made her much depressed. Could not Catherine prevail upon the Tsar 'to show me grace and bring the question of my marriage to a conclusion?' If she were married the gossips would have to cease their rumour-mongering. 'It is quite unbearable the way they inveigh against me.'

Her mother certainly believed the worst. Not content with cutting her off, she now pronounced a curse upon her daughter. In February 1720 Anne wrote in even more anguished tones to Catherine: 'Ei, ei, little mother. . . . Apart from God, little uncle [Peter] and yourself, I have no joy in the world, but only sorrows.' She dared not even go to St. Petersburg now for fear of her 'enemies' there, and though she had written to her mother pleading for a reconciliation there had been no reply. In all, her troubles were too great to express adequately in writing. Could she 'report verbally to your Majesty through some trusted intermediary'?

Catherine replied telling her not to take the calumnies so much to heart, and gave her news of her family. Anne replied appreciatively but full of self-pity. Her mother, so she heard, was angrier than ever with her, believing everything her uncle Vasili had told her. It made her quite miserable. 'It would be better if I were no longer in the world. . . . I humbly beg that you should keep this orphan under your ineffably gracious motherly protection.'

The breach with her mother, the rumours casting doubts upon her virtue, and her failure to find a husband were not to be Anne's only troubles. Soon her own position at Mitau was in danger. The Poles wanted her to leave and she no longer wanted to go. In June she wrote asking Catherine to intercede on her behalf with Peter. 'I manage to live on the income of the villages which have been allotted to me', but she did want the protection of a company of dragoons—she would even pay their upkeep. 'Your Majesty . . . knows how many enemies I have there who might crush me to death. I beg you, my little mother, in tears of grace, not to allow this to happen to poor me.'

But the Polish move succeeded. On 5 August Peter ordered her 'to go immediately to Riga and stay there until such time as we write to you again.' She went, and began to pester Catherine to arrange for her return. She saw Mitau as her refuge now. Since meeting Ernest Biren she had even become fond of it, and of the Courlanders too. She even persuaded herself that they reciprocated her feeling. 'On my departure from Mitau', she confided to Catherine, 'they begged me in tears to ask your Majesty that I should not be separated from them.'

In the spring of 1721 Anne met Peter and Catherine at Riga. They dined together at the end of March and met at least three times during April. What passed between them is not known, but in May she was able to return to Courland—and in the knowledge that Peter had sanctioned a very welcome contribution for her from the Russian treasury.

Anne continued to employ every trick of sycophancy and obsequiousness in order to keep her 'protector' Catherine well disposed. In March 1722, for instance, she sent her a message of congratulation on her birthday:

'All-gracious Lady, aunt and little mother, Greetings. . . . May you live for many years with his Lordship my little uncle. . . . I congratulate your Imperial Majesty . . . on your Majesty's exalted birth-day, and wish with all my heart . . . that God may increase your years in health and happiness together with those of his dear Lordship. . . . I am sending Your Majesty . . . some cloth, and I crave the boon that you may accept it and wear it in health. Truly, my mother, I could not find anything here better than this to send to your Highness. Your Imperial Majesty's niece, Anne.'

Catherine replied pleasantly, expressing her thanks and giving news of Anne's 'dearest mother' who 'though she has been very ill', was 'now never better'. But Praskovya would still not recognize her black sheep of a daughter. Both her other girls were obedient to her wishes. The eldest, now Duchess of Mecklenburg, had even returned to her, having had enough of her husband, but Anne had rejected her authority and must remain under her curse—and not all Catherine's remonstrations could persuade her to change her mind.

Praskovya was crippled by gout now. Unable to walk, she had to be carried about in a chair, and use special contraptions to get in and out of carriages and up and down stairs. Yet she still attended almost every ball and assembly in St. Petersburg. She seemed to derive some malicious satisfaction from it, seeing herself as the embodiment of the old Russian values in the midst of this shameful society. She would sit in her chair, flabby and dropsical, observing the cavortings of the throng from under hooded eyes—a living and magisterial rebuke to all those bared bosoms and foreign gallantries.

By the autumn of 1723 she knew she had not long to live. But she was still not persuaded to lift her curse on Anne. She would have liked the Tsar to have come begging her to do so—she had always wanted to see Peter on his knees. Such a triumph would have been worth the sacrifice. But at the eleventh hour she complied with Catherine's requests at last, and wrote Anne a rather ungracious letter of forgiveness.

'My dearest Princess Anna Ivanovna. Since my illness increases with each hour that passes and I now suffer from it to an extent that I despair of my life, I write to remind you to pray for me to the Lord God, and if He, my Creator should will that I depart this world, then not to forget me in the prayer for the dead.

'I have heard from my most beloved sister-in-law the Lady Empress Catherine Alexeyevna that you apparently consider yourself to be under my interdiction, or, in a word, under my curse. Have no doubt now, for the sake of the above-mentioned Majesty, my well-beloved Lady and sister-in-law, I remove it from you and forgive you everything—even though you did sin against me. Entrusting you to the care and grace of God, I remain your mother, The Tsarevna Praskovya.' Two days later she called her other daughters to her, asked for a mirror, gazed into it for a long time, and expired.

The reconciliation had come too late for Anne to be at her bedside, and when she heard the news, the grief she expressed was deep, but not long lasting. It was a relief to be free of the curser as well as the curse.

She wore deep mourning for the funeral, sobbed loudly at the bier, and was relieved to find her younger sister paying the bulk of the expenses. Then there was Catherine's coronation to look forward to. Anxious to make an appearance worthy of the occasion, and having heard that 'dresses in a particular style will be worn', she made careful enquiries before deciding what to wear. But when the time came she was put into shadow by the general splendour. Her suite seemed small by comparison, her dress still too traditional, and when she received the Duke of Holstein in a fur cap, she made a rather slovenly impression. Still she was in the social swim once more, and having seen the new grandeur of the Russian court, Courland seemed like a backwater again. Her taste for luxury had been thoroughly aroused, and when she returned to Mitau that autumn her standard of living there seemed depressingly inadequate.

With all the expense of the coronation, she was heavily in debt, so she threw herself into another campaign to persuade the Tsar to give her financial help. 'Your Majesty knows that I brought nothing with me to Mitau and that I have received nothing for some time. I have had to live in an empty house suitable only to a person of the middle class, and have had to acquire cooks and carriages, grooms and horses, etc. for my court for myself.' Of her income of 12,680 thalers, 12,254 went on 'basic necessities' and with the 426 thalers remaining she could hardly keep herself in 'dresses, linen and lace, still less in diamonds, silver and horses'. Since the wives of the local gentry had 'no lack of jewels and other finery, my lack of them would arouse no little comment'. The grant Peter had made to her in 1721 had gone on 'essential items for the household and for myself, but I am still indebted 100,000 thalers for a cross, a collection of diamonds, silverware, hangings for the rooms and my mourning apparel, and I cannot possibly repay this amount.' Her credit had run out and she begged Peter for a loan to enable her to pay off her debts, promising to pay back over the next ten years.

Peter died within weeks of receiving this letter and when Catherine succeeded him Anne sent Ernest Biren to congratulate her on her accession hoping he might charm the money out of her. Whether or not he did is not known, though he certainly obtained a personal commission to buy horses for Catherine's stables. But Anne's money problems, and even Ernest Biren, were soon driven from the forefront of her mind.

Suddenly, at thirty-three, she had the prospect of a husband.

Though she had fine dark blue eyes and well-kept hands the bloom of youth had long since disappeared. Her figure had grown thick and her reputation for sullenness and melancholy had made her a laughing-stock throughout the minor courts of central Europe. She would have been content with almost any man prepared to marry her, and yet now she had as a suitor a nobleman of the most glittering reputation—Count Maurice de Saxe.

He had been born in Dresden less than thirty years before, the illegitimate offspring of the King of Poland by the beautiful Aurora, Countess Königsmark. He was of middling stature, strong, good-looking, respected, affable, generous and illiterate. He was a brave and able soldier, had cut a brilliant figure at the court of France, and half the women in Europe were inclined to swoon at the mere mention of his name.

He had arrived in Mitau in the spring of 1726 smothered in perfume, powder and pomade, his huge wig decked out fashionably with ribbons, to press his suit upon the derelict Anne. He was inspired by ambition rather than by love, however. The Duke of Courland was dying and he wanted to succeed him. He had Poland's support—all he reckoned to need now was the support of the Courland gentry, and Anne.

They met first in the spring-time, in her garden, and poor Anne was quite overwhelmed. True, she pretended to a certain reluctance at first but was soon convinced that he was passionately in love with her. He broached the subject of the Dukedom, and she backed him to the hilt. In June when the Courland assembly elected Maurice as heir to the Duke, she was overjoyed. Everything was going perfectly. . . .

Then Alexander Menshikov arrived and ruined everything. The Russian government had decided that Maurice would be unacceptable to them as Duke and when Anne heard that Menshikov had arrived in Riga to supervise the defence of the Baltic lands against the English, she immediately set out to see him. Since her uncle the Emperor had died the year before, Menshikov's seemed to be the most powerful influence on Russian policy, and she hoped to persuade him to change the official line on Maurice. She could not have known that Menshikov wanted to become Duke of Courland himself.

Anne begged him to allow Maurice to be confirmed as Duke, she
pleaded with him, shed tears even, as she confessed her deep desire
to marry Maurice. But Menshikov gave her short shrift. She had
been a widow too long, he told her bluntly; Peter would never have
allowed such a match. Maurice was illegitimate; quite unsuitable.
She grovelled on her knees before him. She, a royal princess, de-
meaned herself before an upstart pie-seller. And it was useless. Her
suit was curtly rejected.

As soon as she got back to Mitau she wrote to Catherine, and to
every influential person she could think of, but before the answers
came Alexander arrived with a strong contingent of troops. Maurice
went to see him, but got no satisfaction. Alexander held all the
trumps. Maurice stayed on, sending to France for money and armed
help. Then Russian troops surrounded his house and broke down the
doors.

When Anne heard he was in danger she sent her bodyguard of
dragoons out to the rescue, and bloodshed was avoided only by a
sensible Russian officer who called a truce.

Meanwhile, Anne's complaints about Menshikov were having an
effect. 'The whole royal family', reported the Austrian Ambassador
in St. Petersburg, 'is exasperated at the insult inflicted on Anna
Ivanovna, and is demanding satisfaction.' They got it. The government decided that Menshikov had mismanaged the whole business.
An official enquiry condemned him for high-handedness, and he was
forced to drop his candidature. But all this did not help Maurice.
Anne rushed off to see Catherine herself, but it was useless. Russia
would produce a candidate for the Dukedom in due course. Anne
must return to Mitau and dismiss her suitor.

She did nothing of the kind. Even in November, when Maurice's
election was officially quashed she continued to fight for him, but in
August 1727 Russian troops marched into Mitau again and Maurice
himself was persuaded to give up. He left with barely a word for
Anne.

She saw him go with a sense of resignation. But she never forgave those responsible for her humiliation. She had learned to hate
them with a strong, uncompromising hatred—Alexander Menshikov
above all—and one day she would be revenged on all of them. There
was only one man, it seemed, whom she could trust and who did

not despise her, Ernest Biren, and she took such comfort as she could from him.

In June 1727 Bestuzhev had been recalled and Ernest took his place as her Chamberlain. He was married now—to Anne's lady-in-waiting Benigna Treyden—a small, quiet, pock-marked woman. Together they formed a workable *ménage à trois*. The Birens had three children, and Anne indulged them as if they had been her own—indeed there were some who thought they were. What is certain is that Ernest's influence over her seemed to increase considerably from about this time.

In 1727 Catherine died. Anne's second cousin, the thirteen-year-old Peter Alexeyevich became Tsar, and the detestable Alexander Regent. Anne found it much easier to kow-tow to little Peter than she had done to Catherine—to address him as 'little father', and 'our light and joy', to fall metaphorically at his 'dear feet' and 'beat her head many times upon the ground in obeisance' before him. Peter II, after all, was a legitimate Tsar of the kind she had been brought up to revere. Alexander Menshikov was quite another matter—and how she rejoiced at the news of his downfall a few months later. The Dolgorukis who took his place seemed infinitely preferable, representing as they did one of the oldest and most distinguished princely houses in all Russia.

But Anne's humiliations did not end with the advent of this new regime. Agrafena Volkonski, a friend and confidante of hers at court, was accused of intrigue, and all Anne's efforts failed to stop a full enquiry; her financial position remained as difficult as ever, the government refused to increase her allowance, giving her to understand that they did not wish extra funds to find their way into Biren's pockets; and the gossip about her continued unabated too. They said she had seduced Peter Bestuzhev, made a fool of herself with de Saxe, and that her attachment to dear Ernest was based only upon lust. It was all quite intolerable. She felt unjustly deprived of pleasure, comfort and respect. Somehow, sometime, she would be revenged on her tormentors. How or when she might gain that opportunity remained the speculation of a dream. But the dream was to come true, and sooner than she ever hoped.

In November 1729 Alexander Menshikov died in exile, and Anne crowed at the news. It was as well for him that he died when he did, for two months later, the Emperor Peter also died, and Anne was asked to mount the throne.

When Peter II died it was obvious that his successor must be a woman—but there was no lack of female candidates: the Princess Dolgoruki whom the Tsar was to have married on the day he died, Peter the Great's first wife Yevdokia, his daughters Anne and Elizabeth, and the Duchess of Mecklenburg besides Anne herself. The Dolgoruki girl was soon dismissed from the reckoning—the Guards would not accept her. Yevdokia was very old now and did not want the throne; the grandees did not like Anna Petrovna's husband Holstein, and regarded Elizabeth as illegitimate. And so the discussion turned to the daughters of Tsar Ivan. Of these, the eldest, Catherine Duchess of Mecklenburg also had a foreign husband, albeit a deserted one. There remained her sister, Anne of Courland.

Of the eight members of the Council, Chancellor Golovkin who had held office in three reigns and wished to survive a fourth said practically nothing and Vice-Chancellor Andrei Ostermann was so afraid of being associated with an unpopular decision that, pleading illness, he took no part at all. Decision then, rested with six men— elegant, wealthy, aristocratic and determined to hold on to power. Four were members of the Dolgoruki family; two were Golitsyns. Of these, Prince Dmitri Golitsyn was the strong man, and it was he who, at five o'clock on the morning following the Tsar's death, first proposed Anne's name. It seemed to him, and his colleagues agreed, that quite apart from her royal blood, Anne had a number of distinct merits. She was no advocate of sweeping change, and was used to modest living. But above all, she was used to taking orders. If elected, she would surely continue to do so, if only out of gratitude to them for rescuing her from Courland. Nevertheless it would be wise to take precautions to ensure that she did, and so they decided to make the offer contingent on her accepting certain limitations to her powers. Anne was to govern only by the advice and with the consent of the Council. She must not marry, name a successor, make war, conclude peace, raise new taxes, nor promote anyone above the rank of colonel without their approval. She must not degrade a nobleman, condemn him to death or confiscate his property without trial by his peers. She was to make no gifts of crown property, nor spend beyond her allowance. Otherwise her crown was to be forfeit.

Such were the conditions attached to the humble petition inviting Anne to the throne. The grandees knew very well that they would have the effect of concentrating power into the hands of a small junta of aristocrats—in other words themselves—and that the mass of gentry would be viciously opposed to the idea. So, when the doors of the Council chamber were thrown open and Anne's name was canvassed to the waiting host of senators and generals no mention was made of the conditions.

However, shortly afterwards Paul Yagujinski got wind of them and at once he sent a messenger to warn Anne not to accept them. This message was intercepted, but one from another source got through, and was probably the first intimation Anne received of the glorious reversal in her fortunes. Nevertheless, when the official delegates—Prince Vasili Dolgoruki, Prince Michael Golitsyn and General Leontiev arrived, she did not baulk at the conditions. The temptation of the throne of Russia, whatever strings might be attached, was not to be resisted. Eagerly, she grasped the pen and scrawled the words: 'By this I promise to observe all the conditions without exception. Anne.' Much relieved, the delegates rushed back to Moscow, though not before Anne had borrowed a thousand roubles from them. She followed three days later.

It was an exhilarating experience to speed over the snowy roads, knowing that a new, delicious form of life awaited her—a life where she could demand respect from everyone, and spend a hundred thousand roubles every year. The past years had been lean indeed, but now there would be fat ones, conditions or no conditions, fat, rich, luscious years, years to be filled with pleasure, romance, and with sweet revenge. Snow-laden boughs and shrubs rushed past her and in her imagination they must have seemed like human forms—the forms of handsome lovers and of enemies suffering the knout. But while she was taking her ecstatic journey towards Moscow sustained by her imagination and potted meat and vodka, the official proclamation of the conditions was casting gloom and despondency in the capital.

The first announcement made in February to the Senate, the synod, the generals and the bureaucrats was met by a stony silence. 'Woefulness was seen everywhere about the city', wrote Archbishop Theophanes Propokovich. Yet it was not Anne herself they were opposed to but those who set out to control her. 'Everyone cursed the grandees' extraordinary impertinence, their greed, their lust for power', continued the Archbishop. Yet no one dared object. The assembled ranks, he wrote, merely stretched back their ears like so many meek donkeys. But then they had good reason to fear the consequences of protest. The grandees of the Council were not fools. If they canvassed opinion now, it was only as a means of making their opponents show themselves. Yagujinski tried to avoid the provocation, but too late. He was invited into the adjoining room where Field Marshal Vasili Dolgoruki was waiting to place him under arrest. Thirty other suspected oppositionists were rounded up that night. But the grandees did not go far enough. The Machiavellian Ostermann was at work from the safety of his sick-bed, trying to form a group to fight the grandees and the conditions. Archbishop Theophanes, Prince Trubetskoi and Prince Cherkasski, the richest nobleman in Russia, were sounded out and all seemed favourably disposed; but as yet it was dangerous to act.

On 10 February, the Councillors welcomed Anne to a village four miles outside Moscow, where she was to stay until preparations had been made for her official entry into the city. They brought her a golden bowl and the Order of St. Andrew. But when they tried to invest her with it, she snatched it from them. Such honours were for her to dispose of now. Nevertheless when Prince Dmitri Golitsyn thanked her for accepting the crown and signing the Articles, Anne not only expressed her thanks for having been elected, but said that she had signed them for the general good and that she was 'resolved to keep them as long as I live'.

Yet the undercurrent of opposition continued to develop. The conditions might have been thought to be a step towards constitutional government, but most Russians did not see them in this light. 'God forbid', wrote one provincial gentleman, 'that we should have ten autocratic families instead of one autocratic monarch.' It was difficult enough to gain justice or patronage from one. Sensing this mood, the grandees began to modify their programme.

Anne as 'a member of the female sex' needed some institution to help her govern, they intimated, but on reflection this need not consist of a tiny cabinet. The council might be enlarged to include a dozen noblemen, with Anne as Chairman having a casting vote. And perhaps there should be a new Senate, smaller than the last, its thirty-six members nominated by the Council of course, and, in addition, a debating chamber for representatives of the gentry, another for merchants and burghers, and so forth. But such constitutional niceties cut little ice with Russians.

All this while Prince Vasili Dolgoruki had been watching Anne like a lynx, guarding her from the outside world and taking particular care to bar all access to her by known or suspected malcontents. But the news filtered through to her in spite of this. First there were whispered hints from her kinswoman, the Countess Saltykova and from her sister Catherine of Mecklenburg that the oligarchs were unpopular. Then Ostermann got word through to Biren who sent his eldest son into her with a note tucked in his shirt; and Archbishop Theophanes smuggled a secret plan of action to her—in a clock presented by the clergy. It was through such clandestine devices that Anne discovered that there was a large body of opinion among gentry, the army and the civil service, that wanted her to be more than a figurehead, and would support her if she tore up the conditions and assumed the autocracy.

Rather than rushing wildly into action, she behaved with sense and with discretion. She declared herself Colonel of the Preobrajenski Guards Regiment and Captain of the Cavalry Company that formed her escort, and handed each man a glass of vodka with which to drink her health—an approach which, in the words of a British observer, immediately 'gained their Hearts'. But otherwise she held her cards close to her chest, played along with the grandees and gave them no cause for suspicion.

On 15 February she made her formal entry into Moscow. Archbishop Theophanes had composed the ode of welcome:

> Away with you, sad night;
> The sun is rising
> The light to bring.
> Away with you sad night.

> If we had gloom and horror
> Anne's sun has shone through
> And given us bright day. . . .

She smiled and passed on to the Uspenski Cathedral where a distinguished congregation took the oath of loyalty to her—as monarch, not as autocrat. The grandees had thought this a major hurdle and when Anne had cleared it, they began to relax. The watch on her became less stringent; it became easier to plot.

Key officers and functionaries were quietly sounded out and a great petition organized begging Anne to tear up the conditions. Its presentation was planned for 25 February. This was to be decisive, and Anne knew it. It would end in glory or in humiliation; in the fall of the grandees or in the ruin of her friends.

Fortified by years of practised insincerity Anne bore up marvellously well under the strain. On the fatal morning she looked every inch an empress. Her double chins and thin eyebrows seemed to indicate a certain weight of mind; her large nose and protruding eyes a certain majesty. Her hair was done up in long thick ringlets like a pair of great sausages and as the petitioners trooped into the hall she stood erect, seeming to dominate all those around her.

The petitioners were led by Prince Cherkasski, his huge head inclined heavily to the left, his even larger stomach biassed distinctly to the right. With him was Prince Trubetskoi and several dozen others. Hundreds more waited outside in the court-yard. Cherkasski started by thanking Anne for signing the articles, but expressed the fear that they might reduce her rights. He asked her to reconsider and to accept his petition which called for a commission of gentry to debate the grandees' plan and make recommendations as to what forms of government might prove most acceptable to the nation.

At this point Prince Vasili Lukich Dolgoruki, who had been thrown off balance by the unexpected turn of events, tried to take control of the situation. 'What right have you got, Prince,' he asked Cherkasski, 'to arrogate to yourself the right of making laws?' As much right, retorted Cherkasski, as any Dolgoruki. 'You have deceived the Empress', he continued. 'You told her the articles she signed in Mitau had the approval of all ranks in the realm. It wasn't

true!' He turned to Anne: 'They drew them up without our knowledge or participation', he began; but Dolgoruki interrupted:
'Would Her Majesty be so gracious', he suggested smoothly, 'as to
tell the petitioners that she would consider their request after dis-
cussing the matter with her Council?' For a moment Anne appeared
to lose her poise, to be oppressed by sudden doubt.

The tension was broken by her sister Catherine who rushed up to
her brandishing a pen saying 'No, no, my Lady. Your Majesty needs
no time to consider such a simple matter. There is no point in a
discussion at this stage; be pleased to sign it now.' She did. Handing
the petition back, she asked the delegation to withdraw and return
with their recommendations that afternoon.

The grandees seemed stunned. But they were given no chance to
recover. Just then, a group of Guards officers rushed in, swept off
their white-beribboned hats and fell to their knees in front of Anne.
'We don't want them to tell you how to rule' cried one of them:
'She should be Autocrat as all former sovereigns have been', said
another; 'Just give us the word', roared a third, 'and we'll take off
all their heads.'

Anne, however, preferred another means of dealing with the
grandees. She signalled to the crowd for silence. 'I would seem', she
said, 'to be in danger. Take orders from General Saltykov', she told
the Guardsmen, 'and from no one else.' Then, in quite a different
tone, she invited the grandees to dinner.

It was a stroke of malicious genius. Saltykov was her man, and
the Golitsyns and the Dolgorukis would be prisoners in her company. But they were not to fall so suddenly. They were to feel their
fate overtaking them only gradually. They did not enjoy their meal.
The Empress seemed very gracious, but they knew that they were
at her mercy, and sensed she was playing cat and mouse with them.
This was her first real exercise in power and she was obviously
savouring it.

At four o'clock the delegates duly returned and asked her to
cancel the articles, dismiss the Council, reconstitute the Senate in
its old form and assume absolute power. Everyone expected that
she would comply, but she insisted on playing the charade out to the
end. She had promised to observe the conditions, she said, because
she thought that was her people's wish, and she affected surprise

when the petitioners denied this. 'Can it be that the points I signed at Mitau were not drawn up by the wish of the people?' she asked, and when cries of 'No!' duly welled up from the hall, she turned to Dolgoruki, the unfortunate diplomatist who had led the delegation to Mitau: 'That must mean that you deceived me, Prince Vasili Lukich.' Neither he nor his companions dared reply. A word out of place now and the Guardsmen, ranged about the hall, might lynch them, and when Anne asked if everyone agreed to her granting the petitioners' wish, even they dared not fail to signify assent. The paper setting out the offending conditions was sent for, and, very slowly, Anne tore it into shreds.

Then she made a speech. She would assume the same prerogatives as her ancestors had done, and whoever opposed her sovereignty would be punished for high treason—at which there was loud applause. She would govern, she continued, with justice and with mildness, and would always have the happiness of her people at heart, using harsh measures only in the utmost extremity.

Doubled guards patrolled the streets, a new oath of allegiance was drafted and messengers rushed out to all the provinces carrying the news. Paul Yagujinski was released from prison and Ostermann, his illness miraculously cured, returned to court. That night the Aurora Borealis was seen, and the entire horizon seemed to be drenched in blood, as if presaging the purge that was to follow.

In fact little blood was shed, but one by one, the grandees of the Council quietly disappeared. Exile, however, could be a very heavy penalty. It could involve the seizure of estates, a fall from noble to the meanest status, and a condemned man's family could be involved in his ruin. No one in society ever enquired after an exile—he became a non-person.

While the Dolgorukis and Golitsyns fell, others rose to prominence. Anne's relatives Vasili and Semen Saltykov received important posts; Cherkasski and others who had helped Anne remove the limits to her power received appropriate rewards, and new faces, including that of Ernest Biren, appeared at Court, though old Golovkin had trimmed his sails just sufficiently to the prevailing wind to be suffered to remain as Chancellor.

One of her first acts was to make a particular show of respect to Peter the Great's first wife, the elderly Yevdokia who had spent so many years a nun. When the two met, they fell weeping into each other's arms, and Anne arranged for the old Dowager to occupy a special box in the Cathedral to watch her coronation.

This was scheduled for 28 April and Anne determined that it should be a most lavish and imposing show. She supervised the arrangements personally, and the result, like the Empress herself now, was pompous, extravagant and touched with elements of barbarous incongruity.

There were Guardsmen in powdered curls and a grand procession across Kremlin Square led by heralds in tricorn hats and frock-like tunics in the Roman style. Carpets had been laid over the cobblestones, and Anne walked over them as if on air, under a canopy borne aloft by half a dozen generals, her long train held by her gentlemen-in-waiting, including the bull-like Ernest Biren.

The milling throng of spectators dropped their hands towards the ground in subject greeting as she passed, and so at last she came to the Cathedral. She kissed the cross which Archbishop Theophanes held out to her, allowed herself to be sprinkled with holy water, and glided on inside.

A glittering company awaited her—the royal princesses, the King of Georgia, all the leading people of the realm were there, each group segregated in its special box. And in the pews around the walls the merchants, the members of the foreign colony and their wives, the foreign envoys, the noblemen and generals sat, all as politely dressed as gallants in a play.

The Empress Autocrat of All Russia stood erect, her eyes stern and protruding beneath her curved brows, the huge cleft crown of state glittering upon her head, the diamond-studded stars of every Russian order reflecting light from her shoulders to her waist. She listened intently as the long list of all her titles was read out:

'Empress and Autocrat of all Russia, Muscovy, Kiev, Vladimir and Novgorod the Great, Tsarina of Kazan, Astrakhan and of Siberia, Lady of Pskov and Grand Duchess of Smolensk'. The even voice droned on, echoing off the high iconostasis and the lofty walls. 'Duchess of Estonia, Livonia and Karelia . . . Sovereign and Grand Duchess of Lower Novgorod, Chernigov, Ryazan . . . and Empress of all the northern regions . . . Mistress of the lands of Iveria, Kartli, Georgia . . . Hereditary Ruler of Circassia and the Dukes of the

Mountains . . .'. She might have listened to such delicious sounds all day. She heard the blessing intoned, Mass sung and the choirs yell out their Alleluias. Then, to the thunder of guns, the beat of kettle-drums and the blare of trumpets, the procession formed up again and passed between lines of Chevalier Guards, out into the sun.

There followed visits to the graves of her ancestors in the Church of the Archangel Michael, and to the Cathedral of the Annunciation. By then the ceremony had lasted four hours and she felt tired. She rested a little before proceeding to the coronation feast.

There at separate tables sat the ministers and the diplomatic corps, the generals and the clergy. In the gallery above, musicians serenaded them. Each guest was served from gold and silver dishes, but for the Empress who sat in solitary state upon her dais, there was no such ordinary service. The Chief Marshal of the Court, two gentlemen-in-waiting, a head carver and the Chief Butler all attended her. Each time she wished the courses to be changed, she would make a sign to the Chief Marshal who informed the Chief Master of Ceremonies, who signalled the Master of Ceremonies, who passed the imperial command on down a line of fifteen colonels who thereupon departed for the imperial kitchens. After a while they would appear again, bearing the imperial platters majestically aloft and slow-march back towards the Empress, each man flanked on either side by two Chevalier Guards with shouldered carbines which they raised to the present when the dishes reached the throne.

The feast was only half over when Anne moved over to the window to survey the common herd at dinner. The mob stood beneath her on the square, gazing at the huge oxen, stuffed with poultry, turning on their spits, then started to rush towards fountains of wine, one red, one white which suddenly began to gush. A dish of gold and silver coronation medals stood close by where she stood. Anne began to grasp handfuls of them, scatter them down over the people below, and watched laughing as they scrimmaged and fought each other for them. The medals bore a motto. It read 'From no one but God'.

Afterwards, she handed out promotions and awards to the more honourable company upstairs. She gave away estates as well, and diamonds too. A large number of foreigners were among the recipients including the mercenary Hesse-Homburg and the Loewen-woldes. Ostermann was made a Count and received estates worth 50,000 crowns a year besides. As for Ernest Biren, he was promoted Chief Gentleman-in-Waiting.

For him it was a great leap up the social scale, if not yet far enough to satisfy his considerable ambition. Conscious of his comparatively humble origins, he had altered the spelling of his name from 'Biren' to 'Biron' in order to reinforce a spurious claim to the arms of the French Dukes of that name. Cardinal Fleury persuaded the real Birons to bear the insult for he did not then want to antagonize the new Empress of Russia. Nor did the Austrians. They agreed to create him a Count of the Holy Roman Empire. So Ernest was a nobleman at last and people began to mutter that here was another Alexander Menshikov—and not even a Russian.

By 2 May, after five days of audiences and junketings, Anne's initial elation had worn off, and she was glad to drive to her Summer Palace outside Moscow. The freshness of the gardens there was a delight after the oppressiveness of the last few days; and she was reluctant to leave them for the great hall where she was to preside over a ball. At dusk, twenty thousand lamps flickered into light and transformed the familiar gardens into a pale, exotic fairyland. On her way home, she discovered that the entire diplomatic corps had lit up their houses in her honour and that the Spanish Ambassador, a gallant Irishman called the Duke de Liria, had gone so far as to have a triumphal arch built across the road and stationed trumpeters there to blow a fanfare as she passed. But that was not all. Moscow itself was ablaze with light, and dominating it, she was delighted to see, flashed a huge portrait of herself complete with her monogram and a list of all her virtues.

There were still three days of official celebrations left. Next day, a wire was stretched across the open space between the Red Staircase and the bell tower of Ivan the Great and when this was done a Persian acrobat appeared and proceeded to dance up and down it to the absolute astonishment of the crowd. This display was followed by a ball at which the guests drew lots to find their partners for the evening. Supper was held in the Golden Hall, where silver fountains played and there was a pool with real fishes swimming in it.

Next day there was a repeat performance and on 5 May, the last day of the festivities, there was dining and dancing in the Hall of the Facets and a final series of fireworks supervised by a colonel of artillery. Thus ended eight days of rejoicing described by the British envoy, Claudius Rondeau, as 'the best in all the world'.

Anne had decided that she should balance these joyful excesses with some simple act of traditional piety—a pilgrimage on foot to the Trinity Monastery some forty miles away. In the event, however, this exercise in humility proved rather less mortifying to the flesh than might have been expected. Since she walked only two, or at most three, miles a day, it took her over a fortnight to complete the pilgrimage, and each evening along the way she repaired to a sumptuous camp which was set up for her.

Her duty to God completed, Anne settled down to a luxurious summer at Ismailovo, where she had spent her childhood. She lived there, reported Rondeau, 'in great splendour'; her dresses were luxurious, her furniture fine and her table a veritable horn of plenty which spilled out hams, roast kid, asparagus and ortolans, salmon and caviare, boar's head done in Rhenish wine, chickens spiked with cloves, jellies, sugarbreads and ice-creams. There was arak, ratafia and brandy to drink, wines from Champagne and from Hungary, hock and burgundy, port and sherry and the fruit-flavoured meads she remembered from her youth. In fact Anne did not eat or drink a great deal—but she did enjoy the exercise of choice, her new-found opportunity to take an intriguing mouthful from a dish—and wave the rest away.

Faced with such an unprecedented range of choice, she found selection very difficult. She engaged architects to design a vast, baroque wooden palace, for instance, to be erected near the Summer Palace, then suddenly changed her mind and ordered the whole complex to be moved to a completely different site. She decided to move to St. Petersburg that winter (and everyone sighed with distress at the cost and inconvenience it would entail), then suddenly she decided she would stay in Moscow (and everyone sighed with relief). Then she decided that she would spend one year in three in St. Petersburg; then that she would never go there; but she did move there at the beginning of 1732 and, having done so, decided never again to return to Moscow.

In these first months of her reign she was in very benign mood. She enjoyed being courted and enjoyed being gracious to those who courted her. That June the Austrian envoy was particularly well received when he made Ernest Biron a Count of the Holy Roman Empire. That had been expected of him, but not the portrait of the Emperor and the gift of 200,000 thalers which the prudent Ernest promptly invested in an estate in far-away Silesia.

Andrei Ostermann was also made a Count. The motto he adopted for his crest, *nec sol, nec frigora mutant*, seemed less than apt, for no one was more sensitive to changes in the political temperature than he. But no one laughed; Ostermann had become too powerful a man to risk offending.

Born the son of a Westphalian clergyman, he had climbed to the top through the exercise of a rather broader range of talents than Ernest Biron's. He was master of several languages and proved adept at gaining the patronage of his superiors (and at betraying them when some advantage was to be gained by it); he could master all the essential details of a diplomatic problem and, by keeping the relevant papers to himself, create the impression of profound indispensability. He could be as servile and ingratiating as any Russian; knew how to avoid commitment in time of crisis, rarely looked another man straight in the eye, and could deliver his opinions with such delicate shades of double meaning as always to leave people with the impression that they had got their way. So Ostermann gained his reputation as a brilliant statesman. Anne certainly thought he was. Rondeau, however, considered him 'false and treacherous', and the German mercenary Manstein, while conceding that he worked hard, called him 'extremely distrustful', a man who could 'neither endure superior nor equal, unless their abilities were palpably inferior to his own'. Ostermann was also mean. He kept his servants in rags, wore repulsive food-stained clothes, and, except on special occasions, kept a very poor, and rather dirty, table.

Despite her faith in him, Anne kept the doddering old Golovkin as her Chancellor—probably at Ostermann's own suggestion for he sensed that the growing number of foreigners with whom Anne surrounded herself would rouse popular resentment. Besides Ostermann and Biron there was the inveterate gambler Gustav Loewenwolde, Marshal of the Court, and his elder brother Reinhold,

Colonel of a new Guards Regiment staffed almost entirely by Livonians and other foreigners. Then there was Ludwig Hesse-Homburg and Baron Mengden too, and even Yagujinski was of Lithuanian, not Russian, origin. Anne it seemed preferred foreigners to Russians.

Yet the alliances and cliques at court did not divide along lines of nationality. Cherkasski aligned himself with Yagujinski in an attempt to trim Ostermann's sails; Ostermann and Biron were soon at daggers drawn. Alliances changed constantly and the intrigues became kaleidoscopic as competition for Anne's favours and attentions grew.

Now she was Empress there was a sudden rush of suitors from abroad. Most of them made discreet proposals through diplomatic channels, but in August the Infante of Portugal arrived. He was seen off within three weeks. Then Maurice de Saxe made another attempt. Anne let him dangle for a time, then delicately let him drop. What need had she for marriage now that she had every man in Russia at her feet?

Lacking beauty herself she surrounded herself with it. She ordered silks and brocades from Western Europe, never appeared twice in the same dress, employed French hairdressers and stylists, and ordered fine new liveries for her expanded staff. She encouraged others to follow her example. 'I cannot express', wrote Claudius Rondeau, 'how magnificent this court is in clothes. . . . I never saw such heaps of gold and silver lace upon cloth, and even gold and silver stuffs, as are seen here.' No expense was spared. A suit of clothes fit to wear at court could cost as much as £2,000 in the money of the time, and there were noblemen, reported Rondeau, who sold off their estates in order to buy fine clothes with which to cut a dash at court.

Anne was in no mood to economize even though, as Rondeau reported early in 1731 'they have not a shilling in the Treasury'. As a result 'nobody is paid which contributes very much to the general complaints.' The complainants included members of the gentry, and to the extent that Anne concerned herself with state affairs—and she worked at them conscientiously from nine till noon each day—she was primarily concerned to propitiate the gentry. After all, it was they who had supported her against the great men of the

Council and they were too powerful a force to risk offending. So, knowing how much they resented Peter the Great's Entail Law which stopped them sharing their estates out among their children when they died, she reversed it. And she did much else besides. She made it illegal for peasants and other people of low class to buy estates with serfs, thus reserving the right solely for the gentry; she put land along the Volga belonging to Tatar chiefs at their disposal; founded a Corps of Cadets from which young gentlemen could be commissioned directly into the army without having the inconvenience, so much resented, of having to serve as privates in the guards. Nonetheless, gentry in government or at court finding their salaries unpaid and faced with ruin were forced to extract ever greater bribes from supplicants and petitioners and to squeeze more and more out of their serfs, while tax-collectors became ever more zealous, oppressive and unjust in their attempts to keep the Empress—and themselves—from bankruptcy.

The burden on the people, which Catherine's government had made some attempt to alleviate, became heavier again, and not only in economic matters. In the name of Orthodoxy Anne launched campaigns of oppression against non-Christians and schismatics. 'Wizards' and 'magicians' were burned at the stake, and a reign of terror was instituted against the numerous sect of 'Old Believers'. The Office of Secret Investigations which Catherine had abolished was revived. The network of spies was expanded; more and more people were placed under surveillance. The number of secret trials increased; so did the use of torture; and 'insulting the Imperial Person of Her Majesty by using offensive expressions' became once more a major offence.

Poverty and oppression were increasing, yet to look at Anne's court one might have thought her country happy and her exchequer full. The Russian cake might be mouldering, but the icing on it was thick, and Anne made it even thicker by becoming patroness of the arts.

Operas were now performed at court and no function was now complete without its specially written music supervised by the celebrated Madonis whom Anne had brought over from Paris at a salary of 3,000 roubles a year. Foreign theatrical companies were also made welcome and the ballet became extremely popular.

Her new Cadet Corps housed in Menshikov's old palace played a particular role in this artistic boom for Anne had decided that young gentlemen of the coming generation should be accomplished courtiers and dabblers in the arts, as well as soldiers. Germans were engaged to teach them languages and history, 'arithmetic, geometry, drawing, fortifications, artillery, fencing, riding and other studies necessary for military action.' But 'dancing, music and other useful sciences' also figured in the curriculum, and beyond that they were encouraged to stage amateur theatricals which in time were to provide Anne with much pleasant, and free, entertainment.

While so many of her subjects languished, Anne would attend dinners wearing cloth of gold and silver petticoats, and go on to the Italian opera where she contrived to make a greater show in the auditorium than the *prima donna* made on the stage. Yet her country's troubles were not blamed on her. Many thought she was a sympathetic woman. Certainly she seemed easily moved to tears. The harshness of her regime was attributed not to her, but to her advisers and especially the foreigners.

In fact Count Biron, the Loewenwoldes, Mengden and Hesse-Homburg, though prominent at court and showered with favours, had comparatively little influence on affairs. Andrei Ostermann, however, had. Anne consulted him regularly, sometimes twice a day. His influence extended now to internal as well as foreign affairs and he dominated the small 'Cabinet Council' which he had persuaded Anne to create. Of the two members besides himself, Chancellor Golovkin was usually absent and Prince Cherkasski was handled easily enough. Paul Yagujinski was the only man to rival him in ability and experience, but he was too outspoken, and his lack of tact was soon to lead to his downfall. He was once ill-advised enough to tease Ostermann in Anne's presence. She had laughed, but Ostermann was not amused. The Empress warned Paul not to offend the man unnecessarily, but he soon got his revenge. Realizing that Anne could refuse Biron nothing, he arranged to set him against his rival. The upshot was that Yagujinski was got rid of as Ambassador to Berlin. His posts as Adjutant General and Marshal of the Horse passed to the younger Loewenwolde. Despite his power, Ostermann tried, chameleon-like, to merge into the background, rarely appearing in public at all. To all appearances

Ernest Biron seemed the most powerful man at court, and Ostermann took care to keep on good terms with him. Biron and Ostermann were reputed not to like each other, but as unpopular foreigners
they recognized the value of a certain solidarity. However powerful
and influential they might be, they felt vulnerable; and it was this
that led them to persuade Anne to move her court from Moscow
to St. Petersburg. Rondeau thought so anyway. 'The favourites
think they shall be there out of the daily hearing of complaints', he
reported, 'and in more security than they can be here.'

Anne arrived in the city on 16 January 1732, attended a service
of thanksgiving for her safe arrival, listened to a series of welcom-
ing speeches, presided over a formal dinner, attended a fireworks
display and finally a ball. The last two items alone cost 100,000
crowns but Anne was in a spending mood.

St. Petersburg was as yet less than half the size of Moscow, and
still consisted mainly of single-storey shacks. But more and more
stone structures were rising up, government offices were worthily
housed now in handsome buildings and Trezzini's great church of
Saints Peter and Paul was almost finished, its graceful spire, awaiting its final sheath of gold, already dominating the city and the
dreary marshes round about. In the middle of it all stood the
Winter Palace. Rondeau's wife was not impressed with it—'a
great number of little rooms', she wrote, 'and nothing remarkable
either in architecture, painting or furniture.' Anne, presumably,
shared this opinion, for she took up residence next door in the
palace that had once belonged to Count Apraxin, and sent for
Bartolomeo Rastrelli, who had designed the triumphal arches
which had welcomed her to St. Petersburg, and various parapher-
nalia for the coronation masquerade. She commanded him to 'build
a great stone Winter Palace' four stories high not counting cellars
and mezzanines. There was to be a great hall that was really great,
a gallery, a theatre, grand formal staircases and a splendid chapel—
all to be richly decorated with sculptures and with paintings.

Rastrelli's palace would be the work of years, but there were
more immediate enjoyments to be tasted: the sight of her entire
court standing respectfully before her while she dined in state as
Louis XIV had done at Versailles, or of her handsome Guards in
peruke wigs and beautiful new uniforms who staged mock battles

on the river ice for her amusement. In the spring she would sit by her window watching the ships and barges pass, and visit the docks to see foreign merchantmen arriving and the gangers struggling up and down the planks, shouting and cursing under their heavy loads of merchandise. She received an envoy from Turkey and another from China, the first ever to visit Europe. He brought her gifts of porcelain, coral and mother of pearl, and when asked if he was not surprised by the court masquerade he was invited to attend, he replied calmly in the negative—everything in Russia seemed but a masquerade to him.

Early in September, accompanied by a vast retinue of eighty boats, Anne went to see another wonder—the newly finished Ladoga canal which her uncle, Peter the Great had begun some fifteen years before. The technicalities involved in cutting a waterway seventy feet wide and sixteen deep a distance of some sixty miles were beyond her comprehension, but she enjoyed the outing and particularly the company of the man who had supervised the completion of the work, Burckhardt Christoph von Münnich.

Manly and charming, he was some fifty years of age with a long narrow face, a sensuous mouth, an eagle nose and shrewd, determined eyes. He came from Oldenburg in Germany, had fought with Prince Eugene at Oudenarde and was promoted colonel at Malplacquet. Engaged by Peter the Great as a military engineer, he had been steadily promoted and now, with Ernest Biron's favour, he had become Field Marshal and Minister for War.

It was he who had introduced German uniforms to Anne's army; he was now Prussianizing its drill and discipline. The birch and pointed rods were liberally used now upon the soldier's backs, and the barking of their German officers, and of Russians trained to ape them, was becoming sharper. That year twenty thousand men deserted from Anne's army—eight men out of every hundred— and more would have done so had they dared.

In January that year men of a regiment employed on public works at Kronstadt complained about their bad conditions. Their corporal embarked on a eulogy of Anne's graciousness, whereupon a soldier called Sedov remarked she ought to be 'bruised over the head with a brick'. He was immediately arrested, handed over to the secret police, interrogated and condemned to death. Anne commuted the sentence—to hard labour for life in Siberia—and ordered those who had born witness against him to be rewarded. Such were the methods Anne's government used to maintain order. It was to have further recourse to them as the situation in the country gave rise to greater discontent.

Russians could not pay their taxes. The assessments were often unrealistically high, and the method of collection such that barely half of what was collected probably ever reached the government—which only made the methods of collection more extortionate. Yet in 1732 poll-tax arrears totalled $15\frac{1}{2}$ million roubles and of the $2\frac{1}{2}$ million roubles expected from customs dues and other indirect taxation, only 187,000 roubles could be collected. The economy was slowing down; harvests were bad; peasants began to mutter that the corn would not grow because a woman sat on Russia's throne. Others attributed their hardships to the hated Germans who ruled Russia, and malcontents turned to arson as a form of inarticulate protest. Fires were started at Kronstadt and in St. Petersburg. But nothing could move the government from its policies, nor curb the galloping expenditure at court.

Senior officers were told to acquire at least three mounts costing a thousand roubles each, the Knights of St. Andrew to appear at their annual dinner wearing golden coats and breeches with masses of lace ruffling, silver-lined cloaks and swords and belts made out of solid gold. Guests at the imperial soirées held every Thursday and Sunday were also expected to dress up to the occasion, and everyone who spent less than two or three thousand a year on suits alone was despised as cutting a very poor figure indeed.

Tastes for sheer magnificence spread from the Empress and her friends to the aristocracy and, as people tried to live up to their fellow Joneses, to the gentry as a whole. Members of society came to vie with one another in the splendour of their palaces and entertainments, the champagne and burgundy with which they plied their guests, the English mahogany furniture upon which they begged to be seated, the multiplicity of mirrors in which they could admire themselves, the richness of their saddlery and the sumptuousness of their upholstered equipages.

Yet the immense sums spent often produced incongruous results. 'The richest coat', wrote one visitor, 'would sometimes be worn with the vilest dressed wig; or you might see a beautiful piece of cloth ruined by some clumsy tailor; or if there was nothing wrong with the dress, the equipage would be a failure. . . . On one side you might see heaps of gold and silver plate. On the other, the grossest filth. . . .' Mere ostentation would ultimately give way to finer taste, but the Russian peasant had meanwhile to foot the huge and wasteful bill.

One of the leaders in this advance to greater luxury was Ernest Biron, now the Lord High Chamberlain. He liked good horses for instance, and Anne had the finest horses imported for him. Indeed he had such a passion for the equine species that it was said that he spoke like a man when he talked about horses and like a horse when he talked about men. But the adventurer from Courland was no fool. He took good care to hold his place against assaults from other aspirants and kept a wary eye on the handsome Marshal Münnich who seemed his likeliest potential rival for Anne's favours.

Biron and Anne still spent much time in each other's company, amused themselves with the 'singing and talking birds' in the aviary, played billiards, hunted in the summer time and in winter went riding in the great stables he had built. Otherwise they would sit about in his apartments with his little pock-marked wife, eating, gossiping, making tapestries or playing with the children. In these informal hours Anne would have her hair done up in a kerchief, and wear a loose robe in red or blue or green—strong colours which both she and Ernest liked. For informal receptions at the court however she commonly appeared in a black dress with a red corsage. In contrast to Peter the Great, Anne disapproved of heavy drinking on such occasions but she positively encouraged gambling.

Cards, *quinze*, *ombre* and faro particularly became very popular and vast sums were staked, twenty thousand roubles won and lost at a single sitting being not at all unusual. Anne herself generally preferred to watch, and when she did play she always took the bank which she used as a means of doling out money to those she favoured, accepting counters which were never redeemed and paying out in solid gold. Mrs. Rondeau, the English envoy's wife, thought this incessant gambling very tedious. There might have been some 'agreeable conversation', she sighed, 'if cards were not known in Russia.'

Still, watching the Empress was an agreeable substitute for conversation and Mrs. Rondeau found her impressive enough, grim and forbidding at first sight perhaps, 'but when she speaks, she has a smile about her mouth that is inexpressibly sweet', and she would chat very affably with her guests almost as an equal. 'Yet', added Mrs. Rondeau hastily, 'she does not for one moment drop the dignity of a sovereign. She seems to have great humanity', she concluded, 'and is, I think, what one would call a fine agreeable woman, were she a private person.' The impression was deceptive. Anne might seem gracious enough in front of foreigners at receptions, but graciousness was less in evidence in the Empress's other dealings.

Anne exercised a rough brand of sardonic humour, and though she may not have hanged her chef for cooking pancakes in rancid butter as was rumoured she could behave quite viciously. The poet Tredyakovski describes how after giving a reading in Anne's presence, he 'had the honour to receive from her Imperial Majesty's own hand a most gracious slap in the face', and once when a poor gentlewoman forced to sing to her all night pleaded exhaustion, Anne sent her to work in her private laundry for a week.

This laundry had become something of a fixation for the Empress. She issued a curiously detailed set of instructions about it. 'Keep a special room', she ordered, 'for washing . . . my linen, and always keep it under lock and key, opening it only when there is some washing to be done. Engage special washerwomen for this—seven or as many as may be necessary—and make sure that they do not do any washing for courtiers or outsiders . . . and that no one who has no business there is let into the room while the washing is in progress.'

It would have been as well if Anne had taken as much care of her subjects' welfare as she did about her dirty underwear. But then private business always had more attraction for her than did public affairs. The years at Mitau had left scars, and having been spied on herself, she now developed a rather sinister passion for spying on others.

She had private correspondence opened whenever she suspected that the contents might amuse her; ordered watches to be kept on anyone connected with the court whose morals she suspected and had them spirited away to monasteries and nunneries when their offences against her code were not serious enough to merit stronger punishment. 'Write and let me know', she told the Governor of Moscow, 'if Kammerherr Yusupov is still married. It is said here that they have separated.' 'Write to me secretly', ran another of her letters, 'when the Belozerski girl got married and where and how she behaves and how Princess Mary Kurakin received her.' No tit-bit of gossip was beneath her attention and she stored it all away for future reference, for use in quite malicious interference in the lives of people for whom she had conceived a dislike.

Among these was the thirty-six-year-old Prince Michael Golitsyn, a relative of the Golitsyns who had once tried to limit her autocratic powers. He was a man of unusual culture, had studied in Italy and France and had earned Anne's disfavour by marrying an Italian girl, and a Catholic to boot. The Empress had him tracked down and brought to Court where she forced him to play the role of her buffoon, thus punishing a sinner and finding amusement for herself at the same time.

Returning to the coarse and cruel amusements she had known in her youth she collected a whole cohort of clowns for her private use, all of them of noble origins. Only one of them, Ivan Balakirev, had any professional experience. Balakirev was the son of a poor landowner, and a dwarf. He had entertained Peter the Great until he had been drafted into the army for his involvement in the schemes of William Mons. Anne had rescued him, though Balakirev was soon to wonder if he had not been happier in the army than at Court. But the clown who gave Anne most amusement was Golitsyn. 'He is the best of all', she wrote to Governor Saltykov in Moscow, 'and has beaten all the fools here. If in time such another one as he should be found let me know immediately.'

Anne's concern for her own immediate family, however, was innocent enough. Her younger sister, Praskovya, had died, and her only surviving relatives now were her elder sister Catherine, who had given her such support during the accession crisis, and Catherine's daughter, called Anna. The child was about fifteen when the Empress set out to find her a husband. Foreign envoys rushed to offer their suggestions, and the choice eventually fell on Austria's candidate, the fourteen-year-old Anton-Ulrich, Prince of Brunswick-Bevern. The boy arrived in St. Petersburg on 6 March 1733. He was short, blond, humble, in all rather unimpressive; but he

Catherine I,
by Karl Moor, 1717

Dwarfs' feast

dding feast of Peter the
at and Catherine I

ЗИМНЕИ ДВОРЕЦ

thplace of Elizabeth:
lomensky near Moscow

Catherine I in regimental uniform

e first Winter Palace in St. Petersburg,
raving by Zubor, 1717

Praskovya, mother of
the Empress Anne

Anne,
by Caravaque, 1730 (?)

Frederick William,
Duke of Courland

Biron

ne's coronation

itsyn wedding procession to Ice Palace, 1740

Triumphal arch

Firework display, 1730

zabeth on horseback, *by Grooth, 1743*

Beztuzhev

Lomonossov

Peter III,
Catherine II's husband

Catherine II

A riverside view of the
Admiralty, St. Petersburg

View of St. Petersburg from
the Moika Canal

Grenadier uniform,
1756–60

Grenadier uniform,
1742–62

Court herald

Life Guard in uniform

was very well received. As for his prospective bride, she was an introspective, serious and rather bashful girl. She seemed too young for marriage, and, to her credit, the Empress, remembering the unhappy marriage arranged for her sister, decided that her niece should not be rushed. There was time, she concluded, for the two to become better acquainted and perhaps in time to form a genuine affection for each other. So Prince Anton was lodged near the palace, given attendants from the Empress's own household and, under the supervision of a reliable duenna, Julia Mengden, brought much into the Princess's company.

On 19 May 1733 the court moved to the Summer Palace. The same day Anne wrote to Governor Saltykov in Moscow giving him another list of people whose correspondence should be seized, or who were to be placed under house arrest. She also gave instructions about the building of a comedy theatre and told him to send her nearly a hundred lengths of damask cloth of a dozen different colours. But within a month her plans were rudely interrupted when her sister Catherine died.

Too upset to attend the funeral, Anne left at once for Peterhof, and when Rondeau called on her ten days later to deliver his condolences she appeared 'very much afflicted and shed a great many tears'. Shortly afterwards Lord Forbes was appointed Ambassador. But though Anne had long been piqued that Britain's representative should be a mere commoner like Rondeau, her satisfaction at having an Englishman of real quality at her court at last was dimmed by her bereavement and Forbes was advised to make no reference to consolation when presenting his credentials for fear this would 'discompose' the Empress. The pain faded slowly, but Peterhof was a very comforting place. 'One of the pleasantest sites', wrote one visitor, 'that can be imagined.' The house itself was rather modest, the apartments being 'extremely small and low', but there were splendid prospects, delightful woods, a magnificent *jet d'eau*, fine gardens where Ernest Biron and his friends played mall, and a long vista out to sea.

From her window Anne could see Kronstadt and the tall ships riding out at anchor there. The shipyards were busy again and the condition of the fleet had much improved, some twenty battleships and over a hundred galleys being fit for service now. It was as well that they were, for Russia was about to go to war again.

That summer the King of Poland died. France wanted Stanislaus Leczinski to be elected his successor, Russia and Austria supported the late King's son. Fifty-seven thousand Russian troops under the old Irish mercenary General Lacy drove Stanislaus out of Warsaw and the Russian candidate sent Anne a fine service of Dresden china as an expression of his gratitude. But with French support Stanislaus set up a rival court at Danzig. The War of the Polish Succession had begun.

It was a war Russia could ill afford. There was a terrible famine that year. Starving peasants fled to the unstable borderlands or crowded into the towns, bringing their diseases with them. Others refused outright to pay rents and taxes. Landlords and bailiffs were murdered and cases of arson showed a marked increase. A pretender had appeared claiming to be the Tsarevich Alexei, the rightful Tsar of Russia, and then another who claimed to be Peter, son of Peter the Great. Rebellion threatened in several Provinces and as grim reports of disorders flowed in, the government reacted in the only way it understood: punitive detachments were sent out to quell riots and put troublesome peasants in chains until their taxes were paid up. The pretenders were arrested and Anne signed the orders for their execution without demur. One was burned to death in public; the other impaled upon a stake.

Good news from Poland where her troops were closing in round Danzig gave more cause for celebration when the new year, Anne's birthday, her name day and the anniversary of her accession all came round again. Courtiers knelt to kiss the imperial hand and toss off their bumpers of Hungarian wine—the only occasion in the year they were permitted to drink so much, that privilege being reserved at all other times to Prince Kurakin whose drunken antics happened to amuse the Empress.

Rastrelli's new winter palace was almost ready. There was a throne room decorated with glass and leather, and a heating system powerful enough to keep rows of orange trees and myrtles in full bloom. Russia had never seen so wonderful a thing, said Archbishop Theophanes, and it enraptured Mrs. Rondeau. 'The beauty, fragrance and warmth of this new-formed grove, when you see nothing but ice and snow through the windows', she wrote, 'looked like enchantment.' Several splendid balls were immediately held there. Gilded coaches drew up at the doors, glittering crowds swarmed up the staircase; plump belles and beaux supped tea and coffee, danced, and played innumerable games of cards. Sometimes the company assembled in carnival attire and peered out through misty windows to admire fireworks let off from the jetty on the island opposite.

Anne presided happily over her private fairy-land—a faery queen content to leave affairs to Ostermann—and to Ernest Biron, who was already emerging from his cautious place in the political wings to take a more obvious part in state affairs. Prince Cherkasski would shortly be displaced, and now the two Germans conspired to have their potential rival, Marshal Münnich, sent away.

He went to Poland to take over command from General Lacy who was given charge of another force sent to take up a watch on the Rhine. Russian troops had never marched so far west before and Anne waited impatiently for the panting couriers to arrive carrying despatches. In fact Lacy's troops did no fighting at all, but Münnich found a hard fight on his hands at Danzig. Courtiers sneered at his failure to push the matter to a quick conclusion. He complained that he had too few troops at his disposal. The fleet was sent to help him, but still the siege continued.

In May the court moved into the Summer Palace and found a new diversion—Dutch spinning tops. The craze lasted for weeks and special couriers had to be sent to Amsterdam for quantities of suitable twine to keep everyone supplied.

Anne also sent away for every conceivable kind of craftsman, artist and inventor who might help to make her existence more comfortable and amusing. The cabinet-makers Michel and André Crinieux were engaged and Rochebot, a specialist in making 'beds in the French fashion'. A new Italian band arrived, the artist Phillippe Bazancourt was brought from France and so was the celebrated Landet, the first *maître-de-ballet* to the court, who started another craze teaching everyone to dance the minuet.

In July came the long awaited news that Danzig had fallen. The heavy Russian casualties and the fact that Stanislaus had managed to escape were not allowed to detract from the round of self-congratulatory celebrations. They were curtailed, however, when Ernest Biron had a fit of colic, followed by a fever. Suddenly afraid that he might die Anne became quite distraught, and wandered about with tears in her eyes saying Ernest was the only person she could trust. Suspecting Ostermann wanted to see him dead, even though he appeared 'to be very sorry', she sent him away on some invented mission. But it was all unnecessary. Ernest recovered; Anne regained her composure and the celebrations were resumed.

The climax came at the end of August with a great banquet and masquerade ball held in the Summer Gardens. The ladies, Mrs. Rondeau observed, 'were dressed in stiffened-bodied gowns of white gauze decorated with silver flowers, and quilted petticoats of different colours.' They wore no wigs but 'only their own hair, cut short, and curled in large natural curls' and topped with chaplets of flowers. The Empress took her seat in the grotto with the royal princesses, her niece, and her cousin Elizabeth, while three hundred guests ranged themselves in front of her at tables set out under the long green silk tent supported by pillars hung with flowers which stretched almost the entire length of the long walk. The gentlemen had drawn tickets for their partners and 'every man sat by his partner at table', a mixing of the sexes which still made most older Russians feel uncomfortable.

Two courses each of six hundred dishes were served besides a dessert, and after they had eaten the company amused themselves in the gardens until evening when everything was prettily illuminated and the ball began, the musicians being hidden away behind a hedge so that 'it appeared as if the deity of the place . . . supplied the entertainment'.

The high point came when French officers taken prisoner at Danzig were led in to be gloated over. Anne at first rubbed salt into their wounds by telling their commander, the Count de la Motte, that she considered he had treated his Russian prisoners very badly. She had the power, she said, to take revenge. However, as she was a generous person, she would not—and summoning up some ladies who spoke French, told them to console the prisoners for the remainder of the evening. Gallant Frenchmen subsequently let out on parole were to find no lack of hostesses eager to experience true *politesse*, and in the weeks that followed not a few Russian husbands were cuckolded.

Anne herself, however, had no taste for Frenchmen, and, apart from Ernest Biron, seemed to prefer the company of women these days. Her staff of female attendants grew steadily in numbers and each member was hand-picked for her talent to amuse and given nicknames—'Mother No-Feet', 'Long Darya' and 'Catherine the Cat'—conforming to their personal characteristics. That October she wrote to Governor Saltykov ordering him to find exotic 'Persian, Georgian or Lesghian girls' of specified height who 'must be clean, good, and not stupid' to add to them, and when one of her performers took sick, a prodigious gossiper she had known since her childhood, she ordered Saltykov to find someone who resembled her. 'I believe she will soon die', she wrote, and 'I want someone to replace her. You know what We want—someone about forty, who is chatty.' In this way Anne made sure she always had people on hand to keep up a ceaseless show of song and witty or malicious chatter—her private eighteenth-century equivalent of a pop radio programme.

She continued to amuse herself supervising the lives of certain selected subjects too. 'Let me know if Prince Fedor Shcherbatov is taking his wife with him of his own free will', she ordered. 'If he doesn't want to take her, then tell him that he must, and no lame excuses.' Have that person watched; have this man's correspondence opened—Anne made full use of her autocratic powers, and spent with greater freedom than ever. That year's bill for the royal stables totalled 100,000 roubles—as much as was spent on maintaining Russia's entire diplomatic service; a quarter of a million went on the building of new palaces—half as much again as on the entire central state administration. Anne treated Russia as if it were her private estate, and she was a careless landlord. While grain was exported to pay for the luxuries imported for her court, people in famine areas were allowed to starve. Yet she tolerated no criticism of her extravagance. When Count Alexander Rumyantsev was offered the Finance Ministry and he protested that he could not in all conscience undertake to raise so much money for the court while people were so poor, she had him arrested, stripped of his honours, and banished to Kazan. An Empress Autocrat anointed by God could not, after all, be wrong.

Anne had begun her reign with some sense of her obligations as an Empress, and had come only gradually to neglect affairs and sink into the morass of luxury. It took five years for the full extent of her corruption to become evident, yet it was not the product of power alone. The roots ran deep into her past. The narrowness of her upbringing, the disappointments of her youth, the long, unhappy years at Mitau had made half her life a wasteland in which nothing would grow except the Dragon's Teeth of cruelty and vindictiveness. Now, at last, they produced a bumper crop. She had been kept poor and now she spent as none of her predecessors had spent; she had once been made to crawl before others, and now she made others crawl to her. Her own suffering had anaesthetized her sensitivity to the suffering of others, and her sadistic streak found a new vent now in a taste for other's degradations. True, her enemies of former years like Alexander Menshikov were now beyond her reach, but she found substitutes on whom to vent her spite.

Anne had grown up with a taste for tumblers and grotesques, the sight of ugliness and physical impediments. She had her professional clowns and satirists at court now—Jean da Costa the Portuguese Jew, Balakirev the dwarf, and 'Pedrillo' the Neapolitan violinist who found he made a better living as a *buffa* figure at the palace. But the antics of professionals was not enough for Anne. She treated ordinary courtiers, too, as clowns. There were the two gluttonous noblewomen Natasia and Asisia who were made to swallow down endless successions of pastries, and, best of all, there were the proud and sober noblemen she made fools of—Prince Alexei Apraxin, Prince Nikita Volkonski who was appointed Keeper of her favourite dog, a greyhound, and made to feed it at appointed hours with jugs of cream, and Prince Michael Golitsyn who was stationed outside her door, ready to rush in whenever she called with a flagon of *kvass*.

Nor did their wives escape. Volkonski's spouse was given charge of the Empress's pet white rabbit; and a full scale witch-hunt was launched against Prince Michael's wife whom he had been forced to leave in Moscow. On 16 January 1735, Anne asked to be informed where she was living. 'Question the Catholic priests as to what subsistence she has and who supplies it', she told Governor Saltykov. 'And if she is not in Moscow, find out where she has gone and at whose expense.' The unfortunate woman was eventually hounded to an untimely death, but there seemed to be no end to the degradation heaped on her husband and his fellows.

Anne ordered Golitsyn and Volkonski to be 'married'; she made them sit in straw baskets outside her room and cackle and flap about like hens each time she passed them by on her way to chapel; she made them stand up in line against the wall like dunces, trip each other up so that they fell heavily upon the floor, pull each other's hair, and fight until the blood flowed. And when they did this 'Her Majesty', as one observer reported, 'looked on in raptures, exploding with laughter at the spectacle.'

Balakirev the dwarf once refused to play her games, protesting he was ill. He was taken out and thrashed with rods. Even Ernest Biron found the grotesque farces staged under the threat of whip and bastinado too much to stomach, but even he dared not protest; so the degrading scenes continued.

Such amusements were only for Anne's private hours, however. Outsiders like Elizabeth Justice, who had just arrived from England and who was to publish her account of her experiences in Russia in the 1740s, were still given the impression that the Empress was 'always merciful', just as Jane Rondeau was assured that Anne was possessed of 'the most amiable qualities' and showed 'unaffected horror at any mark of cruelty'. On more than one occasion the Empress was observed to 'melt into tears at a melancholy story', and it is true that she was genuinely sentimental. Tyrants usually are.

As rumours of Anne's true nature leaked out, members of St. Petersburg society, or such of them as could yet read, rushed out to buy a new book portraying Messalina and other evil females hoping it might throw more light on her character. But the firework displays staged on public occasions still threw up pictures of her attended by 'Charity' and 'Justice', holding a horn of plenty and the motto 'Beyond Praise'.

In February 1735 Anne was 'graciously pleased to declare that she will remit the last half-year's poll-tax to all her subjects.' The concession was not quite as generous as it seemed. The people could not pay the poll-tax anyway. She was merely writing off a bad debt. But the famine and the poverty in the countryside were not allowed to diminish the merry-making of the court. Sledging was a favourite sport at the pre-Lenten carnival that year, and since 'great numbers' of people broke 'their legs and arms' in the process, it was a diversion interesting enough 'to have Her Majesty for a Spectator'. After Lent came the Easter festivities, with the usual congratulations, the exchanges of Easter eggs, the prostrations before icons, and the resumption of entertainments over which Hesse-Homburg, the new Grand Master of Ceremonies racked his brains.

In March the Empress suffered another 'little attack of the Gout', but by April she was back to form again, ordering the fire-bells to be rung about the city to see how much consternation they might cause. Three days later the heavens answered her. Lightning struck two St. Petersburg churches and burned one down to the ground, and Anne, mortally afraid of thunder-storms, was panic-stricken. But she recovered sufficiently by coronation day to entertain all her ministers at Court.

It was there that to Ostermann's 'unspeakable grief' his arch-enemy Yagujinski appeared again, recalled from Berlin to take up the posts of Cabinet Minister and Chief Master of the Horse in succession to Loewenwolde, who had died that month. The two men still hated one another, but having taken the bold step of trying to balance Ostermann's power, Anne was not persuaded to devote any more time to government business.

That summer she visited Peterhof again, inaugurated Rastrelli's great new 'Samson' fountain and went shooting and walking in the gardens. But the forest fires burning now for the second year, de-tracted from her pleasure. 'It is so smoky here', she wrote to General Ushakov, 'that one dare not open a window. . . . We are very surprised that no one sees to holding back these fires.' The fires, so much a feature of Anne's reign, symbolized the smoulder-ing discontent within the country, and at last the government took some action to reduce the discomfort. Retired army surgeons were posted as medical officers in the larger towns and food was distri-buted to starving peasants from government stocks—a measure which had the added value of allowing landowners to keep their labour-forces alive at the state's expense. But such remedies were too slight to cope with the aftermath of two successive famine years. The number of peasants fleeing from cruel or over-demanding landlords was still increasing, and many of them turned to robbery as a means of subsistence, making the highways so dangerous for travellers that the forest had to be cleared on either side of every major road in order to cut down the bandits' cover, while the number of army units deployed in collecting taxes, tracking down brigands, catching runaway serfs and dragging dissident priests off to punishment had to be considerably increased.

Meanwhile the new Italian opera was making a great stir in the capital. It was supervised by Francesco Araja who had only recently arrived at court fresh from triumphs in Naples, Rome and Florence. He gradually assembled a whole array of talent—Marigi the male soprano from Bologna, the tenor Filippo Georgi from Rome, his wife Caterina, a soprano, and the lively Rosina Bon. Araja's first production was entitled *La Forza del' Amore e del' Odio*, but the opera itself, although 'very well done' was rather less appreciated than its comedy interludes. Anne also preferred *Commedia dell' Arte*, and German burlesque still more—chiefly because they almost always ended with someone getting a beating. Only gradually did she surrender to more sophisticated tastes, particularly to Girolamo Bon's ballets in which Antonio Fusano danced the comic leads and which boasted a *prima ballerina* who was to earn a certain posthumous notoriety as Casanova's mother.

The theatre was taking strong root in Russia with Anne's encouragement. She had built a fine new theatre with a thousand seats and in winter went there twice a week. And the Empress's troupe was not the only one in St. Petersburg. Singers, dancers and comedians from the West were flocking into Russia now, confident that they would find a patron, and hopeful impresarios issued beguiling advertisements for their shows. One enterprising puppeteer offered 'the worthy comedy entitled *On the Crime of our Prime Forebears Adam and Eve*' in which he promised that 'views of Hades and of beautiful Paradise will be depicted . . . together with various wild beasts and delightful songbirds.'

The vast new Palace Anne had ordered to be built in Moscow was ready now, but it waited empty for her. Her new Winter Palace in St. Petersburg with its seventy suites, its ceiling painted by Caravaque, its gilded galleries, and its sumptuous theatre had sufficient attractions to hold her now. She ordered the royal portraits to be brought up from Moscow. She would never return there again.

On Wednesday 28 January 1736, the night before her birthday, the Empress, accompanied by Ernest Biron, went to a performance of the Italian opera in her theatre. Elizabeth Justice was there as well and left an account of the affair. Anne, wearing a huge, hooped 'French Night-Gown of plain Padua' and a fine lace 'Aspadilly cap' with a crotchet of diamonds to one side took her seat in the centre of the pit between her niece, the Princess Anna, who was dressed in crimson velvet, and her cousin, the Princess Elizabeth who wore a gown of gold and silver cloth. Both of her companions glittered with diamonds and the rest of the audience glittered too, the ladies in evening gowns in the French style, the men with velvet suits sewn with pearls. The unmarried girls wore their hair long and braided up, a broad piece of silver or gold lace on their foreheads, sleeveless jackets and gaudy petticoats. Everyone arrived in fur cloaks for it was bitterly cold—so cold that, as Rondeau reported, every day 'a great many poor people and travellers' were brought 'to the police, frozen to death.' Not that St. Petersburg society did not like to wear their furs even in the height of summer, to keep out the heat as they claimed, but in reality to show them off.

Among this general splendour it took the arrival of so unusual a figure as a Persian Ambassador with a retinue of three hundred splendid servitors that April to create much of a stir about the capital. He wore a golden tunic, a turban stuck with diamonds, a great pearl necklace, and large, fierce whiskers. Anne received him and his gifts—rolls of silk flowered in gold and silver, a huge pearl, and an elephant complete with howdah.

But for once she was too preoccupied with serious matters to spare very much time for elephants and silk. Yagujinski, her counter-balance to Andrei Ostermann, had just died; a scandal was blowing up over the Minister for Commerce who was accused of maladministering the state's monopoly in the rhubarb trade to his private advantage. And, most serious of all, war had broken out against the Turks. Anne's ambassador to the Porte had been imprisoned in the fortress of the Seven Towers at Istanbul, and Russian troops under Marshal Münnich were already marching south to Azov and the Crimea.

War had been foreseen and it was expected to be popular. The Turks and Tatars were, after all, traditional enemies of Russia. But popularity did not guarantee success, and Anne knew failure would bring shame and might bring danger. Marshal Münnich, it seemed, carried her popularity and her glory in his hands. She prayed fervently and crossed herself innumerable times as she waited impatiently for news of victories.

Things began very well. The citadel of Azov was besieged, and troops attacked the Perekop, the gateway to the Crimea. Its moat was crossed, its walls were scaled and its towers of crumbly sandstone taken. Within weeks, it seemed, Anne might accomplish what her uncle, Peter the Great had failed to achieve—capture the whole length of the Black Sea's northern shore.

The good news reached St. Petersburg on 5 June and better followed. An officer arrived from General Lacy bringing her the keys of captured Azov. Then the citadel of Kinburn fell. On 2 July, the Empress boarded her gilded barge and sailed across the river to attend a service of thanksgiving in the Cathedral. Four days later she gave a huge banquet to celebrate the capture of Azov, at which everyone drank to 'success at arms' and 'the health of the good soldiers'.

And her good soldiers continued their triumphant progress. Anne was at Peterhof when she got the news that the Crimea had actually been conquered, that the Cossacks had burned down Bakhchiserai, fabled residence of the Khan himself. She was ecstatic.

Meanwhile, in June, a great fire had broken out in Moscow and on 12 August another struck St. Petersburg, burning with such violence, reported Rondeau, who was once more in charge of the British Mission, that 'some thousand houses were consumed to ashes ... which puts everyone here in great confusion.' Suspected arsonists were rounded up and some were later burned alive on the sites of their supposed crimes. Two million roubles worth of damage had been done, and, as if this were not enough, eleven days later lightning struck one of the largest warships at anchor in Kronstadt, whereupon the soldiers and sailors stationed there 'instead of dowsing the fire ... only looted and robbed like bandits.'

None of this seemed to put the Empress much out of humour, but then the tone of the war reports began to change. The troops, it seemed, were suffering heavy losses. Only two thousand men had been killed in battle, but thirty thousand were dead or sick because of malnutrition, exhaustion and disease. The Tatars had not been able to withstand the invasion, but they had evidently burned down all their crops and granaries in their retreat. As a result, the condition of the army had become so bad that 'there were even officers', it was reported, who 'died of hunger and misery of all kinds.' Facing the inevitable, Marshal Münnich ordered a withdrawal.

As usual in the shadow of failure, the generals made haste to exonerate themselves and accuse each other. General Keith blamed Münnich for marching the troops in the heat of the day rather than at night; General Lacy blamed him for not informing him about his movements; Hesse-Homburg accused him of being too slow, and for good measure rated his fellow generals and inferiors for incompetence as well.

The bickering, recrimination and intrigue that raged among the general staff made the Empress quite confused, but she was furious with Münnich for failing to hold the Crimea. She ordered a court of enquiry to be set up to investigate the condition of Münnich's army, but General Lacy, a shade more honourable than his colleagues, contrived to decline the chairmanship of the enquiry, and the quarrelling continued. Anne became quite infuriated with the generals 'who so ill requite our grace and favour by their mutual wranglings', and when Münnich wrote to Biron asking to be relieved of his command on grounds of ill-health sheer fury overcame her.

'We cannot conceal from you', she replied, 'That we find this action of yours quite insulting. We have never heard of . . . a commander-in-chief wishing to act in such a way towards his sovereign in time of war, and when the greatest service is expected of him, particularly when he has no lawful and justified reason, and moreover with the use of such extreme expressions such as you use in your letter to our Chief Gentleman-in-Waiting', Ernest Biron.

But at last he came to St. Petersburg and she forgave him his offence. He withdrew his resignation, and, in return, was not only entirely cleared of blame, but rewarded with considerable estates in the Ukraine. The cause of this sudden reversal of fortune was due in part to Biron's desire to keep him as a counter-weight to Ostermann, and partly to Anne's susceptibility to the Marshal's particular brand of charm.

He was tall, slender and though in his early fifties still quite handsome, with a very fair complexion. As the ever-observant Jane Rondeau described him he was also 'very genteel and graceful in all his motions'. He danced well, put on 'youthful airs' and was very gallant in female company. He would listen to a lady 'with dying eyes', then suddenly snatch up her hand and 'kiss it in raptures'. Seeing him do the same with several other ladies, however, Mrs. Rondeau became somewhat disenchanted. She came to suspect that his tenderness was affected and to imagine that 'ambush would be his favourite art of war, as sincerity is a quality I take him to be a stranger to.' Moreover, she added bitterly, he tried to be altogether too gay for one with 'the German stiffness—and to see a man of that cast attempt the flutter of a *petit maître* is like seeing a cow frolicsome'.

The Empress, however, proved susceptible to his charms, and all complaints forgotten, he was clasped to the imperial bosom once again and restored to an eminence second only to dear Ernest's.

And Münnich was not the only beneficiary of the season. Ernest's children were included too. On 2 January 1737 Anne wrote to Moscow, still the shopping-centre of the Empire, ordering some wooden toys for them—'three carriages . . . whose doors should open, and sledges and carts, and some large wooden horses. Have them well packed so that they do not break'. And enemies were remembered as well as friends. Field Marshal Dolgoruki and Prince Dmitri Golitsyn, the venerable aristocrats who once tried to impose limitations on her powers, were further punished by imprisonment in the notorious Schlüsselburg gaol where the latter soon died. Prince Vasili Dolgoruki was sent into exile in the Arctic, and various of their brothers, sons and nephews were punished too.

But Anne's memory stretched back beyond her accession in 1730. Peter the Great's secretary, Makarov, was held under arrest in Moscow while he was 'investigated' by General Ushakov and his minions of the Secret Affairs Office. And as Ushakov, under Biron's supervision, set about tracking down all Anne's supposed enemies and his own, midnight arrests, interrogations under torture, and sentences on perjured evidence came to be counted in their thousands. The slow purge in operation throughout the reign seemed to be developing into an all-out campaign to crush every independent mind and cut down the most respected elements of the Russian aristocracy.

Cases already dealt with were revived and the sentences increased. In 1738 the Dolgorukis were again accused of treason and when Prince Ivan eventually confessed to using 'improper language' about the Empress, he was broken on the wheel and then beheaded. Prince Vasili and two cousins were also beheaded; others were sentenced to spend the remainder of their lives in solitary confinement. There was muttering about a 'German plot' to crush all Russians.

Anne, meanwhile, had been enjoying life. On her forty-fourth birthday she attended the first night of a new work, Araja's *Abizaire*. The loggias of the court theatre were packed to overflowing; the stalls were thronged. The singers—Caterina Georgi, the castrato Morigi, la Catherla, and Crichi from Bologna—were accompanied by an orchestra of virtuosi forty strong augmented by the best oboe players from the Guards bands, and 'the court honoured the staging of this first opera with frequent applause and full acclamation.'

That winter there was another new craze at the court. A chute was constructed between the top story of the palace and the courtyard down below, and water was sluiced over it till it was covered with thick ice. The ladies and gentlemen of the court then seated themselves in sledges and flew down it. Anne herself did not join in. But she enjoyed watching. As Jane Rondeau commented, 'sometimes if these sledges meet with any resistance the person in them tumbles head over heels; that I suppose is a joke.' She was with child and terrified of being ordered down, not merely out of 'dread of breaking my neck, but of being exposed to indecency too frightful to think on without horror'. At last someone noticed she had never been down, but Anne, for once, relented, and Mrs. Rondeau was excused.

A serious influenza epidemic which swept the city during March brought that particular mode of jollification to an end. Biron escaped it and so did Anne, though she did catch a streaming cold. Then spring came and the war began again.

There had been hopes of reaching peace that winter. Representatives of both sides had met to negotiate a settlement but the Turks were not ready to make concessions, and since so much had already been spent Anne was unwilling to end the fighting without winning some glittering prize or other. True, Russia could hardly afford to continue the war, but this was disregarded. Plans were made to borrow money in Holland and raise more taxes at home, and so in April 1737 Münnich had marched to war again.

That summer Anne inaugurated a great new church to house the holy icon of Our Lady of Kazan—an icon which Ivan the Terrible had recovered from the Muslim Tatars and which symbolized the righteousness of the Russian cause against Islam. But Anne never allowed her piety to restrict her entertainment, nor her indulgence of the faithful Ernest Biron.

When the old Duke of Courland, expected to die at any moment for almost a decade now, finally gave up the ghost, Anne immediately declared Biron candidate to take his place and ordered the Governor of Riga to secure his election, if necessary by force of arms. It was done. Biron had achieved what de Saxe and even Menshikov had failed to accomplish. The upstart whom the gentlemen of Courland used to sneer at, became their sovereign prince, a potentate whom even the Emperor Charles VI himself greeted as a 'Serene Highness'. His wife now had a status equal to the royal princesses; could sit now in the presence of the Empress and have her hand kissed on public occasions. And the Birons had their own court now—a court within a court, with their own ladies and gentlemen-in-waiting, and their own liveried pages. Yet Biron remained Anne's Chamberlain and his wife first lady of the bedchamber. They had bigger fish to fry in St. Petersburg than in a backwater like Courland.

When he first arrived in Russia, Biron had kept out of the political limelight, but his influence had increased steadily and now he exercised power openly—power far beyond his office. Almost everyone now thought that he ruled Russia's affairs and directed Russian policy.

The Birons had grown very arrogant. 'His every glance', wrote Prince Shcherbatov, 'set the most noble and eminent man trembling with fear.' As for his wife, she was 'haughty and sour', wrote Jane Rondeau, 'and had a harshness in her looks and manner that forbids the respect it would command.' She was thought to influence affairs as well. 'It is by their frown or smile', wrote Mrs. Rondeau,

'that the whole empire is happy or miserable.' All major prefer-
ments, all disgraces meted out were attributed to them. 'There are
so few that one or both these do not make subservient to them, that
they have the whole people at their command.' He seemed proud
and passionate, violent in his favours and vehement in his dislikes.
Yet, unlike Ostermann, he was sincere—too sincere perhaps, show-
ing 'a contempt for Russians', said Mrs. Rondeau, even 'to the
greatest of them so publicly, on all occasions, that I fancy it will
one day be his ruin.'

As the Birons climbed in status, so did their children—two sons
and a daughter. They were a stupid, unattractive brood, badly
brought up and notoriously spoiled. Peter Biron, now known as
'His Illustrious Highness Prince Peter of Courland', was made
Chief Master of the Hunt and Colonel of a regiment of cuirassiers
before he reached the age of ten; Karl was made a Knight of the
Polish Order of the White Eagle. Anne indulged them as if they
had been her own, played ball and shuttle-cock with them, and
encouraged them in all sorts of mischief. She laughed out loud when
they poured wine over courtiers or pulled off their wigs. When
Karl, ignoring his tutor's warnings, gorged himself on unripe plums
and suffered the results, she had the tutor gaoled. And they could
do no wrong in their father's eyes either. When a General complained that one of them had slashed his legs with a riding whip
Biron told him coolly that if he did not like his son's behaviour, he
was free to resign his post and retire from court.

He showed no more indulgence to Courlanders than he did to
Russians. No Courlander, wrote Manstein, dared 'open his mouth
without running a risk of being arrested and sent to Siberia.' In
Russia Biron was said to rule the court, the cabinet and the country.
Anne was said to 'think with his head'. Those who wanted prefer-
ment danced attendance on him like gnats around a flame, scurried
off to do his bidding and begged like dogs for any scrap he might
care to toss at them from his rich table. No one nowadays dared to
cross him. His spy network stretched everywhere.

Ernest Biron was not only powerful now, he was immensely rich.
He had estates in Courland, Silesia, Lithuania and the Ukraine, and
he lived up to his income. He kept nearly four hundred servants,
commissioned Rastrelli to build him a fine new palace; and filled

his stables with the finest horses in the world. His saddles—over two hundred of them—were studded with brilliants; his plate was said to be the best in all St. Petersburg. His wife's jewels alone were worth two million roubles and she was reputed to spend up to 100,000 roubles on a single dress.

Where the Birons led, others tried to follow and as aspiring gentry also built extensions to their houses, enlarged their stables and their staffs, and became increasingly conscious of their personal appearances, it became possible for almost any foreign pedlar in fashion to make a fortune by staying in St. Petersburg for as little as a year or two—always provided that he watched his debts. Many Russian noblemen were living far beyond their means these days—and becoming none too particular about paying off their creditors. And as their aspirations rose along with their debts, more and more noblemen took care to ingratiate themselves with those who had patronage at their command—and became even more dependent on Ernest Biron's favour. Servility, flattery and cheating increased along with ostentation; the standards of honesty which Peter the Great had tried to introduce went completely by the board.

The gentry's rapaciousness and cruelty increased along with their corruption and their luxury. And as they tried to bleed their peasants for yet more money in order to maintain their luxurious living standards, their peasants protested in the only ways open to them—by evasion, flight and fire-raising.

The fires that broke out in Russia in 1737 were almost unprecedented in number and in scale. In May the ancient town of Yaroslav went up in flames, and a vast and frightening conflagration swept through central Moscow, destroying the Kremlin stables, the arsenal, fifty churches, countless shops and nearly three thousand houses. Anne lost fifteen million roubles' worth of property in the blaze and a few days later fire struck St. Petersburg, attacking the quarter adjacent to the Summer Palace, where she was staying at the time. It did little damage and did not spread, but on the morning of 25 June a much more serious fire occurred, in which the houses of Princess Elizabeth, Prince Cherkasski, Secret Police Chief Ushakov and many notables all went up in flames.

'The frequent fires that have happened of late in this country puts everybody here in the greatest terror and consternation', wrote the British envoy Rondeau. 'Nobody can imagine the continual frights we are in for fear of being burnt, and the great misery vaster numbers of poor people are reduced to. . . .' Thousands of buildings had been destroyed. Others were so badly damaged as to be unsafe and had to be demolished. But then the lack of housing became so acute that the demolition had to stop. The fires produced a serious shortage of food and other necessities of life as well. Prices rose sharply and the thousands who could not afford them were forced to steal or starve.

But the fires did result in some improvements, especially to St. Petersburg. A commission was set up which prescribed better building standards, wider streets and the erection of bridges. Important buildings were to be built of stone or brick and roofed with tiles or iron instead of wood in future. New palaces, new squares, new avenues of trees would soon rise, more beautiful than the old.

The Empress, meanwhile, seemed as indifferent to the burning of her city as Nero was to the fate of Rome. While the homeless starved and suffered she sat for Tiorano the portrait-painter, who depicted her surrounded by trophies and chained captives. She did nothing for her people except offer the hope of a victory against the Turks, and even this was far from certain.

In June, Münnich's army set siege to the fortress of Ochakov. Next month, to almost everyone's surprise, it fell. Kinburn was also taken, and Lacy's force devastated the western Crimea. But Münnich had lost more than a third of his men; and the campaign turned out to be as inconclusive as the last. The generals returned to St. Petersburg in August somewhat thinner for their exertions, but an autumn and winter at court soon fattened them up again.

It was a winter of spectacle and above all of music. Violin concertos and 'symphonies' for all sorts of instrumental combinations were written by Madonis, the new Director of Music at the court. There was a new opera by Araja in which la Piantonida took the leading role, and a ballet supervised by Landet danced by young members of the nobility dressed magnificently at the court's expense. Music was more popular now than ever it had been. Suddenly it became almost *de rigueur* for a young socialite to take singing or dancing lessons or learn to play an instrument. The young

Princess Kantemir learned to play the clavier and to master the most taxing arias, Peter Repnin, one of Anne's gentlemen-in-waiting, played the flute, and the three Trubetskoi boys formed a piano trio.

It was the Italians, sponsored by the elegant Reinhold Loewen-wolde, who made the biggest impact on cultural tastes, but Ernest Biron had protégés of his own in this sphere too. He had already engaged the Neubers who staged roustabout shows in the style of Punch and Judy, and now he brought in a company from Leipzig to play comedy and farces, forcing the talented Fuzano and his troupe out of Russia.

Fireworks had been popular ever since Peter the Great's time, but they had become increasingly elaborate—an art form in their own right. Architects, sculptors and stage designers laboured for months to produce pictures of baroque elegance with which to light up the winter nights. By use of ingenious devices and complex timing arrangements they could create whole cities of enchantment sparkling in the sky. And they showed no sign of begrudging such efforts spent to create spectacles of such brief duration. Artists of that time were less self-regarding than they are today. Composers wrote for a single performance and playwrights for a single staging. They produced art for the moment; they did not demand remembrance.

Butter Week passed off with its usual carnival, then Lent and Easter, and in April the coronation ball extended that year until the unusually late hour for Anne of 11 p.m. For the season of the long white nights, the most beautiful of the year, the court moved into the Summer Palace, and, in July, out to Peterhof for a month. Then came the annual reviews of the Guards regiments and the Cadet Corps in St. Petersburg, and, come October, the court would move back into the Winter Palace to lead an indoor life as the days grew cold and the ice formed on the Neva.

In a word, the routine was as usual. One might never have suspected that Russia was at war. Yet at the beginning of 1738, apparently indifferent to the cost and suffering of the previous campaigns, Anne sanctioned another. She realized it would place a huge strain on the exchequer, but that April she appointed a new minister to the governing council, 'a very ingenious man' called Artemius Volynski. No doubt he would put things right.

Born in 1689, Volynski had been Ambassador to Persia, governor of two provinces and had sat in on occasional cabinet meetings since 1735. No one doubted his ability or experience, but he owed his promotion above all things to being Ernest Biron's protégé.

Volynski was to be Biron's man on the Council, a counterweight to Ostermann, but, as it turned out, he had ideas of his own,—a firm resolve, so it was said, to put Russian interests before foreign ones—in other words to make himself more powerful than Biron and Ostermann. On reaching the top, however, he became somewhat disillusioned, and not least about the way business was conducted. 'Our sovereign', he said later, 'is a fool. When you report you get no decision from her at all.' Anne had long since lost any enthusiasm for directing affairs, she did not want her ministers to trouble her. True, she wanted victories against the Turks, but that was left to Marshal Münnich.

The Marshall had marched south yet again in search of the enemy army, but final success seemed as elusive as ever. While Volynski struggled with the state finances and sensible men yearned for peace at almost any price, Anne consulted her astrologers, watched burlesque in the theatre, laughed at the grotesque farces staged in the privacy of her apartments, and went hunting.

Anne spent 18,000 roubles a year on hunting. There was a special workshop to assemble her guns (each one plated with golden figurines), a special hunting carriage, a hunting staff of thirty-six, and a fine collection of dogs including borzoi hounds, pointers from England and over thirty pairs of basset hounds from France. Coursing within twenty miles of St. Petersburg was banned so that there should be sufficient hares for her to pot at; and when the Empress chose to shoot at something from her window the palace aviary always had birds on hand ready to release for sacrifice. The special hunting strip in the park at Peterhof had been cleared of game by now, so bears, and wild boars, foxes, stags and numbers of other animals were introduced to bring the community of the hunted up to number, for Anne took no pleasure from chance sightings and long chases; for her the sport meant the certainty of being followed by a suitably large and varied bag when she rode home at end of day.

She still found sport in torturing human beings too. A woman called Anastasia Filatovna, whom Anne had known years before and who had a reputation as a talker, described the treatment she received at the Summer Palace in June 1738. On being presented the Empress examined her as she might have done a horse. 'She's very old', she commented, 'not what she was. She's grown so yellow.' Poor Anastasia muttered an apology and offered to apply some make-up. The Empress then asked her if she thought she herself had aged. She received the predictably flattering answer and ordered Anastasia to start talking. Eventually the woman tired. She begged permission to stop, and was refused; she fell exhausted at the Empress's feet, but Anne merely laughed, told her to come closer, then dragged her up by the sleeves and barked at her to carry on. She did, but eventually she could think of nothing else to talk about. 'Tell me about bandits, then', cried the Empress. Anastasia protested she knew nothing about bandits, but for Anne this was no excuse. The woman was forced to chatter on long into the night. Next morning she was brought into the Empress's bed-chamber once again, and the charade continued, until, at last, the Empress became bored.

But as harsh as she could be to her retainers, she could be lavishly indulgent to those she loved, particularly to Biron's uncontrollable sons Karl and Peter. She had a little fort built for them at Peterhof that summer, put Guardsmen at their disposal, and brought the entire diplomatic corps to watch the mock fight in which little Peter had the satisfaction of bloodying a good many innocent noses without fear of being touched himself. Meanwhile a thousand miles away war was being waged and men were dying. Münnich claimed another victory, but his army was decimated by an epidemic of the plague and by the autumn it was obvious that the Turks were still in no mood to sue for peace.

The campaign was a failure. The Bashkirs of the eastern border were in revolt, and then the Kirghiz of the south-east joined them. Large forces had to be diverted to cope with them. Then in January 1738 a new challenge to Anne's authority came from inside Russia. A new pretender had arisen in the provinces and, promising to end the war with Turkey, attracted a good deal of support from peasants and runaway soldiers. The movement was crushed. The 'low people' involved were subjected to torture, the affected villages razed to the

ground and the leaders were executed, though not before their
tongues were pulled out to prevent them making a last appeal to the
watching crowd.

But not only armed rebels were punished without mercy. Even
peaceful protesters might expect the knout these days. Old Believers
were still persecuted, and special inquisitions set up to deal with a
whole crop of 'New Christs'. A Russian naval captain was burned
alive for becoming a Jew, and a Cossack executed for converting to
Islam. And not a few poor people had their nostrils torn out, or
were sentenced to hard labour for their impertinence in petitioning
the Empress.

In the words of a contemporary nobleman, Anne 'did not spare
her subjects' blood'. She would 'sign a death sentence by torture
without a shudder'. An aristocrat to the very marrow, Anne was
successor to a very harsh tradition and as confident of her own
rectitude as ever she was of God's existence. Hardened by unhappiness in youth, spoiled by flattery, and grown proud and
arrogant with power she was completely cut off from the common
people and completely insensitive to them.

The darkness of the peasants' lives only seemed to make the
court shine brighter. Receptions, balls and banquets followed each
other with monotonous regularity. The court glittered as it had
never done before and if Anne was its sun, Biron's planet glowed
almost as strongly. In June 1739 'His Illustrious Highness' celebrated
his accession as Duke of Courland and his name day, when on two
successive days all the 'best people' congregated to offer him their
congratulations; and then he held another levee, accompanied by
Italian music, to honour his wife on her birthday. His power in
Russia was now unchallengeable. Of the lesser stars, Ostermann
still schemed in the background, Volynski fought off his frustrations,
and Münnich worried about winning his war. He had arrived in St.
Petersburg in February for his son's marriage—a truly grand affair
with horse-guards, trumpeters, and running footmen, and a
galaxy of ministers and generals—and to attend a cabinet meeting
to discuss the war and the involvement of Russia's ally, Austria, in it.

There was plenty of other activity at court, however. In March
Anne ordered three hundred new liveries for her pages, heyducks
and footmen. Increasingly bored at the sight of the green cloth

uniforms laced with gold, she had thought long about the new design, and the result was predictably gaudy and magnificent— yellow cloth laced with silver and black velvet. Ernest Biron promptly ordered fine new liveries for his own staff, and they both approved designs for another special uniform to be worn by the staff of the great riding school which Anne attended every Monday, Thursday and Saturday to take a little gentle exercise on horseback. This uniform consisted of yellow buffalo-skins with silver galloons and blue waistcoats—and had to be worn by everyone who attended, Ministers included.

Meanwhile, observant passers-by noticed unusual activity at the palace—a veritable invasion by hordes of craftsmen and seam-stresses. Great preparations were obviously under way, and the cause as it turned out was the forthcoming marriage of her niece, Anna.

The Empress had hummed and hawed for years now about whether Prince Anton of Brunswick-Bevern would, after all, be the right choice. People might find precious little to say for the Prince, but they had little to say against him either. Anyway the Princess herself was a rather insipid girl. According to Jane Rondeau she was neither handsome nor genteel. 'She is very grave, seldom speaks, and never laughs.' Though she had plenty of time to become acquainted with the Prince, it seemed that she had conceived no great liking for him—but then she liked so few people or things very much. She was roused to great passion only over the hairstyle the Empress ordered her to wear. Otherwise she remained cold and shy, and would shut herself away for hours with French and German story books, more especially those romantic ones in which oppressed princesses expressed their emotions to the oppressors. She did not, however, regard Prince Anton as the shining knight come to deliver her from the dragon. Still, the Princess was nineteen, her reputation had been maintained intact; it was time for her to take a husband and produce a son and heir.

Anna found difficulty making up her mind, and in a sense it was Ernest Biron who resolved the matter for her. If Prince Anton was not suitable, he suggested, perhaps his own son Peter might be. True, Peter was several years younger than the Princess, and grossly unpleasant, but he had a princely title and was a favourite of the

Empress. But then Prince Anton was the nephew of the Emperor Charles VI of Austria, an ally who must not be alienated, and furthermore the Princess was adamant in her dislike of Peter Biron. In her eyes, even Prince Anton was preferable.

This was a severe blow to Ernest Biron, and it was not the only one. He had received a suggestion that the Duke of Holstein's son should marry his daughter. The Duke was very poor and a dowry of 100,000 roubles had been mentioned. Biron evidently thought he could persuade the Empress to give it him but for once he calculated wrongly. 'That sot' as Anne referred to Holstein—'that sot is mistaken in imagining that he can wheedle me into giving him the money', she said when Biron broached the matter. It was evident that her hatred of Holstein exceeded even her fondness for dear Ernest and there the matter ended, though she did try to make amends by suggesting that the Crown Prince of Hesse-Darmstadt might prove a suitable husband for his daughter. However nothing was to come of that proposal either.

Meanwhile arrangements for the marriage of Anne's niece had gone ahead. The date was fixed for 3 July 1739 and shortly before this a special Austrian Ambassador, the Marquis de Botta, arrived at court. Anne received him in splendid style in the great hall of the Palace attended by her court, the diplomatic corps and scores of palace lackeys dressed in their brand-new gaudy liveries.

She then proceeded to the long gallery to receive Prince Anton's thanks. He was dressed 'in a white satin suit of cloth embroidered with gold', and wore his long fair hair in loose curls. 'I could not help thinking', commented Jane Rondeau, 'that he looked like a victim.' Others, however, imagined the Princess to be the victim. The story had got about that she had once attacked Volynski and tried to scratch out his eyes, screaming 'You arranged this, you damned Ministers.' But now she seemed acquiescent—there was consolation, after all, in the thought that she was not to marry Peter Biron. She flung her arms round the Empress's neck and burst into tears. The Empress for good measure burst into tears as well, and taking their cue from her, the Princess Elizabeth and the other ladies also fell about 'in an agony of tears'. Somehow engagement rings were exchanged and the couple were kissed, wished well, and allowed to depart.

The wedding itself was a predictably rich affair which Rondeau felt bound to report in great detail to his masters at the British Foreign Office. 'It is not to be expressed', he wrote, lest they should labour under any doubt about it, 'the Magnificency of the cavalcade nor the fine clothes and the equipages.'

The procession set off from the palace at eleven in the morning. It was led by the groom in a bright silk caftan. He and his suite rode in a succession of state coaches, each attended by two negro running footmen wearing black velvet suits which 'so exactly fitted to their bodies', Jane Rondeau noticed, 'that they appeared naked.' There followed the nobility and Ernest Biron whose coach was attended by twenty-four footmen, eight running footmen, four heyducks, four pages and two gentlemen-in-waiting; and behind him, accompanied by twice as many attendants, came an eight-horse chariot bearing the Empress and the bride.

Anne wore a great hooped gown of silver cloth, a diamond stomacher and had her hair curled up in complex tresses glittering with diamonds. Beside her, the orphaned bride looked singularly unimpressive. Thereafter the procession gradually diminished in magnificence. There were seven coaches carrying Princess Elizabeth and her suite, then the Duchess of Courland and her daughter, and, after them, a long procession of noblemen's wives each in a fine coach and with attendant hordes of servants.

The ceremony took place in the Cathedral of St. Mary of Kazan, and was conducted by the Archbishop of Novgorod and the Bishop of Vologda. Afterwards, everyone returned to the palace for the reception. For this, the Empress changed into an even richer gown in brown and gold, and replaced her diamonds with pearls. She made her entrance leaning on Biron's arm.

The decorations were as exotic as they were numerous. The tables were littered with a profusion of yellow, white and golden candles, ten thousand artificial flowers made out of feathers in 'the Italian style' and a further 8,570 'Chinese' paper flowers. The apparel of the guests was worthy of the setting—one courtier wore a uniform studded with brilliants said to be worth 150,000 roubles— and the feast was as heavy as it was lavish. The ball which followed lasted until midnight, when the bride was led off to the newly decorated bridal chamber, put into a white satin nightgown trimmed with fine Brussels lace and deposited on a great four-poster bed to await the groom.

Some guests had not got to bed until three in the morning and were already exhausted when they arrived next day for a reception, ball and supper in the hall of fountains. The Empress, however, seemed to be in excellent spirits, and when everyone sat down to supper she walked about between the tables talking to the guests. Among the diversions which followed were a Pastorale at the theatre and on the Friday a masquerade ball with the novelty of quadrilles.

There were four sets of dancers, the first, led by the bride and groom wearing orange dominos, cockades and ribbons; the second in green and gold was led by Princess Elizabeth and Peter Biron; the third, of older people, was led by Biron's wife and Saltykov in blue and pink; and the last by the two youngest Birons in pink and green and silver. It was extremely hot. The dancers sweated profusely under their heavy costumes, and were relieved when it was time for the supper laid out for them in the gallery which had been decorated with banks of grass to look like a rustic glade. The junketings continued until the Sunday when there was another masquerade and fireworks. 'Thus ended this grand wedding, from which I am not yet rested', wrote Jane Rondeau. And what was worse, 'all this rout has been made to tie two people together, who, I believe, heartily hate one another.'

Meanwhile the war with Turkey continued. That June there was a sudden surge of optimism at court when news came that the Turkish Vizier had been deposed. But peace was still a mirage—until, in August, Münnich reached the river Pruth, and unexpectedly found himself facing the elusive Turkish army. The battle of Stavuchany lasted twelve hours and ended with an astonishing Russian victory. The news reached St. Petersburg early in September. Anne was overjoyed. She gave the messenger a gift of 4,000 roubles, went to special thanksgiving services and threw another 'rich dress' ball. The court buzzed with excitement; there was even talk of taking Constantinople.

But then Austria made a separate peace with Turkey and Münnich was ordered to call a halt. His victory had come too late; it had been decided that Russia could not fight on alone. Instead a peace was hastily concluded. By it, Russia regained Azov and Turkey recognized part of the Caucasus as a Russian sphere of influence. It was a meagre result for years of war and the loss of a hundred thousand men.

Even so Münnich reckoned he deserved a rich reward. He asked to be made Lord of Moldavia, but was refused; he asked to be created 'Prince of the Ukraine'. But Anne was only amused. 'The Marshal is really too modest', she commented. 'I would have thought he would have been satisfied with nothing less than the title Grand Duke of Muscovy!'

The war had ended, but victory brought no immediate respite to the Russian people. The state's finances were in disorder, the value of money had fallen by half, and fires, disorder and rebellion still plagued the countryside. In these circumstances the tyrannical regime had a need for scapegoats, and scapegoats were duly found. In November, the Dolgorukis were executed publicly in Novgorod. The official charges included conspiracy to treason and uttering 'harmful and malicious words' about the Empress and Princess Elizabeth, but their main offence was hardly mentioned—what they or members of their family had done years before in trying to limit Anne's powers.

Russia was an unhappy country, but it was just beginning to be regarded as a power to be reckoned with in Europe, as it had never been in Peter the Great's time. Ordinary Russians cared little about that, but Anne was delighted when, that December, France for the first time deigned to send her an Ambassador. He was the Marquis de la Chetardie, and Anne did her very best to impress him. Detachments of horse guards and an Admiral were sent to fetch him from his residence; lines of immaculate Guardsmen lined his route from the Palace gate to the audience chamber, and he was greeted by the sounds of drums and music.

Russia was becoming a member of the club of civilized European states at last, as Peter the Great had always hoped it would. And however angry he might have been to see so many of his projects neglected, so much corruption and futile show, he might at least have been satisfied with the development of his Academy of Sciences. That very year a Department of Geography had been inaugurated and the task of making the first comprehensive map of Russia was begun. The history he had ordered was also completed and the scientific side of the Academy's activities progressed from strength to strength. Anne showed little personal interest in all this, but that winter the Academy embarked on one project which managed to engage not only her interest, but her enthusiasm.

The winter of 1739–40 was unusually cold, and the scientists of the Academy embarked on a programme of experiments to test the properties of ice that was available in such abundance. Knowing this, a court Chamberlain called Alexander Tatishchev thought of combining it with a new entertainment for the court—building a palace of ice on which artists and artisans as well as scientists could exercise their skills. In the end it turned out to be a setting for another of the Empress's macabre jokes for which poor Golitsyn was again the butt.

The Prince, still only a court page, was in his forties now and long since a widower. But the Empress insisted that he should take another wife. Indeed she chose one for him—Avdotaya Ivanovna, nicknamed 'Bujenina' after Anne's favourite dish—roast pork done in a sauce of onions, vinegar and spices. Avdotaya was of Kalmyk origin, extremely ugly and wanted desperately to find a husband. The Empress not only answered her prayers but agreed to pay for the wedding, deciding that it should be made the greatest comic spectacle ever seen in Russia.

A rocket whistled into the air and exploded with a loud report above the city. Within seconds a whole sheaf of rockets was set loose; fountains of coloured fire began to flame, catherine wheels to circle madly. All St. Petersburg was lit up in brilliant flashes of light. The New Year 1740 had arrived.

The Empress attended the usual round of functions, but her own special comedy was due to be staged a few days later. Already the city was alive with excitement and despite the bitter cold, large crowds gathered on the frozen river, hoping to catch a glimpse of what the hundreds of craftsmen were up to concealed behind thick lines of guarding troops.

Then one morning a huge and astonishing procession formed up in the streets. Goats, pigs, cows, camels, dogs and reindeer were seen harnessed to various strange vehicles each of which contained a representative pair from each of the 'Barbarous Races' in the

Empire. There were Lapps and Kirghiz, Tunguses and Tatars, Bashkirs and Finns—each couple in 'national dress'. But the centre-piece was an elephant with an iron cage on its back. The cage contained Golitsyn and his unlovely bride.

To the accompaniment of cymbals, bells and the occasional roaring of an angry beast, the procession passed the Palace and eventually arrived at Ernest Biron's covered riding school, where a banquet had been prepared for the captive bridal pair and their guests. By the Empress's express command each couple was served with its own traditional dishes—including such culinary delights as reindeer meat, horse-flesh and fermented mare's milk. There was entertainment too. A poet named Tredyakovski declaimed an ode composed specially for the occasion entitled: 'Greetings to the Bridal Pair of Fools', and each pair of guests was made to dance its own 'national dance' for the amusement of the onlookers. Then the procession formed up again to accompany the bride and groom to their home for the night—the palace made of ice.

No other material had been used in its construction—walls and steps, baroque balustrades, cornices and columns, even the decorative figurines and window-panes were made of ice. So was the furniture—a huge four-poster bridal bed, chairs, tables, chandeliers, a clock, a commode, a set of playing cards, with the markings coloured in, and a statue of a Cupid. Outside there were other marvels of engineering and the sculptor's art—flowers and trees complete with perching birds, ice cannon which fired real charges, a pair of dolphins which breathed out flames of fire (thanks to a device inside which pumped out naphtha), and a life-sized model of an elephant equipped with a machine to squirt out water to a height of two hundred and fifty feet. Everything had been done to excite the eye and astonish the imagination—and all at a cost of only thirty thousand roubles.

The Empress accompanied the bridal pair inside, saw them undressed and laid upon their bed of ice. Then she withdrew. From her bedroom she had an excellent view of the Ice Palace, and next morning she saw Golitsyn and his wife emerge apparently none the worse for their experience. The stove installed inside their chilly bedroom, as the scientists of the Academy took careful note, had proved effective.

On 14 February the peace with Turkey was officially proclaimed. The Empress, wearing gold brocade, rode in state to a service of thanksgiving, and then inspected twenty thousand troops who had been drawn up on the ice outside the Winter Palace, before going inside to receive the plaudits of the notables. Chancellor Cherkasski made a speech praying that Russia by following Anne's footsteps—and God's will—might create things pleasing to the Lord; there were illuminations and a masquerade with 'Turkish' music, while wine and food and coins were distributed to the crowds which had gathered in the cold outside.

The honours and rewards doled out on this occasion presumably reflected Anne's sense of priorities. Ernest Biron received an immense golden goblet, studded with brilliants, and half a million roubles. His wife, whose contributions to the war effort can only be the object of surmise, was invested with the Order of St. Catherine, and their two gallant sons with the Order of St. Andrew. Prince Anton who had, after all, made a visit to the front, was promoted to the rank of Lieutenant-General, Ostermann received a fine ring and a pension of 5,000 roubles, and Volynski got 20,000 roubles in cash. As for the fighting generals, the worthy Lacy got a sword, a pension, and the patent of a Count, while Münnich himself was awarded a pension of 5,000 roubles and the Order of St. Andrew which put him on a par with Biron's sons. The entire officer corps were also given something—permission to retire on the completion of twenty years' service, though since over half of them immediately tendered their resignations, this generous measure had soon to be withdrawn.

With the war over, the men at the top could once again give their entire attentions to intriguing against one another. Münnich and Ostermann hated one another; Ernest Biron distrusted both of them; while Volynski worked against all three. Apart from the nonentity of a Chancellor, Volynski was the only Russian in any position of real power. Otherwise foreigners seemed to run everything, including the Empress. Even lower down the scale they took a huge proportion of the better jobs. No less than forty per cent of the general staff were foreigners—more even than in Catherine's reign. Russians felt they faced unfair competition and Volynski set himself up as their spokesman.

He had proceeded cautiously at first, but then he dismissed two foreigners who complained to the Empress and he was summoned into her presence to explain his action. Volynski used this occasion to launch into a general diatribe against all foreigners. Russians in the army and the bureaucracy, he claimed, were losing their 'courage, their willingness and their zeal to serve their sovereign', because their routes of promotion were blocked by outsiders. It was time the system was reformed, he said passionately; high time that Russia was ruled by Russians. Anne seemed to be impressed. She told him to draw up a paper setting out his proposals in detail and promised to give them serious consideration.

But Ernest Biron had already smelt danger. He went to work on Anne and she had depended on him for too long not to listen to him now. When Volynski returned with his paper, which, among other things, called for the dismissal of Ernest Biron, his reception was a good deal cooler than he had expected. Anne, in fact, was very angry. She accused him of treating her like a child; said it was not his place to tell her what to do. Volynski withdrew in some confusion and was arrested shortly afterwards.

Volynski's own arrogance and past indiscretions provided Biron with material to bring about his downfall. Only recently he had been involved in an unseemly row with Tredyakovski, the court functionary and poet, who had been ordered to compose some suitable verse for Golitsyn's wedding. Volynski had found a reference to himself which he thought insulting, and had boxed the poet's ears. When Tredyakovski protested, Volynski gave him two black eyes, whereupon he trotted off to complain to Ernest Biron. But Volynski followed him into Biron's ante-chamber, had him arrested, stripped and birched for his impertinence, and thrown into gaol. On the day of the wedding carnival he had to release him, but as soon as the poet had recited his piece, Volynski had him taken back to gaol and beaten up again.

When Ernest Biron found out he was furious—not so much because the worthy poet had been beaten up as because the man had been dragged away from his own ante-room. In due course 360 roubles' worth of compensation was paid out to the poet, who was later appointed Professor of Rhetoric and Poetical Ingenuity at the Academy, but the incident was also exploited as ammunition when Biron approached the Empress to demand Volynski's arrest.

At first Anne was reluctant, and when Biron threatened to leave her if she took no action she burst into tears. But she gave way in the end. On 12 April Volynski was arrested. Three days later the investigation began. He confessed to ill-treating Tredyakovski and to calling Ostermann and others dangerous. Later, under torture, he was also persuaded to betray the names of his friends and to admit to being implicated with the Dolgorukis. The court dismissed his plea for mercy, and finding him 'guilty' of 'seditious and traitorous crimes', sentenced him to death.

Anne hesitated before she signed the warrant, but she signed all the same, salving her conscience by refusing to let him be impaled. By the time the execution took place on 27 June the once proud and arrogant Volynski had been reduced to a bandaged, trembling wreck. They cut out his tongue, then severed his right hand, and, finally, his head. His friends suffered with him. Their estates were distributed among the clients of Ernest Biron.

Anne went to Peterhof as usual that summer. Since it was feared that the Swedes might make a sudden attack ten battalions of the Guard were bivouacked in the grounds and a fast coach was kept in constant readiness by the door. But the precautions turned out to be unnecessary and the Empress was able to indulge her passion for hunting undisturbed. Between 1 June and the middle of August that year Anne managed to dispose of nine stags, sixteen roe deer, four wild boar, a wolf, sixty-eight wild duck, sixteen 'great sea birds' and no fewer than 374 hares—besides Volynski and his friends.

She cut short her hunting to rush back to St. Petersburg where on 12 August her niece, the Princess Anna, gave birth to a baby boy. The Empress was present at the delivery, and as soon as the child was born, she had it taken to her own apartments, and entrusted to the care of the Duchess of Courland, whom she reckoned to be the most experienced matron available.

The new heir to the throne was called Ivan after the Empress's father, and she doted on the child, spent hours cooing over it, watched the nurses feed and swaddle it, smiled at its every gurgle, fretted over every cry. But if Anne was happy, Biron was sunk in gloom. He had been hoping somehow to link his own children with the imperial family and with the birth of a direct male descendant of Tsar Ivan that prospect became even more remote than it had been before. He shut himself up in his apartments for several days and refused to see anyone. Ostermann also stayed in his apartments putting out that he was seriously ill, though whether the illness was real or pretended no one knew. Some said he really did have palsied feet, others that he was piqued because Biron had got another of his protégés to take Volynski's place on the Council of Ministers. The man was Alexei Bestuzhev, the son of Anne's chamberlain when she had first arrived at Mitau.

The birth of a potential heir also triggered off a new bout of religious fervour in Anne, a fervour which she expressed by urging more active missionary activity backed with armed force to be carried out among the Muslims, Buddhists and pagans in the empire. Religious intolerance seemed to be one area of policy where the Empress took an active personal lead. But she was not to do so for much longer.

Early in October she had just finished dinner in the Birons' apartments when she fainted. They put her to bed and sent for the doctors who diagnosed another attack of gout from which she had been suffering of late. But the trouble soon seemed to be more serious than that, so they decided it must be gall-stones, then that she had kidney ulcers, and finally that she had complications arising from a change of life. Whatever it was, her condition deteriorated rapidly. There were more fainting fits, then serious vomiting; finally she began to spit blood, and at once the Muscovite nobles began to gather at the palace like crows around a piece of carrion.

Anne had not yet issued instructions about the succession, and the great men at court and government made hasty calculations as to which allegiance would bring the best prospects of personal advancement. Should they support the Princess Anna or her infant son, and if the latter, who was to be Regent? Ostermann eventually plumped for little Ivan; Biron had already done so. He handed Anne the necessary paper, she signed it, and it was published next day. The question of the Regency remained open, but by 11 October she seemed very much better, and there seemed to be no urgent need to answer it. Biron however, was letting no chance slip. His man, Bestuzhev, set about collecting signatures to a petition calling for him to be declared Regent. Two hundred signatures were obtained and Biron took it to the Empress demanding a decision. Ostermann, on the other hand, advised her to do nothing. Anne vacillated. She did not want to disappoint Biron, but she knew he was unpopular and that even greater odium would attach to him if he were Regent. Anyway, she would not admit that she was as dangerously ill as her advisers imagined her to be, so she saw no need for an immediate decision. But on 15 October she suffered a relapse and the terrible truth dawned on her at last.

Realizing that she could procrastinate no longer, on 16 October she signed the order nominating Ernest Biron as Regent until such time as Ivan should come of age. Next evening the final agony began. By ten o'clock she was dead.

Anne was only forty-six when she died. She had reigned for ten years and her reign has been called prudent, beneficial, even glorious. It is true that it had its glories. A war was won, Russia's prestige abroad was as high at her death as ever it had been and the arts had experienced something of a boom. But the common people did not care for art or glory. They wanted their bellies filled and to be left in peace, and these were the last priorities of Anne's government. There had been time over the past ten years when half Russia seemed to be waging a guerilla war against her; there had been a great number of bloody executions and tens of thousands of her subjects had been exiled to Siberia.

It had been a cruel regime and often wantonly cruel, in a way that Peter the Great had rarely been. Peter had used cruelty as a means to making Russia better educated, strong and rich; Anne used terror to keep down opposition to policies which had no great moral, visionary purpose, and sometimes just to vent her private spleen. Anne may have been scarred by the unhappiness and disappointments she suffered in her youth, but she was vindictive, cruel, perverted and there were very few who mourned her. Yet though she had too many victims to attract much love there were some who loved her.

When the doors of the crowded anteroom were opened the Princess Anna was seen weeping over the corpse, while Ernest Biron was streaming tears and throwing himself from side to side in paroxysms of grief.

Calm gradually descended. Priests arrived to chant over the body, Prince Trubetskoi read out the will and some while afterwards Ernest Biron showed himself to have recovered something of his former spirit by sneering at Prince Anton.

In the weeks that followed a new manifesto was read out in every church throughout the Empire. And when they heard its first words: 'By the Grace of God, We Ivan VI . . .' people sighed with relief, blessed the Lord, and prayed that better times were on the way.

Interlude

His Royal Highness Ernest Biron began his regency of Russia with a judicial disbursement of rewards. Prince Anton was given nominal command of the armed forces; Marshal Münnich received 100,000 roubles. But within a year both of them had turned against him and in April 1741 Biron and his family were packed off to Siberia. Prince Anton and his wife the Princess Anna took over the regency supported by Marshal Münnich's bayonets. Before long, however, Münnich's services were also dispensed with, and some time afterwards, on a winter's night, the Regent Anna's second cousin and a group of Guardsmen forced their way into her apartment and arrested her and her child the baby Emperor. Tsar Ivan's reign was abruptly ended. The glorious reign of Elizabeth Petrovna had begun.

PART III
Elizabeth

ELIZABETH was born on 18 December 1709—the day her father, Peter the Great, arrived back in Moscow after his astonishing victory over the Swedes at the battle of Poltava. The auguries could hardly have been better. The birth of a sturdy, well-formed child of royal blood just at the moment of Russia's greatest change in fortune delighted Peter; it seemed to symbolize the dawn of a new era.

True, he had 'not found time', as he put it, to marry Catherine before the child was born, so, like her sister Anna Petrovna, Elizabeth was technically illegitimate. But she grew up in an atmosphere of security and love, surrounded by plenty, and doted on by her parents.

They gave her a Karelian and a Russian nurse, and a French governess besides, so that Elizabeth was brought up to appreciate the ways and manners of the West as well as Russian folk traditions. It was a combination of cultures which her cousin, later the Empress Anne, could never quite reconcile, but Elizabeth was to feel at home in both. She became a fervent church-goer and a fluent speaker of French; a passionate Russian patriot and an accomplished dancer of the minuet.

Fair-haired and blue-eyed, Elizabeth was attractive, vivacious and full of *joie de vivre*—always with 'one foot in the air' as one contemporary described her. Yet even as a child she was a public person. She made her first appearance at the age of two as a brides-maid at her parents' wedding; was decked out in pink flowers and put on show at Peter's riotous masquerades; and from the time she was four Ministers and dignitaries would gather at the Palace every year to offer their congratulations on her birthday.

By the age of twelve, Elizabeth had 'a beautiful figure', a bearing 'full of grace', and was a fabulous dancer—an almost ethereal spirit whose feet hardly seemed to touch the ground. She was a centre of attraction at every carnival, firework display, launching and festivity. Yet she remained unspoiled. Peter was proud of her. One day he hoped to make her the bride of Louis XV, King of France.

Elizabeth was happy, and she was fortunate—not least in having an elder sister close enough to her in years for good companionship, and yet able to pilot her through the difficulties of puberty and the trials of the princely marriage-market. She was not quite twelve when the Duke of Holstein arrived to pay court to her sister and the ensuing summer was wonderfully exciting for her. These were days full of sweetness, sun and music. The Duke brought his private orchestra to serenade them with the strains of Tartini, Schütz and Telemann; there were picnics, dinners, parties in the Summer Gardens, trips to Peterhof where there were ponds to fish and woods to scamper in—and admiration everywhere.

Elizabeth reflected the joy she felt. With her hair decorated with pearls and other jewels in a style that 'would have done honour to the best Paris hairdresser', and wearing little wings made out of coloured gauze and whalebone (the mark of a princess not yet come of age), she looked like a rather mischievous angel. And she played the part as well. She would sit prim, wide-eyed and innocent in church—and at parties, when not handing wine out to the guests, she would lurk in corners with her sister ready to pounce on any unattended glass and drain it.

On 28 January 1722 Peter declared Elizabeth to be of age. He led her out of her mother's apartments into the adjoining hall and there, in front of a grave assembly of notables and clergymen, he cut off her little wings. She grasped his hands and kissed them, rushed to hug her mother, then raised a glass of wine in tribute to the company, to which all the gentlemen present responded by raising theirs to her.

By the time she was fifteen Elizabeth had grown into a very beautiful young woman—indeed the Duke de Liria thought her more beautiful than any woman he had ever seen. And though she was still shy in the company of boys, she was considered ripe for marriage. Her prospects seemed bright enough: offers were to pour in from Europe's minor princes, and even the Jacobites wanted her as the bride for Prince Charles Edward Stuart. But Peter set his sights much higher. He wanted to match her with Louis XV, King of France. Yet despite her graceful bearing, her charming manners and her almost fluent French, Versailles, and virtually every other major European court as it turned out, looked askance at her. Elizabeth had been born out of wedlock after all—and to a peasant woman.

In 1725, when her father died and her mother became Empress, her prospects of a brilliant match receded further. That spring Elizabeth was bridesmaid at her sister's wedding, and her mother was anxious to see her, too, become a bride. But though Russian diplomatists pressed the French hard on Elizabeth's behalf, offering a handsome dowry and a military alliance as inducements, they succeeded only in having her name included on a short-list of seventeen princesses, and in the end the decision went against her. King Louis married the Polish candidate. The Duc de Bourbon was then canvassed, but he too rejected her, and though there were plenty of would-be suitors among the lesser fry, those candidates that the Russian government did not regard as unsuitable Elizabeth herself turned down. At last Holstein produced his kinsman Karl, the Prince-Bishop of Lübeck, and since both Elizabeth and her mother seemed to take to him, an engagement was arranged. But before the marriage could take place her fiancé died of smallpox. Elizabeth at seventeen was destined to remain a spinster.

Meanwhile, in May 1727 her mother had died, and Elizabeth duly took the oath of loyalty to her nephew Peter. According to her mother's will, she was to succeed if he should die without issue. She was also given a seat on the Supreme Privy Council along with her sister and brother-in-law, but that was only for appearance's sake. She wielded no influence or power, and within four months of her mother's death the new regime expelled her sister and the troublesome Duke of Holstein from the country. Within a year, soon after giving birth to a son, her sister died. At eighteen Elizabeth was left alone. Ever since her parents died the great men of the realm suddenly seemed to have less time for her, and now the limelight that had always followed her faded right away.

Catherine had left her two country estates and the house and park at Tsarskoye Selo, so she was materially provided for. She had her own household and her own staff, but life which had always been so easy for her suddenly became difficult and even dangerous. As Peter the Great's daughter she had a claim to the throne, so she was a person to be feared by those in power. And there was no one she could trust—her mother's uncouth relatives counted for nothing, Menshikov was always a ruthless self-seeker, and his successors, the Dolgorukis, saw her from the first as a potential threat. They made her unwelcome at the court, set spies on her, and wondered how they might dispose of her for good.

Eventually, however, they concluded that they had no need to. At eighteen Elizabeth only wanted to enjoy life apparently. She hunted and hawked on her country estates, went sledging in winter, danced and sang with the local peasant girls, and took lessons in love from any ostler or page who caught her fancy.

Now that the protective cocoon of her family had finally dissolved away the fledgling was taking exuberantly to wing. Feather-brained and pleasure-loving as the world saw her, the Dolgorukis ceased to regard her as a threat. Instead, they brought her back to court and began to think in terms of marrying her off to their kinsman Ivan.

In March 1728 the court had moved to Moscow, the city of her birth. She loved its rolling hills and squalid brilliance, and, better still, her nephew, the young Emperor, had a passion for hunting which he invited her to share. They went beagling and bear-baiting together, attended balls and boxing-matches, and by August, according to Jane Rondeau, Elizabeth was 'in high favour' again, for she was 'very beautiful' and seemed 'to love all that can please the Tsar'.

So far from meddling in state affairs, her days were entirely given up to the pursuit of pleasure, and there were those who thought that she took her pleasures beyond the bounds of moderation and even decency. 'The behaviour of the Princess Elizabeth gets worse and worse with each day', commented the Duke de Liria. 'She does things without shame, things that would make even the humble blush.' Certainly she took lovers—perhaps as many as half-a-dozen by the time she reached her twenties. Some thought that her nephew, the young Emperor himself, was among them.

Elizabeth showed contempt for modesty, confessed more than once that she was 'content only when she was in love', and tolerated no restraint. When the Dolgorukis proposed that she marry their Ivan, she refused. Marriage would have set limits to her freedom and her choice of lovers. Yet though her scandalous behaviour shocked traditionalists, it made her tolerable to the ruling Dolgorukis. Elizabeth was dissolute, a coquette, a leader of fashion—a person of no political importance.

She was the brightest star in society, but in a society with only a few years' experience of western ways and whose manners were still rough. People continued to wear clothes that 'seemed to have been the show-dress of the family for at least three generations', as an English visitor observed in 1729. They danced clumsily, never letting go the hand, and clicked their heels out of time to the music. Elizabeth herself might be the epitome of gracefulness, but most members of Russian 'society' were clumsy bears who preferred quantity to finesse. Dinners were heavy, lasted several hours, and ended in clouds of smoke as the gentlemen lit up long clay pipes. At one such banquet Jane Rondeau's arms were 'quite fatigued' handing round plates, each laden with enough 'to have dined me for a week', and the guests 'drank in proportion'. Yet young girls were usually given nothing at all. When Claudius Rondeau offered something to the host's daughter her ancient father rudely interrupted him: it was not customary for unmarried girls to eat 'before folks', he had yelled out from the far end of the room. 'But I warrant she's taken care to line her inside well before she came out, and will stuff like a devil when she gets home.' The old ways died hard, young ladies were still barely tolerated in Muscovite society, and Elizabeth was fortunate in being an orphaned princess allowed to behave as she pleased.

And she meant to keep her freedom. When the ambitious Dolgorukis pressed her to marry their Ivan again, her pretty chin jutted out determinedly and her rosebud lips stayed firm; she refused him with as much politeness as she could muster. But the Dolgorukis were persistent, and some thought it doubtful if she could fend them off forever.

Then, at the beginning of 1730, Peter II died. Elizabeth was staying in the country when her personal doctor, Armand Lestocq, burst in with the news. According to her mother's will she should have been proclaimed Empress now, but the Dolgorukis would not have her. After all, she had refused to accept their kinsman Ivan as her husband. Lestocq urged her to take power—to go to the barracks, assemble the Guards, to show herself to the people. But Elizabeth was afraid. If she mounted a *coup d'état* which failed, she would be disgraced, imprisoned even. Besides, what use had she for responsibility and power? She wanted to be free from officialdom and protocol; free to gallop through fields and forests with her favourite groom Gabriel by her side; free to enjoy the caresses of her current lover Alexei Shubin, a Sergeant of the Guards. She seems never to have regretted her failure to make a bid for the crown in 1730. 'I was too young then,' she said years afterwards, 'the people would never have stood for me.'

When her surly cousin Anne of Courland became Empress, Elizabeth was not seen much about the court. Some said that she was ill, some that she was sulking, others that she dared not appear because she was pregnant by Sergeant Shubin of the Guards.

Elizabeth was certainly besotted with Shubin; she even wrote him love poems in the crudely sentimental style so popular at the time:

> 'It is not within my power to dowse the fire
> 'I suffer in my heart—and who can remedy the fact
> 'That we are always parting
> 'And life's boring without you?
> 'Better we had never met
> 'Than always to suffer so
>   'About you.'

The trials of separation were soon ended, however, and by the Empress Anne herself. According to Rondeau, she wanted to encourage Elizabeth's promiscuousness as a means of discrediting her. So Sergeant Shubin was released from regular duties and attached to Elizabeth's household. But then jealousy got the better of the Empress. Her cousin was beautiful, popular, a magnet to men. Why should she be allowed to enjoy the sort of love she herself had sought so long in vain? In January 1731 Alexei Shubin was arrested, stripped of all his possessions and transported to Kamchatka.

Elizabeth wept, and not only for the loss of her lover but because the Empress was thinking of banishing her as well—to a nunnery. It was the obvious way to deal with a potential rival, but the decision was not taken. Ernest Biron dissuaded her and so Elizabeth was left at liberty. But she was watched very closely from now on. Note was taken of every movement she made, of every visitor she received. Elizabeth knew it; but she was learning to be at least politically discreet.

Much though she mourned her lover Shubin, she soon found consolation with another. One day she heard a splendid new voice singing solo with the choir of the court chapel. The singer was presented, and his manner and appearance proved as seductive as his voice. He was tall and dark, had fiery black eyes, jet black hair, an intriguing Ukrainian accent, and a most appealing smile. His name was Alexei Razumovski.

Elizabeth decided then and there that she must have him for her own. She asked for him to be transferred to her household, and the request was granted. Alexei was given a room, an allowance, a daily jug of vodka and several more of beer. In return, he sang to his mistress, played the *bandura* to her, and became her lover—or her 'leading descant' as she called him in her *billets-doux*.

The affair with Razumovski injected new joy into her life, but there were still enough irritations to put up with—the Empress's thinly-veiled hostility towards her, the shame of having to take an oath of loyalty to the Empress's unnamed successor, and then, when the Empress at last decided to recognize her status with a court reception and a birthday ball, the fire which broke out during dinner and sent everyone rushing out into the cold. Rumours about her affairs and her supposed pregnancies multiplied all the time as well—until eventually she was to be credited with eight children, though no evidence has come to light to support the contention that she had any at all. But even worse than the rumours and the constant spying was the parsimony with which she was treated by the government.

Elizabeth was brought up to take luxury for granted, but she could not live luxuriously on her income of 40,000 roubles a year, and the Empress refused outright to give her more. Anne remembered the way Elizabeth's father had treated her over money, and felt that her cousin should taste something of the impecunious obscurity she herself had suffered. Elizabeth could not borrow either. In later years she was to claim that she did not dare to because if she died no one would have repaid her debts and so her soul would have gone to hell. In fact, however, she did try to borrow, only no one would extend her credit. Her only course, therefore, was to cut back her expenditure.

Not that all her pleasures were expensive ones. She liked to sing folk-songs with the village girls, to watch them do their wonderful embroidery, to munch roasted nuts and butter-cakes with them. And though she resented having to wear black cotton skirts and simple blouses in order to save her best clothes for public appearances she did not need to dress as richly as she did with her fine complexion, her huge blue eyes, her fine teeth, pretty mouth and incandescent gaiety. Men were ecstatic about her. 'The colour of her face is amazing,' wrote the Duke de Liria, 'the eyes are flamy, the mouth full, the neck most white, and the figure extraordinary.' And she was extraordinarily lively too. She danced like a nymph, rode like a demon, and drove her *troika* like a madwoman at the Butter Week masquerades.

In her mid-twenties now she still seemed the giddy young thing, all froth and exuberance. But, as Jane Rondeau commented, though 'in public she has an unaffected gaiety, and a certain air of giddiness that seems entirely to possess her whole mind . . . in private I have heard her talk with such a strain of good sense and steady reasoning, that I am persuaded the other behaviour is a feint.'

She certainly needed to be circumspect with the Empress so resentful of her. At times Elizabeth's beauty and popularity seemed like a canker gnawing at the Empress's soul. When a Chinese Ambassador arrived at court Anne was incautious enough to ask him whom he considered to be the prettiest woman in the room. 'It would be difficult in the star-light to say which star was the brightest', he replied, but when the Empress insisted, he bowed towards Elizabeth: 'Among such a number of fine women', he said, 'I consider her to be the handsomest. If she'd not quite such large eyes, nobody could see her and live.' The Empress could hardly mask her pique, and when, at the New Year Ball in 1737, a firework broke a window at which Elizabeth was standing and the flying glass cut her forehead open, the Empress's eyes lit up as if in triumph. But the wound healed quickly and left no noticeable scar.

The Empress seemed to be waiting for some excuse to punish her, but Elizabeth was careful. She congratulated the Empress on every conceivable occasion—her birthday, her name-day, the anniversaries of her accession and of her coronation, on every little victory reported from the war—and she congratulated her with every show of sincerity and respect. She referred to herself as 'Her Imperial Majesty's obedient slave', attended banquets to mark the birth- and name-days of Anna Leopoldovna, the Empress's niece, betraying no sign of resentment that the girl was given precedence above her, even managing to smile. Elizabeth took care to be subservient in word and deed, to obey the Empress's every spoken wish, to flatter Ernest Biron, and keep politically detached.

So long as she did this, she knew the Empress dared not touch her. But it was not always easy, especially once the secret police began to meddle in what she regarded as her private affairs.

Elizabeth had placed a member of her household in custody, but the man, evidently an employee of the Secret Police, was subsequently released on orders of the Secret Police Chief and the Empress had scolded her for being so high-handed. Elizabeth replied on 16 November 1736 in measured tones, trying, as she put it, 'to establish my innocence'.

According to her, the man in question had taken 'many bribes from the peasants . . . delayed many petitioners' and was an embezzler into the bargain. 'In one case' he had 'crossed out what I had written' so that money due to be paid to her was paid to him instead. He had also committed 'uncountable other impertinences, which it would be impossible to itemize here'. His arrest may have been ordered 'without your Imperial Majesty's permission', but surely 'any landowner' had the right to punish his own servants. No doubt the Empress had been misinformed about the case, and she, Elizabeth, certainly never had the least intention of acting 'contrary to the will and order of Your Imperial Majesty', so if the culprit was now returned to her custody, she would 'personally report every tiniest detail' about his investigation to the Empress.

Financial dishonesty might be the norm in Russia, but Elizabeth could not afford to harbour an embezzler when she had a staff of seventy to maintain on her limited resources. She kept her own ladies- and gentlemen-in-waiting, her own pages and ostlers, housekeepers and seamstresses, two chaplains, a splendid chef called Fuchs, a personal courier, musicians, Alexei Razumovski, and half a dozen other singers, a blacksmith, an escort of Guardsmen, a clerk of works, and a miscellany of maids and lackeys. By court standards the staff was small—far smaller than Anna Leopoldovna's with whom she had to keep up appearances, but clothes and food also had to be found for all of them, and her expenses did not end there.

In 1736 she engaged Zemtsov, a talented young Russian architect, to make alterations at Tsarskoye Selo, and an English gardener called Lambert to improve its gardens. The cost was considerable, and with the Empress's agents in her chancery determined that she should live within her means, there were almost constant difficulties. Her people indenting for supplies often received only a fraction of what they needed, work was sometimes brought to a standstill for lack of funds, and on at least one occasion the household had to do without its customary supply of beef. Such petty restrictions were frustrating for a princess with generous impulses and a taste for grandeur. How she managed to find enough rich dresses and sufficient resources of good temper for her appearances at court no one could imagine.

Gradually, public sympathy for her began to grow. People imagined that she was oppressed, and they admired her for her charm and patience in adversity. They saw her as a Cinderella, and as a patriot who tried to protect her fellow-countrymen from the all-powerful Germans at the court. And as Anne's vindictiveness became ever more apparent; as the midnight arrests, the secret trials, the exiles and the executions multiplied, more and more Russians began to pray that Elizabeth might take the Empress's place—and Elizabeth herself would not have refused the crown now if it had been offered. But it was not to be. In 1740 Anna Leopoldovna gave birth to a boy, and it became obvious to everyone that Elizabeth would be passed over once again.

When the Empress took to her bed in what proved to be her final illness, Elizabeth was twice refused permission to see her. When she was finally admitted, the interview was extremely short. What passed between them is not known, but when, on 18 October 1740 the Empress's will was read out, the four-months-old Ivan was proclaimed Emperor.

Biron became Regent, and he began his rule in a conciliatory way. He promised to make promotions upon merit and to restrict the ostentation of the court; he took pains to speak Russian instead of German when he appeared in public—and to ingratiate himself with Elizabeth. He sent her a gift of 20,000 roubles, then another of 50,000 with which to clear her debts, granted her an allowance of 80,000 a year, and then tripled it. This was a fraction of the half a million Biron drew himself, but it meant that Elizabeth had no more need to scrimp.

Biron's generosity was not disinterested, however. He wanted to enlist Elizabeth as a potential ally against the Tsar's parents, the whining, obstreperous Prince Anton and the fractious Anna Leopoldovna. More than once Biron lost his temper with them. He reduced Prince Anton to tears several times and publicly threatened Anna that if she continued to 'give herself airs' he would pack her, and her child, off to Germany and invite Elizabeth's brother-in-law, the Duke of Holstein, to the throne. But to Elizabeth he was all consideration.

He consulted her frequently, held conferences with her which sometimes lasted hours. Cynics thought he was trying to persuade her to marry his odious elder son, and to use her influence with the Duke of Holstein—now a widower—to persuade him to marry his daughter. Success in either of these directions might have secured the throne for his descendants, but if this was his plan it came to nothing. In November 1740 Ostermann smeared his face with lemon juice and took to his bed pretending to be ill with jaundice while Marshal Münnich organized a *coup* in favour of the little Tsar's parents. Biron was arrested and spirited away to Siberia where so many of his victims had gone before.

Life under Biron might have had its perils for Elizabeth—the pressure to marry, the unwelcome attentions of the Regent's scarfaced brother Karl—but with Anna Leopoldovna as Regent, Elizabeth was in greater danger still. She was watched day and night, shadowed wherever she went by a team of secret agents under an officer called Chicherin. The new regime had good reason to be afraid of her. The Regent Anna Leopoldovna was half German, had spent half her life abroad, and, like the Empress Anne, seemed to favour foreigners. This was enough to earn her a certain degree of unpopularity, especially among the gentry. Elizabeth on the other hand was popular in the country and she had men about her now who were totally devoted to her and what they thought should be her cause. The two Shuvalov brothers, Michael Vorontsov, and her devious physician Dr. Lestocq were prominent among them, and though they were few, they were ambitious.

But much more important, Elizabeth had become the darling of the Guards. Some officers had known her since childhood and loved her as the last surviving child of their hero Peter the Great, and she made many friends among the young men by standing as godmother to their children, giving them gifts and entertaining them. The court might sneer at her 'assemblies for the Preobrajenskis', but many Guardsmen had come to like her generosity, love her beauty, and trust her Russianness. When they had marched to the Palace to bring down Ernest Biron, some of them had imagined they were acting on Elizabeth's behalf and were bitterly disappointed at the outcome. She must have known this but she made no attempt to exploit their goodwill. Action meant blood, and Elizabeth was squeamish.

The new regime heaped humiliations on her. Despite Biron's generosity she was soon in financial difficulties again, and when she asked for 32,000 roubles to pay off her debts the answer, delayed for weeks, was 'No'. When she persisted they asked her for detailed accounts of every debt and item of expenditure. As a result they noticed that her household had consumed no less than 1,500 gallons of wine and spirits in one month, and that she owed 11,000 roubles more than she had thought. They paid up eventually, but with every show of reluctance and then in quantities of copper coin which Elizabeth is said to have thrown into the river in disdain.

And when Ostermann refused to allow the new Persian Ambassador to pay a courtesy call on her, Elizabeth was stirred to outright fury. She rounded on Count Apraxin who brought her the message and the envoy's gifts: 'You can tell Count Ostermann from me that *he* may think he can pull the wool over everybody's eyes, but *I* know perfectly well that he's trying to humiliate me on every possible occasion. . . . He forgets what I am and what he was.'

At first, however, the Regent herself seemed reasonably well disposed towards her—at least she invited her to frequent gossip sessions at the Palace. But the two women were surrounded by people only too anxious to feed their fears of one another, and their friendship did not prosper. Elizabeth became even more reserved, and the informal meetings eventually ceased.

The Regent left affairs more and more to her clique of German advisers, and spent rather less time on state business than on her coiffure and on designing an elaborate new hairstyle to be worn by the ladies of the court. The hair was neither to be powdered nor curled, but folded over the ears with a chignon at the nape and a strand fastened to the cheek with glue. The whole confection was to be decorated with flowers and held together by twenty feet of ribbon wound round the head one regulation inch above the forehead and tied up with bows, the remainder being left to hang loose over the back.

Such were the preoccupations of the Regent Anna, and when Marshal Münnich, who had brought her to power, threatened resignation over the conduct of affairs, she placidly allowed him to resign. Henceforth Ostermann ruled Russia virtually single-handed while Anna occupied her hours playing cards, chattering to her ladies, complaining about her husband's timidity, and administering snubs to certain courtiers for whom she had conceived a dislike.

At last she took it into her head to marry Elizabeth off to her husband's brother, Prince Ludwig of Brunswick-Wolfenbüttel. When Elizabeth refused, she pleaded with her, then applied pressure, and finally offered her a bribe. All Livonia and Courland would be hers, she promised, if only she would marry the man and move out of Russia.

Elizabeth began to tire of the constant nagging. She wanted to be left alone in luxury and indolence, but they would neither let her alone, nor keep her in the style she thought appropriate. Perhaps the only way out was to take power into her own hands, as some of her friends had hinted she might. The Regent and her husband certainly seemed a contemptible pair, complaining about each other to all and sundry, accusing each other of having affairs. Elizabeth did not care if Prince Anton was in love with Julia Mengden, or if the Regent was consoling herself with the Saxon envoy Count Lynar. But she could not but be impressed by their incompetence. They had let their one reliable friend, Münnich, go, and now everything was in the hands of the unpopular Ostermann. They even seemed lax about their own security these days. Perhaps a palace coup was possible after all.

But when the Swedish envoy Nolken promised his country's support if she made a bid for power Elizabeth became frightened. Ostermann was so suspicious, and who was there of any importance whom she could trust? She might be popular among the Guards, but how many of them would risk their lives for her? So, when the French envoy, the Marquis de la Chetardie, urged her on as well she pondered—and did nothing.

But by the spring of 1741 her supporters among the Guards were becoming restive. Early in June she was talking to a group of them in the Summer Gardens when one of them blurted out: 'Little mother! We're ready and waiting. Just give us the signal.' Elizabeth seemed panic-stricken. 'Keep quiet for God's sake; someone might hear you.' Then she added in a whisper: 'Don't bring misfortune on yourselves or me, my children. Split up and walk away quietly. The time has not yet come. I'll tell you when it does.'

Impatience grew and nerves began to fray as weeks passed and still Elizabeth refused to give the signal. Time and again she would grow hopeful listening to her supporters—and then baulk at the prospect of blood. It seemed she was prepared to rush into nothing except a love affair.

When, as Nolken had predicted, Sweden declared war on Russia giving her a splendid opportunity, she ignored it, and when Lestocq brought her news that de la Chetardie, the French Ambassador, was ready to finance the operation, she hesitated still. She wanted to be certain of success; but there is no certainty in politics. Besides, she was afraid. Spies in long fur coats followed her wherever she went. She had to be careful what she said, whom she talked to, whom she met. She felt very lonely and very afraid.

So autumn came and people who had expected her to make a move that spring, and then in the summer, revised their opinions of her. As Edward Finch M.P., the British Minister, reported, 'we may say of her as Shakespeare makes Julius Caesar say ... that her Highness is too fat to be in a plot.'

Elizabeth seemed to have lost her opportunity. Contrary to expectations, the Swedish war seemed to be bolstering rather than sapping the strength of the regime. The Russian army was successful, and crowds came onto the streets to cheer its victories. Yet as her prospects deteriorated, her motivation suddenly increased. For weeks past, the envoys of Austria, Saxony and Britain—countries opposed to France and Sweden, aware of Elizabeth's involvement with Nolken and de la Chetardie, had been pressing the Regent to have Elizabeth shut away in a nunnery. Rumour of this reached Elizabeth and made her shudder. After all, as Finch once remarked, there was 'not an ounce of nun's flesh about her'. Then, shortly afterwards, she was refused admittance to the infant Emperor Ivan, on whom she had always taken care to pay regular and respectful calls. There may have been nothing sinister about her exclusion at this time, but Elizabeth, who was used to reading auguries at the Russian court by now, took it as a signal of danger, and when she heard that the Regent Anna was preparing to proclaim herself Empress the following December, she felt compelled to act.

Ostermann suspected as much and told the Regent so. She seemed sceptical, but at last agreed to confront Elizabeth face to face. It was 24 November 1741 and a reception was being held in the Winter Palace. The Regent Anna retired to her apartments early and sent for Elizabeth.

She came to the point as soon as she arrived. 'What's this I hear about you?—that you're in correspondence with the country's enemies, and that your doctor is plotting with the French Minister?' At this Elizabeth assumed an air of outraged innocence. How could the Regent believe that she would break the solemn oath she had taken to the Infant Ivan? 'Madam,' the Regent continued, 'I'm going to ask the King of France to recall Monsieur de la Chetardie, and I must ask you never to receive him again.' Elizabeth dissembled. It would be more appropriate, she said, to tell the Frenchman not to see her. But as she spoke she must have realized that her retainer Lestocq must be in danger, perhaps others of her friends as well, and the spectre of the nunnery loomed large again. She began to weep, and suddenly the Regent took pity on her. At last they fell into each other's arms, Elizabeth swearing loyalty, Anne proclaiming her trust in her.

That night, at home, Elizabeth's retainers—Vorontsov, Alexei Shuvalov and his brother Peter, her music-master Schwarz, and Alexei Razumovski—urged her to act at once. But she seemed to be drained of all courage. 'Of course the attempt requires a lot of daring, Madam,' persisted Vorontsov, 'but where is such daring to be found except in a descendant of Peter the Great?' Yet even flattery failed to move her. Elizabeth wanted certainty. She wanted each one of her supporters thoroughly checked out and a detailed plan of action drawn up before taking any action. She even insisted on it. But time was far too short for all this now—and just then news arrived that the three Guards battalions stationed in the capital had orders to leave for the Swedish front within twenty-four hours. Those battalions contained her most ardent supporters. Once they had gone, she would stand no chance at all.

Lestocq had already begun to use the 49,000 ducats supplied by de la Chetardie. Bribes had been distributed, and twenty Preobrajenski grenadiers had been drawn into the plot. Elizabeth was told of this, but she hesitated still, until at last Lestocq himself came in. He handed her a card. It bore a sketch of the imperial crown on one side, and on the other the figure of a nun surrounded by hanged men. The message was plain enough but Lestocq took the trouble to explain it: 'Your Highness must choose between these two alternatives *now*. You must either decide to be Empress, or else allow yourself to be put into a convent and see your faithful servants die in torments.' The others pressed her too. It really was to be now or never.

Elizabeth went into her private chapel, and, taking up a silver cross, fell to her knees before an icon. She stayed there for some moments, and when she emerged, she nodded to her retainers. At once the conspirators swung into action.

The twenty grenadiers arrived. Elizabeth asked them straight if she could depend on them. 'We would die for you, little mother', they replied. They were told to return to barracks and enlist their comrades to the cause—as quickly and as secretly as possible. Elizabeth would join them in an hour. The soldiers trooped out; she returned to her icons to fortify herself with prayer.

The seconds ticked by merging into minutes. Half an hour passed; then an hour. The clutch of nervous men in the adjoining room became impatient. At last Lestocq went in and interrupted her. It would be dangerous, he insisted, to wait a moment longer. She came out without protest. They helped her into a heavy cuirass, arranged her cloak over it, and pinned on the Order of St. Catherine. Then they took her out onto the porch where a sledge stood waiting.

The horses' breath gusted out like steam in the cold night air as shadowy figures helped her in. Lestocq took the seat beside her; two others climbed up behind. Then the driver cracked his whip, and the horses' muffled hooves began to pad out along the dark, snow-covered street. Alexei Razumovski watched them go. He noticed that his mistress was still clutching the silver cross in her hand. He prayed that it would keep her safe.

On the morning of 25 November the Marquis de la Chetardie was penning a report to his masters in Paris. The outcome of any attempted *coup d'état*, he wrote, must now be regarded as extremely uncertain. It was impossible to tell whether Elizabeth could attract sufficient support any more. The Frenchman was quite unaware that the issue had already been decided.

At two o'clock that very morning some two hundred men, mostly Preobrajenski grenadiers, had gathered on their gloomy barrack square. It was bitterly cold, and they passed round flasks of vodka to keep themselves warm, not daring to light a fire, or even to stamp their feet, for fear of rousing comrades loyal to the regime. For hours, it seemed, they waited straining their ears for the tell-tale swish of an approaching sledge.

At last, quick, muffled steps were heard, and a moment later a great sledge swept in through the gates. They rushed up to it excitedly. There were whispered cries of 'Welcome, little mother' as Elizabeth dismounted and, seizing a half-pike from an officer standing by her, marched towards the mess hall. The others followed—all except Lestocq who suddenly thought of the alarm drums and hurried off to make sure they were all slit open.

Meanwhile Elizabeth was addressing her supporters: 'Children,

I have decided to save you and all Russia from our German tor-
turers tonight. Will you follow me?' 'We'll follow you to the
death, little mother', they clamoured. 'As for the Germans, we'll
hack 'em all to pieces.' 'No!' she interrupted, 'There will be no
bloodshed. What we are about to do we shall do only for the good
of our country.' Then, holding her silver cross in outstretched
hands, she sank to her knees. They knelt too. 'I swear before heaven
that I am ready to die for you. Will you swear that you are ready to
die for me?' It seemed a romantic proposition, and the response was
impassioned. 'We swear!' they roared.

All this while more men had drifted in to join her, and there were
now some three or four hundred, all fully armed. Some were sent
to enlist other regiments to the cause, some to arrest notables loyal
to the regime. The remainder set out for the Winter Palace. Elizabeth went with them.

By the time they reached the end of the Nevski Prospect, it was
reckoned that her sledge was making too much noise, so they helped
her out, and she went on by foot. But the pace was fast, her cuirass
was heavy, and her cloak dragged in the snow. They urged her to
go faster, then took her by the arms and virtually carried her along.

At the gates of the Winter Palace the sentries challenged them.
They were ordered to call out the rest of the guard. When they
appeared, still rubbing the sleep from their eyes, Elizabeth addressed them: 'Wake up, my children. You know who I am. You
know that by rights the crown belongs to me. So will you follow
me?' Four officers and a guardsman made as if to grab her, but when
a rebel soldier lunged at them with his bayonet, Elizabeth turned
the point aside. She would have no bloodshed. The loyalists were
quietly bound and gagged; new guards were posted, and Elizabeth
led the rest of the insurgents on into the Palace.

They rushed up the staircase and along deserted corridors,
securing the Empire room by room. And at last they came to a pair
of double doors with a pair of sentries lounging by them. They
offered no resistance and, flushed with excitement now, Elizabeth
crept inside.

As she approached the bedside of the Regent Anna, lumps of
snow dropped from her cloak and melted into little puddles on the
floor. She shook the Regent by the shoulders. 'Time to get up,

sister', she whispered. Anna stirred, and muttered irritably in her sleep. Then her eyes blinked open. She realized immediately what had happened.

There were no protests, no recriminations, no complaints. The ex-Regent merely begged that no harm should befall her little son, Ivan, and that her companion, Julia Mengden, be allowed to stay with her. Elizabeth agreed. The ex-Regent and her friend were led out under guard; nurses followed carrying the infant Emperor and his new-born sister. 'Poor things', Elizabeth observed as they passed by, 'it's your parents' fault, not yours.' Then she turned away to hear from breathless messengers how the rest of the operation was progressing.

Prince Anton, his relatives and Baron Mengden had all been found at the Palace. Elsewhere in the city, Chancellor Golovkin, Count Loewenwolde, Marshal Münnich and the dangerous Ostermann were safely under guard; most of the garrison had declared for the new regime. Elizabeth, it seemed, was safe.

Dawn came late, and the streets were almost silent. Soldiers lounged about at street corners, and occasionally a small group of Elizabeth's supporters would rush past on their way to pull in the smaller fry. They came to Field Marshal Lacy's house and asked him which side he supported. 'The party in power', replied the shrewd old Irishman. He was allowed to go to the Palace to congratulate Elizabeth.

By the time he arrived, the ante-rooms were thronged with dignitaries. Elizabeth had returned home briefly to receive Alexei Razumovski's congratulatory embrace, but was now holding her first levee. She stood on the dais looking magnificent in the uniform of a Guards Colonel. Her eyes were bright, her face pink with ecstasy under her white peruke, and her rosebud mouth flashed brilliant smiles as courtiers queued up to kneel and kiss her hand.

Sounds of commotion began to drift in from the street outside and the windows were flung open. Elizabeth stepped onto the balcony—and the crowd below roared out their cheers. At last, after all the dull nonentities who had occupied the throne, after all those arrogant and crafty Germans, someone young and exciting ruled the destinies of Russia. Elizabeth was the saviour they had longed for all these years; she had charismatic charm; she was everybody's darling. Her bosom heaved with satisfaction. The neglected princess had come in from the cold at last.

The Guards continued to administer the new oath of loyalty to seemingly endless lines of functionaries; messengers rushed out to take the good news of Elizabeth's accession to every quarter of the Empire, and the new Empress began the task of government.

Unlike the Empress Anne, she was generous in victory. When the Adjutant-General, Count Saltykov, was thrown to her feet, one of her supporters commented, 'You go on your knees to her now, but yesterday you wouldn't even have looked at her.' It was true, but Elizabeth smiled graciously; the Count was saved.

She made sure that others kept their revenge in check as well. It was not easy. Feeling against foreigners was running very high, especially in the army. People thought to be of foreign origin were beaten up in the streets; one or two officers were lynched by their men. For a moment it looked as if xenophobic fury might lead to widespread mutiny and even massacre. Elizabeth put her foot down. The guilty Germans were already under lock and key, and she would tolerate no more disorders on pain of death. The fever subsided almost at once.

Every day, long-forgotten faces reappeared in St. Petersburg. The Dolgorukis and Golitsyns, long out of favour, were brought back to court; Elizabeth's own relatives, who had lurked in the shadows for over thirty years, emerged into the light again, and political prisoners of previous reigns were released in their hundreds. It took months to trace some of them, and almost two years were to pass before the unfortunate Shubin, once Elizabeth's lover, was rescued from the Siberian outback and promoted Major-General. But by then he was a broken man.

Those who had helped her to take power were generously rewarded. The Preobrajenski grenadiers were all promoted—each private became a lieutenant, the corporals majors, and the sergeants colonels—and allotted a minimum of twenty-nine serfs apiece, at which they showed their joy by getting drunk every day, roistering in the streets, and robbing passers-by. Peter Shuvalov became a Count, Vorontsov an imperial gentleman-in-waiting, and Alexei Razumovski Chief Master of the Hounds. Armand Lestocq who had done most to bring her to the throne was granted a stipend of

7,000 roubles a year and the title 'Excellency'. But as a foreigner the rank embarrassed him. 'My promotion will inevitably surround me with enemies', he told Elizabeth. 'I shall be banished in the end.'

Elizabeth leant heavily on his advice in structuring her government, and it was he who recommended Biron's erstwhile protégé Alexei Bestuzhev to take Ostermann's place as Vice-Chancellor. Bestuzhev was an ugly man—thin-lipped, sharp-chinned, large-nosed, and with an incredibly broad and sloping forehead. He was an epicure, an amateur chemist, and something of a hypochondriac as well, being the inventor of a nerve tonic for which he claimed great powers. He was not likeable, but he was educated, experienced in diplomacy and supposedly able. He got the job, and he drafted most of the orders that passed under Elizabeth's pen in the weeks that followed. The noted gourmet and hunting-man Prince Alexei Cherkasski was confirmed as Chancellor.

But personalities were only part of it. The whole shape of the administrative machine was changed as well. The so-called 'Secret Council' was abolished, though a cabinet or 'conference' of heads of state departments presided over by Elizabeth soon replaced it. The Senate was revived; so was the post of Procurator-General. The idea was to show Elizabeth as the restorer of her father's works— not that she could distinguish between the essence and the trappings of Peter the Great's achievements much better than her mother could.

Her choice as Procurator-General was the noted German-hater and devotee of Peter the Great, Prince Nikita Trubetskoi. And it was hoped that he would counterbalance the power of the Vice-Chancellor, for although the Prince was Bestuzhev's son-in-law, the two were known to dislike one another.

Meanwhile the members of the previous regime were being dealt with. Anna Leopoldovna, Prince Anton and their children were imprisoned in the fort of Dünamunde; Anton's relatives were moved to Riga, and preparations went forward to put their Ministers on trial.

Ostermann, the principal figure, was accused of ignoring Catherine's will; of propositioning Elizabeth to marry a foreign prince; of persuading Anna Leopoldovna to assume the title Empress, and of using State funds without consulting the Cabinet. Münnich was also charged with ignoring Catherine's will, and with both helping Biron to become Regent and getting rid of him. Sufficiently grave, though lesser, charges were compiled against Golovkin, Loewenwolde, Mengden and the rest.

As usual in Russia, the onus of proof lay on the defendants. Guilt was assumed from the fact of arrest; the functions of prosecution and judge were barely distinguishable, and the proceedings were held in secret. Münnich is said to have expressed surprise that since those responsible had taken so much trouble in preparing the indictment and the questions put to him, they had not bothered to prepare his answers too. He might have been forgiven for adopting so cynical an attitude, for whatever crimes were on the charge-sheet, they were really being tried for constituting a threat to the new regime, and for being Germans.

The court sentenced Andrei Ostermann to be broken on the wheel, Münnich to be quartered and eight others to be beheaded. Execution was fixed for 18 January. That morning six thousand troops took up their posts by a specially erected scaffold in St. Petersburg, and at ten o'clock the condemned men appeared. They came on foot—all except Ostermann who was allowed to ride in a sledge on account of his gout. The list of charges was read out, Ostermann's black hat and his wig were removed, and while the rest awaited their turns, he was led to execution.

Suddenly, the Secretary to the Senate ordered the executioner to hold his hand and began reading from another document: 'God and the Empress grant you life!' Elizabeth had commuted the sentences to exile; there would be no bloodshed after all. Ostermann immediately asked for his wig and hat to be returned; Münnich joked with his guards and handed them some coins; Golovkin broke down, and Loewenwolde became hysterical.

On his way into exile, Münnich happened to pass his old rival Biron returning now from exile to his estate at Yaroslav. Neither acknowledged the other.

Now she was established in power Elizabeth set about bringing the war with Sweden to an end. She expressed her willingness to come to terms. But the Swedish demands were harsher than expected and placed her in a quandary. The Swedes had encouraged her to make her bid for power and they expected a reward. But she was Peter the Great's daughter and she could not start her reign by surrendering territory won by the army which had made her Empress. To make matters worse, the French Ambassador tried to mediate. De la Chetardie was witty and brilliant; she enjoyed his company. He had done even more to bring her to the throne, and though she had repaid the 49,000 ducats he had spent on her behalf and given him presents worth a million and a half roubles besides, she still owed him a moral debt.

De la Chetardie did his best to exploit it. He begged her to make some concession to the Swedes. It was all a question of saving face, he explained. He realized that such a step must be unpopular, but asked her to 'consider the position in which the King, my master, is placed, Madame—a position into which he has been placed only by the wish to see you on the throne. Surely you will do all you can to help him, by giving him the means to hasten the conclusion of a peace.' Friendship and obligation were weighed against patriotism and filial duty, but in the end Elizabeth refused. She was too conscious of her duty to her father's memory, she said. She did feel guilty however—until the Austrian Ambassador, de Botta, handed her a document his Government had intercepted. Originating from Paris, and addressed to the French envoy at Constantinople, it turned out to be an assessment of Russia's situation based, apparently, on Chetardie's reports. It suggested that Elizabeth's coup had weakened Russia and that the Turks should be encouraged to attack her while she was still embroiled on the Swedish front. The Frenchman had betrayed the Empress's trust in him. She no longer felt guilty; she felt furious.

Realizing that he was no longer welcome, in the summer of 1742 de la Chetardie left Russia. But the war continued. The Russian army beat the Swedes at Helsingfors and captured all of Finland. When peace was concluded in 1743 Sweden ceded Finland to Elizabeth, and allowed her to dictate who should be declared heir to the Swedish throne. It was a heartening beginning.

Meanwhile preparations had gone forward for Elizabeth's coronation. It was planned to symbolize Russia's new power and grandeur after sixteen years of foreign rule. All her rivals, and her friends, were to be outshone—Louis XV who had once refused to marry her, her neighbour Frederick the Great, and her ally Maria Theresa who had just acceded to the throne of Austria.

Precedent demanded that she be crowned in Moscow, and in February 1742 the entire court left St. Petersburg bound in that direction. This was a vastly complex operation involving the movement of stores and furniture as well as personnel, though Elizabeth herself took only three days on the journey. She stayed a few days at Vsesvyatskoye just outside the city before proceeding into Moscow itself.

Her entry was triumphal. Seventy-one guns were fired and vast crowds cheered as she appeared in a veritable wedding-cake of a carriage drawn by eight Neapolitan horses and flanked by dozens of attendants. Triumphal arches had been erected in her honour, lavishly decorated with paintings and sculptures of Biblical, classical and Russian heroes. Neptune, Mars and Jupiter were attended, somewhat inappropriately, by angels; Gideon was pictured in the company of Saturn, Boris and Gleb with Samuel and David. There were representations of all the Virtues too—Courage, Truth, Steadiness, even Economy, and extravagant mottoes such as 'May Elizabeth live a hundred years' were everywhere.

Beyond the arch on Tver Street the Vice-Governor was waiting to receive her. A further eighty-five guns boomed out their welcome, troops of infantry fired off their muskets and Archbishop Ambrosius of Novgorod delivered an address which filled nearly sixteen pages of print and must have lasted the better part of an hour. At a second arch, students of the Moscow Academy clad in virgin white and bearing laurel branches sang ten verses of a particularly unctuous song of welcome, and at a third arch erected in the Street of the Butchers, the merchants of the city welcomed her. That evening everyone of importance arrived at the Kremlin 'in rich dress' for a ball which lasted until midnight. It was then that Elizabeth announced that 25 April would be her coronation day.

During the intervening weeks she attended lengthy conferences to decide the forms of service to be used and the order of the entertainments. She held long discussions with her architects about how to transform dirty, labyrinthine Moscow into a glittering capital for the day; spent hours pondering the various styles of dress that might be worn; and sent to St. Petersburg for masquerade costumes, ordering them to 'be packed carefully so that they will be in a fit condition to be used'.

By dawn on coronation day Kremlin Square had been covered with fine carpets and hung with crimson cloth. There were troops galore in resplendent uniforms, and expectant and excited crowds. At last the great cavalcade made its appearance—solemn Ministers with the Regalia (still to be seen in the Kremlin armoury) and the graceful Elizabeth herself under a gold and silver canopy borne by the most handsome of her courtiers.

She enjoyed every moment of the ceremony, was fervent in every response, loud in every hymn, devout in every prayer, and patient throughout every sermon. The violent Alleluias, the gilded carriages, the beautiful Guardsmen, the odes composed for her, all gave her delight. And yet 'the most glorious Monarch, the invincible Sovereign Empress and Autocrat of all Russia' as Elizabeth was now, was still child-like and superstitious. That morning she had given her private chaplain a small sealed packet to place on the Cathedral altar. It contained a note which read: 'Long live the Most Pious, Autocratic, Great Monarch and Empress of all the Russias, Elizabeth Petrovna.' It added, as if confiding a secret to the good Lord Himself, a declaration of intent to make her nephew her successor.

There followed a round of celebrations unparalleled even by those of the Empress Anne's coronation eleven years before. There were receptions galore, four masquerades within six days and another five before the end of May. There was splendid music, including some exotic Turkish melodies arranged by the violinist Schnurpfeil, and some splendid productions in a brand-new opera house. Among the highlights were two 'allegorical ballets' produced by Fusano, their titles as opulent as the occasion: *The Golden Apple at the Feast of the Gods and the Judgement of Paris* and *The Joy of the Nations over the Appearance of Astrea on the Russian Horizon and the Restoration of a Golden Age*, in which 'Astrea', of course, represented Elizabeth and the 'Golden Age' was meant to represent her reign. This second ballet was followed by a Grand Opera first performed in Dresden in 1738, Johann Hasse's *La Clemenza di Tito*, and the rather indigestible programme was completed by a work of the Academy's Professor of Allegory, Staehlin, entitled *Russia Afflicted and Consoled* in which, again, the consoler was meant to symbolize Elizabeth. The decor was by Girolamo Bon, the music by Domenico dall'Oglio from Padua, and the leading part was sung by the beautiful Rosina, the designer's wife and the composer's mistress. At least one member of the audience thought Rosina's acting rather crude, but Elizabeth was so moved by the performance that, according to the librettist, Staehlin, she 'could not hold back the tears'.

Yet Elizabeth was never to forget that she was the 'Pious Autocrat'. Even at the opera or at a masquerade she always had an abbot and a bishop or two in attendance and when she went on pilgrimage —and she made several that summer—she took whole armies of clerics with her. She was a veritable blessing on the Church. She showered money on it; fixed a maximum price of five roubles on Bibles, banned her Muslim subjects from building any more mosques, and ordered foreigners who had adopted the Orthodox faith never to leave Russia (thus saving them from the temptations of returning to their old religions and losing their souls).

Her religious enthusiasms were apparently shared by her lover, Alexei Razumovski. The two went everywhere together, did everything together, billed and cooed over each other like a pair of imperial lovebirds. The unashamed pleasure they took in each other's company, their public displays of mutual affection, proved so much of an embarrassment to the Church that it pressed her to legalize the relationship. She is said to have married him at a clandestine ceremony that autumn. But the marriage was morganatic. There was no question of Elizabeth bearing a child that would succeed her. She had already decided that her nephew should be her heir.

The fourteen-year-old Karl Peter Ulrich, Duke of Holstein, had been brought to Russia in the greatest secrecy earlier that year, and she had awaited his arrival with 'benevolent impatience'. She had never seen him, but he was an orphan, her beloved sister's child, and she determined to be a second mother to him.

Young Peter turned out to be an unprepossessing, callow youth— pale and thin, with lank, fair hair, an awkward posture, a protruding lower lip, and a receding chin. He also had an extremely shrill and high-pitched voice. Elizabeth promptly attributed his shortcomings to poor health and entrusted him to the care of the fashionable Dr. Struve. The cure did little for him but the Empress persevered.

She gave him a tutor to teach him Russian, another to instruct him in the true religion, and made him a Colonel of the Guards.

That November he was baptized into the Orthodox faith and proclaimed heir to the throne. His first important public appearance proved to be something of an ordeal. Despite all the coaching he had received he was confused about the ritual, uncertain of the language, and extremely nervous. Elizabeth had to mother him right through the ceremony—tell him where to stand and when to kneel, and prompt him with whispers when he forgot his lines.

She doted on the boy, yet even she could not but recognize that he had serious shortcomings. He could barely stumble through the simplest steps of a quadrille and was altogether very idle. 'I have noticed', she remarked, 'that my nephew passes entire days without doing anything', and concluding that young Peter had 'a great many pretty things to learn', she determined to improve him. She engaged the admirable Landet to teach him how to dance, obtained reports on various teaching systems fashionable abroad, and appointed Professor Staehlin to teach the boy how 'to pass his time with pleasure and advantage'.

She followed his progress assiduously and was always ready with encouragement. Observing his interest in uniforms and parades, she at once concluded that his intellectual strength could best be developed through studying the military sciences. She had a vast bureau made for him crammed full of accurate working models of every conceivable instrument of war, each with a printed sheet of explanatory notes and instructions for use. But though Peter took the toys to pieces readily enough, he seemed rather less interested in putting them together again afterwards, and the notes were never read.

The learned Staehlin sighed. Exertions of a cerebral kind came very hard to Peter, and even Elizabeth, who was ever ready to lavish gifts on him at the least sign of progress, tut-tutted. At last she had to derive such satisfaction as she could from his gradual growth of confidence and his ability to draw and copy neatly.

Care for the future Emperor's education did not divert Elizabeth's attention from that constant preoccupation of eighteenth-century female autocrats: improving standards at court. In order that they should conform to the very best of western practice, people were instructed to appear in 'good and not in verminous dress'; field marshals and full generals were to maintain at least eight and not more than twelve lackeys, while major-generals had to be attended by exactly four. There was innovation too: everyone at court, even her female attendants, was given rank. Gentlemen-in-waiting were created brigadiers, the *chefs de cuisine* majors, while concierges and bakers all became lieutenants. In this way, everybody knew his own and everybody else's place, a man's status was obvious on sight, and the number of petty squabbles over precedence was drastically reduced.

The political intrigues, however, did not diminish. As the British envoy Finch reported, 'the new councillors . . . are already quarreling together and forming into different parties.' Lestocq and Trubetskoi were soon at each others' throats; Bestuzhev and his friends mistrusted Count Rumyantsev and his friends, and both disliked General Buturlin. Foreign diplomatists forecast Russia's doom. The new men, they said, were inexperienced and incompetent; Elizabeth was weak; Ostermann was irreplaceable; the dissolution of the Empire was only a matter of time. Like so many experienced diplomatists before and since they were to be proved wrong on almost every count.

Much as she loved Moscow, at the beginning of 1743 Elizabeth moved back to St. Petersburg. The place had changed beyond recognition since her childhood. Once a primitive fortress village built upon a marsh, it was now almost a city—elegant, Italianate, two miles across from end to end, and according to Jonas Hanway, a British visitor of the time, 'very healthful and abounding in all the necessaries and many of the pleasures of life.' True, some quarters were jerry-built and oats still grew in the fields outside the Winter Palace. But there were charming canals, cobblestoned wharves, broad prospects paved with timber, and a number of impressive buildings. New ones were rising all the time. The city, artificially created by her father, was breathing lustily of its own accord.

One of Elizabeth's concerns in coming north was to see the navy. The fleet was her father's creation and she decided to review it every spring as he had done. She did not understand naval affairs, but if she lacked her father's practical abilities she certainly appears to have inherited something of his restless energy. That summer she visited Peterhof, Tsarskoye Selo and Strelna, as well as Kronstadt. She seemed always to be on the move, though in search of pleasure rather than of work. But then taking pleasure was her *métier*, and with so many grand fêtes and opulent picnics to attend, so many *divertissements* at country houses where gondolas sailed by and clarinets cooed out serenades across the water, who could blame her?

At court the arts were flowering as never before. Virtuosi of all kinds were flooding into Russia. Francesco Araja had returned from Italy with a fresh contingent of instrumentalists and singers, the artist Guiseppe Valeriani, a pupil of Piranesi, arrived from Rome to work on stage designs, and the celebrated Baldassare Galuppi, originator of the concerto style, was brought to Russia to take over the court choir. But best of all, Elizabeth enjoyed the grand hunts at Tsarskoye.

The pleasures Elizabeth derived from hunting, however, were not quite the same as those of the Empress Anne. Anne had usually hunted from the safety of a carriage, the game being driven past the muzzle of her gun at almost point-blank range. Elizabeth, on the other hand, liked to mount some splendid horse and speed out like the wind with her beloved Alexei by her side. For her there were always excitements to the chase, and if the quarry proved at all elusive she was quite content to exchange caresses with the Master of the Hunt until the followers caught up.

Late in July, however, Elizabeth's round of pleasure was rudely interrupted when Lestocq rushed in with news of a plot to free Ivan and throw her off the throne. Within moments the palace was in a state of seige. Doors were locked, engagements cancelled, and extra guards rushed in. A commission of investigation was appointed and the arrests began. For months to come the atmosphere at court was to be tense with suspicion and intrigue.

One of the principal figures involved was the Countess Natalia Lopukhina, an attractive woman and an old rival of Elizabeth's. She had once dared to appear at a court ball with her hair dressed with pink roses in the same way as the Empress's. Elizabeth had torn the offending flowers out of the Countess's hair and slapped her face. But though she saw Natalia as 'a little fool' who 'only got what she deserved', the Countess's grudge had rankled, and she had another grudge as well: Elizabeth had exiled her lover Loewenwolde.

The Countess's letters to Loewenwolde had been intercepted, and these had produced the first glimmering suspicion of the existence of a plot to liberate ex-Tsar Ivan. Upon further investigation, the Vice-Chancellor's sister-in-law, Anna Bestuzheva, was also found to be 'involved'—and the Austrian Ambassador, who had instructions from the Empress Maria Theresa to do what he could for the imprisoned ex-Regent and her family. The Ambassador himself enjoyed diplomatic immunity but the two ladies and a number of their relatives and associates were arrested and interrogated.

Try as they might, however, the inquisitors failed to produce more evidence of a working conspiracy to restore Ivan to the throne than a number of rumours and some authenticated reports of gossip about the Empress of a critical, not to say bitchy, kind. As the new British envoy, Sir Cyril Wych, reported, 'the terrible plot was found to be little more than the ill-considered discourses of a couple of spiteful passionate women.' Yet Elizabeth had seen too many successful *coups* at court to take the matter lightly. Anna Bestuzheva and Natalia Lopukhina were accordingly sentenced to death.

Elizabeth kept the orders confirming sentence on her dressing table until the eve of execution. Then she commuted them. The culprits were merely to be flogged, have their tongues clipped, and sent into exile. The Empress left town before the sentences were carried out.

The affair was soon seen to have wide-ranging political and diplomatic implications. One of the accused was a close relative of Vice-Chancellor Bestuzhev's, whom Lestocq and his friends were known to dislike and hoped to implicate. Lestocq was said to be in the pay of the French (as well as of the English, the Prussians and the Poles), and the French were certainly anxious to disrupt the Austro-Russian alliance—and discrediting the pro-Austrian Bestuzhev and the Austrian Ambassador was an obvious way to do it.

In the event, relations with Austria did become severely strained as the result of the 'Lopukhina affair'. When Elizabeth demanded that de Botta be punished Maria Theresa retorted that extorted evidence was worthless, and the two Empresses were to remain estranged for some considerable time to come. But Elizabeth refused to get rid of Peter Bestuzhev, as Lestocq and his friends had hoped she would.

All this time, the atmosphere at court had been heavy with tension and mistrust and Elizabeth found the experience extremely upsetting. At times, Alexei Razumovski seemed to be the only person she could trust among all the warring cliques and jealous women at court, and she expressed her feelings to him by means of sentimental *billets doux* in verse.

> 'Oh, those sly and evil people,
> 'People who are jealous of me
> 'People who hate love,
> 'Make it difficult to live.'

The only antidote to the conniving and the veiled hostility, she was sure, was love, and

> 'It would not be possible
> 'To live without you.'

Alexei was not clever like the others; and wealth and honours had not spoiled him. Elizabeth adored him and he was content with her adoration.

Totally unashamed of his humble origins, Alexei decided to bring his family to court. It was not an entirely successful experiment. When he presented his mother to her, Elizabeth was the epitome of kindness and generosity. But the old woman found the glitter of the court utterly confusing. Wits propagated the story that when she first arrived at court dressed and powdered for the occasion, she caught sight of herself in a mirror and fell to her knees, thinking that so fine an apparition must be the Empress herself. So the old woman returned to her simple homestead in the Ukraine. Her second son, Cyril, who was still young enough to be adjusted to the *grand monde*, was sent on an extended Grand Tour of Europe. Alexei, however, remained at court.

He continued to accompany Elizabeth everywhere, and everywhere she showed him signs of tenderness. He was her pet, her idol, her Adonis. Alexei breathed geniality and life into the atmosphere at court. He represented the freedom and the gaiety of the open steppes and of his Cossack ancestors. She loved him, and since he was a Ukrainian, she loved all things Ukrainian. Ukrainian food, Ukrainian music and the dashing Ukrainian costume all became popular at court. One day, she promised Alexei, she would let him show her the Ukraine.

For the moment, however, work had priority, and she was working very conscientiously—actually reading documents before signing them, listening attentively to reports, presiding over ministerial meetings, making peace between her warring cohorts of advisers, protecting Bestuzhev from Lestocq, and Vorontsov from Bestuzhev. She acquainted herself with the outlines, if not the intricacies, of every major issue, and concerned herself particularly with the administration of justice. 'Subjects with a grievance', she ordered, 'should not be impeded by anyone—of whatever title, rank or worth', and peculation must stop too. Her father had had the same objectives; but bribery and corruption were ingrained into the system, into the very fabric of society, and she was to have no more success than he had done in extirpating them—except perhaps at court where no one was to take so much as 'a chip' without her personal authorization.

The control of Court expenditure was necessary enough with a budget deficit of a million roubles—a deficit due partly to her reducing the poll-tax by ten kopeks, for which the peasants blessed her—but economy was not pressed to the point of restricting her own comforts.

Elizabeth continued to be surrounded by opulence, by grandeur and by dignity—and yet despite this she found it difficult to keep up any prolonged pretence of *hauteur*. She could still flash with temper, beam a sudden, unaffected smile, or swear like a fishwife. If her afternoon nap ever happened to be disturbed, albeit by the slightest noise, the culprit could expect a sharp slap on the face or a blow from a well-aimed slipper. But she was as quick to forgive as she was to lash out. She laughed easily, cried easily; Elizabeth was a passionate woman, and true to her passions.

One of her particular passions, seen in everything except decision-taking, was for speed. In January 1744 when the court migrated to Moscow again, she travelled in a magnificent covered sledge, luxuriously equipped with beds and chairs, a stove, a card-table, so that she could travel by night as well as day. It needed a dozen specially-fattened horses to move it. Yet though the teams were changed every few miles, the pace she demanded was so furiously fast that animals fell dead from exhaustion on the way.

One of the purposes of this particular journey was to introduce her nephew Peter to his prospective bride, an obscure German princess recommended by Lestocq, the Prussians and the French—Sophia Augusta of Anhalt-Zerbst. The Anhalt-Zerbsts were known to be poor, and the Empress had sent them 10,000 roubles to cover the expenses of the journey. The princess, accompanied by her mother, Joanna, arrived at Moscow on the evening of Thursday, 9 February. The Empress received them in the Annenhof Palace.

The thirty-four-year-old Elizabeth, who was wearing an immense hooped dress of silver *moiré* and diamonds in her hair, made a great impression on the girl. 'It was quite impossible', she wrote in retrospect, 'not to be struck by her beauty and the majesty of her bearing. She was a large woman ... but not the least disfigured by her size' and 'her face was also very beautiful.'

Meanwhile, Elizabeth was appraising the girl. She seemed to be about fifteen, had a rather long, thin face, a good complexion, and splendid chestnut hair. But the interview was too short for Elizabeth to form an adequate impression. The visitors were tired after six weeks on the road, and she had allowed them to withdraw after a few minutes. But she was intensely curious about the young princess she had chosen to be her nephew's wife. Later that night, while the newcomers were at supper, she crept up to their apartments and peered at them through a hole in the door.

Next day she put on a brown gown embroidered with silver, smothered her neck and bosom with jewels and accompanied by the gorgeous Alexei, went to invest her visitors with the Order of St. Catherine. From there, it being the first week of Lent, she went to church. And then, having appointed tutors to instruct the girl in religion, Russian and dancing, she left on a pilgrimage to the Troitsa Monastery.

She had left strict instructions with Countess Rumyantsev and the other ladies-in-waiting she had attached to Sophia's suite to make regular reports about the girl, and extremely satisfactory they turned out to be. Sophia was evidently obedient, serious, intelligent, and a much keener student than young Peter. Within ten days she was managing to say a few things in Russian. The more Elizabeth learned about her, the more satisfied she was with her decision.

Then Sophia fell ill. Even though the physicians suspected small-pox, Elizabeth rushed to her bedside, and she maintained her vigil by it while they bled her, despite her fear of blood. Sophia, it seemed, aroused all Elizabeth's maternal instincts.

In May she took Sophia and Peter on another pilgrimage to the Troitsa monastery. But however fond she had become of the girl, she disliked Joanna, the girl's mother, and Vice-Chancellor Bestuzhev soon gave her grounds to distrust the woman too. Bestuzhev had been busy intercepting correspondence again and had discovered not only that de la Chetardie, who had recently returned to Russia, seemed to be conspiring against Russia, but that Joanna was involved with him.

Elizabeth at once descended on her and ordered her into an adjoining room. She emerged some time later red-faced and obviously angry. Joanna followed red-eyed and in tears. Then Elizabeth suddenly noticed Sophia and Peter scrambling down from the window seat like frightened fawns. Her face broke into a smile, she kissed them both, and, ignoring the girl's mother, swept on out of the room.

Then she dealt with de la Chetardie. At the crack of dawn on 6 June the Secret Police Chief arrived at the French Residence with an escort of fifty Guards. The Ambassador was roused from his bed and ordered to pack his bags. France had finally lost the foothold she had gained in 1741; indeed the whole disposition of Russian foreign policy was changing.

Prussia was one of the countries more immediately involved. When King Frederick heard that Russia and Austria had fallen out over the Lopukhina affair, he had sent Elizabeth a fulsome letter proposing an exchange of portraits. He wanted, he said, to let his eyes linger over the features of 'the greatest, most beautiful, and most accomplished sovereign that Europe has seen'. Elizabeth responded by calling Frederick 'the most perfect sovereign in all the world' and treating his ambassador, Mardefeldt, with particular favour. The pro-Austrian Bestuzhev, however, presented the Prussians with a stumbling block, and since he would not accept their bribes, they engaged Sophia's mother, Joanna, to intrigue with Lestocq to bring him down. But Bestuzhev had got the better of them. The correspondence he had intercepted had enabled him to expose Joanna as well as de la Chetardie, and within days he was promoted Chancellor.

That autumn, after Frederick's troops had invaded Bohemia and occupied Prague, Elizabeth, though still angry about Austria's supposed involvement in the Lopukhina affair, agreed to accept an Austrian ambassador to her court again, and relations with Prussia were sent on a downward drift which was, eventually, to end in war.

On 28 June 1744, after two months of intense instruction, young Sophia was baptized into the Russian Church and given a new name. Elizabeth had chosen to call her after her mother. Henceforth Sophia was known as Catherine; one day she would be known as the Empress Catherine II, as Catherine the Great.

Despite her anger with the mother, Elizabeth was still fond of the child. She was moved to tears that day as Sophia delivered her responses in such clear, bright tones, and returning from the ceremony, she presented her with a necklace and a diamond brooch worth a hundred thousand roubles. Next day, St. Peter's Day, was the day fixed for the betrothal. The ceremony took place in the Kremlin, and was accompanied by as much pomp as a coronation. There followed eight days of masquerades, fireworks, operas and illuminations. Then Elizabeth and the court left for Kiev, for the tour of the Ukraine she had promised Alexei she would make one day.

The Ukraine was his birth-place and it was the scene of her father's greatest victory. But there were patriotic and religious excuses for the tour as well. Kiev had been the capital of the original Russian state, and its ancient monasteries and seminaries were famed throughout the Orthodox world. Elizabeth called the trip a pilgrimage. It was probably the grandest the world had ever seen.

She took a vast suite with her requiring twenty-three thousand horses distributed at thirty staging posts to carry them. The expedition was provided with every comfort and plentifully supplied with food and drink—twenty-two barrels of meat, ninety of poultry, eight of sucking-pig, two of wild boar, and considerable quantities of butter, hams, molasses, mushrooms and wine, besides twenty-seven gallons of double-strength vodka. Other necessities had to be found along the way.

At the borders of the Ukraine the 'pilgrimage' was greeted by a parade of Cossacks with flowing mustachios, dark blue cloaks and colourful baggy trousers. They took over Elizabeth's escort and rode by her carriage the rest of the way, sabres drawn and horse-tail banners flying in the wind. However, this time Elizabeth's progress was more leisurely than usual. There were frequent halts at luxurious camps, walks and excursions, shooting expeditions, even concerts and dancing, and at every village along the way crowds of rustics turned out to cheer her. The warmth of these receptions delighted her—so did the delectable companionship of the adorable Alexei.

Towards the end of August they approached Kiev. The clergy met them at the outskirts carrying religious banners and icons, whereupon the pilgrims left their carriages and were conducted towards the city on foot, following the cross. Further on, a chorus of theological students, dressed as heroes, monsters and Greek gods welcomed them. One of them, representing 'St. Vladimir', legendary founder of Kiev, presented Elizabeth with the keys of the city. Then she was helped into a chariot adorned with the figures of a two-winged Pegasus, and was driven through the Golden Gate of Yaroslav I, towards the city centre.

Elizabeth spent the next fortnight visiting the famous Monastery of the Caves, worshipping numerous relics, including the miraculous icon of the Virgin supposedly painted by St. Luke, seeing catacombs and attending sumptuous masses where everyone wore full court dress. The faithful Alexei was always at her side, and, thanks to his exertions as the impresario of the expedition, wild proofs of her popularity were given everywhere. It seemed that she had never been so happy. But the climax was yet to come—an entertainment to cap all entertainment.

It took place in the open air above the majestic Dnieper River. The performance began at seven. By two the following morning Elizabeth had seen ballets, choruses and prologues, a mock battle in which the Cossacks beat the 'Poles', a real fishing scene, a performance of Sumarokov's *The Piety of Marcus Aurelius* . . . and the entertainment still continued. At last Elizabeth ventured to ask when it might finish. They replied in astonishment that they were only half-way through, and when she indicated that she was fatigued the organizers were so obviously distressed and begged so earnestly to be allowed at least a few fireworks that she had not the heart to refuse them.

One of the very first rockets flew over her head, frightened the horses and set fire to a tent. For some minutes there was pande-monium. But no serious damage was done, and Elizabeth could not bring herself to feel annoyed with such a child-like people who wanted so desperately to please her. 'Oh God', she was heard to pray when the time came for her to leave, 'do but love me as I love this gentle, guileless people', and when, in later years, reference was made to Kiev she would often weep in happy recollection.

That autumn on her way to St. Petersburg she heard that her nephew Peter had fallen ill. Smallpox was diagnosed. She turned back immediately to Moscow. Smallpox had always been the scourge of her family. Somehow she nursed her nephew through it. But the sickness left scars, and those scars were to affect his rela-tionship with Catherine.

Not even Peter's illness, however, could erase the memory of the delights she had experienced, nor detract from her continuing pleasure in the company of Alexei Razumovski. Wits called him the 'Night Emperor' and Elizabeth could refuse him nothing. She cancelled public functions when he was indisposed, took time off to nurse him for the gout, made him a Count, gave him her old palace in St. Petersburg and another near to Moscow. She cooked meals for him in the privacy of his apartments, obtained a special dispensation to exempt him from the frequent fasts observed at court, and forgave him at once when, in a drunken fit, he gave Peter Shuvalov a flogging.

Alexei's drinking was beginning to pass the bounds of modera-tion—but so was Elizabeth's vanity. Since the excursion to the

Ukraine, the court resumed a routine stiff with protocol. There was a reception every Sunday, an opera or a theatrical performance every Monday, on Tuesdays a masquerade, on Thursdays a comedy. There were grandiose banquets at which the sexes were segregated at vast 'E'-shaped tables, forming her monogram, and two grand balls a week. Such functions were usually confined to certain ranks, attendance was compulsory, and while minimum standards of elegance were insisted on (and court functionaries fixed seals to the coat-tails or skirts of any outfit considered too old or unfashionable), other rules were stringently applied to prevent any woman competing with the Empress in appearance.

Now that the gloss of youth was wearing off, now that her hair had to be tinted and her complexion needed rouge, no one except the Empress was allowed to wear crystal, or hoops larger than a given size, while she herself changed as often as six times a day, and hardly ever wore the same dress more than twice. Even so, she felt it increasingly difficult to face competition from the young, and showed an increasing tendency to wear men's clothes which showed her tiny feet and splendid legs off to the best advantage. While harlequin costumes were banned at the fancy dress balls she gave because she considered them indecent, and pilgrims' dress was banned because it mocked the church, Elizabeth herself would appear as a French musketeer, a Colonel of the Guards, a Cossack or a sailorman. And as these pleasures began to pall, she took to more recherché entertainments. Not only did she derive particular enjoyment from the sight of the boys of the Cadet Corps portraying female roles in their performances of French plays, but she began to hold exclusive 'metamorphosis balls' where all the gentlemen had to wear whaleboned petticoats and clumsy crinolines, and all the ladies had to dress as men.

The result was both ludicrous and vulgar. On one occasion, a lugubrious Court Chamberlain called Sievers was dancing a polonaise with young Catherine when the Countess Hendrikov tripped over his dress and all three came tumbling to the floor. As they tried to struggle to their feet, they became entangled in poor Sievers's crinolines and Catherine ended up 'choking with laughter' under the Chamberlain's hooped skirts. Only Elizabeth herself seemed to carry off the disguise with complete success. She looked gorgeous in men's clothes—but then this was the object of the whole contrivance.

Elizabeth was proving just as corruptible as her female predecessors had proved themselves to be, and the imprisoned Ivan VI, the infant Tsar she had displaced, was a haunting reminder of her corruption and her guilt. Ivan was separated from his parents now, and surrounded by the most stringent security measures. His guards knew him only as 'Grigory' and ultimately as 'the prisoner without a name'. Every month the prison governor sent in a report on him. But Elizabeth's sense of guilt did not become obsessive. She dared not free him, for fear that he would be exploited by oppositionists at home and abroad, who were imagined to be only too anxious to disturb the peace and put her family in danger. And if Ivan was not to blame for his predicament, nor, so she persuaded herself, was she. She was Russia's legitimate ruler, after all. She should have succeeded Peter II. The situation was unfortunate, but in her opinion the responsibility lay with the Empress Anne, and with Ivan's mother, Anna Leopoldovna. Her mind never dwelt for long on little Ivan, and he was never allowed to diminish her appetite for pleasures.

Pleasure—and particularly physical pleasure—seemed to be her reason for existence, and only her passions for religion and for sports saved her from falling victim to her excesses much sooner than she did. She hunted and hawked in summer, took regular exercise at the St. Petersburg Riding School in winter, and if the prospect of yet another pilgrimage or fast made her courtiers sigh with desperation, they provided excellent cures for late nights, excitements and overladen stomachs.

Elizabeth emerged from these periods of deprivation refreshed and ready for the high life once again. Unlike Anne who had dined regularly at noon, supped at six and gone to bed at ten, Elizabeth, like her mother in her latter years, would commonly decide to dine at supper-time and go to bed at sunrise. When she retired, at whatever time of the day or night, the thoroughfare outside her window was closed to traffic lest she should be disturbed by noise. Even so she often felt bored at the prospect of sleep and when she was in such a mood she could place a considerable strain on the resources of her entourage.

Her ladies-in-waiting often had to sit up with her half the night chatting to her and tickling her feet. When they had withdrawn, the 'Emperor of the Night' or some other favourite of the hour would get his summons, and only then would her old retainer Vasili Chulkov take his place at the foot of her bed while she surrendered herself at last to slumber. Chulkov was another of her genuine admirers and as such a great comfort to her. In earlier years if she woke up to find him still asleep she used to proceed, full of the joys of early morning, to pull the pillow out from underneath him and tickle him under the armpits; and nowadays he could still be relied on, when need arose, to stroke her shoulders and call her his 'white, white swan'. Even Empresses needed reassurance, and Elizabeth needed more of it than most.

Gossip and gambling remained features of the life of Russian high society, and a turnover of fifty thousand roubles at an evening playing cards was by no means unusual nowadays. Yet the court under Elizabeth was never quite as philistine as it had been under her predecessors. Elizabeth showed a certain respect for learning if only out of regard for her father's memory, and when Alexei Razumovski's younger brother Cyril returned to Russia in 1745 fresh from his improving studies at western universities, she immediately recognized 'the skill he has acquired in the sciences' by making him a Count and President of the Academy of Sciences.

The appointment turned out surprisingly well. The Academy had been neglected in recent years and the enthusiastic young Ukrainian breathed new vigour into it, increasing its income and engaging eminent scholars to occupy its Chairs. He also sponsored the publication of Russia's first monthly periodical 'for the utility and amusement' of gentlefolk, and patronized Russian talents like Vasili Adadurov, author of the first Russian grammar, and Lomonosov, a fisherman's son who had come barefoot to St. Petersburg in the reign of the Empress Anne, studied at the Academy and in Germany, and was now formulating a theory on gases, doing important work on meteorology, geology and the formation of icebergs, developing a new vernacular style in poetry, and experimenting in the art of portraiture in mosaic.

The secular sciences were beginning to form strong roots in Russian soil, and learning even became respectable at court. Yet though Baron Stroganov, a gentleman of the bedchamber, translated a French version of Milton's *Paradise Lost* into Russian, though the court theatre was no longer confined to performances of lightweight ballets and Italian comic operas, though Racine, Molière and Corneille (done in atrocious French accents by the boys of the Cadet Corps) were now staged, barely half the court could read, and Elizabeth herself was not personally inclined to improve her rather limited education. She could write perfectly well, though like so many of her eighteenth-century contemporaries she spelt phonetically, and was forever confusing p with b and o with a. She could read perfectly well, too, but she considered it to be a dangerous occupation, tiring for the eyes and generally conducive to ill-health. And though she maintained a necessary interest in international affairs, she was never absolutely sure where England was.

She was quite confident of her tastes in art and architecture, however. The Summer Palace started by the Empress Anne was now complete. It was a splendid baroque structure with huge windows facing onto a spacious courtyard in which courtiers could pass the time of day and wave to their friends as they glided by in gondolas. Inside, the floors were paved with parquet and the walls were a mass of mirrors, delicate plaster-work and gilding. Yet the place was hardly ready for habitation before Elizabeth began to think of improvements. Caravaque, Bon and Valeriani were engaged to decorate the ceilings; then a new wing was added; finally, she regarded it merely as a temporary residence while Rastrelli erected a palace intended to be of a magnificence unsurpassed in all of Europe.

Peterhof, where the court moved in the early summer of 1745, did not satisfy her either. Leblond's charming structure was too cramped for her now that the Grand Duke Peter and his fiancée needed so much room. Alterations were made, and finally she told Rastrelli to raise the roof-line, add extensive wings and galleries—in short to regard the existing building merely as a core for something altogether grander. The pavilion of Monplaisir was also extended, while the palace of Tsarskoye Selo was to be rebuilt six times at a total cost of one and a half million roubles. In brief,

Elizabeth was entering upon a phase of building mania. No wonder ambassadors thought her court to be the most expensive in Europe. She spent more than any other monarch. But she was also proving herself to be Russia's greatest patroness of the decorative arts.

One of her immediate priorities was the addition of a new wing to the Golovin Palace in Moscow intended to accommodate the Grand Duke Peter and Catherine once they were married. She was looking forward to the wedding with mounting excitement, even though she felt repelled by her nephew's ugliness. Peter's illness had given him an unpleasantly swollen, puffy look and left him badly pock-marked. It had also necessitated the shaving of his head, and ever since he had taken to wearing a particularly huge ungainly wig which made him appear even uglier and even more ridiculous.

Elizabeth made conscious efforts to overcome her disgust. The poor boy, she told herself, was her beloved father's only male descendant. His lack of grace, his unpleasant characteristics must, like his German accent, be attributed to his misfortune in being brought up among foreigners. Anyway, his prospective bride who was acclimatizing so splendidly to the Russian scene would no doubt help him overcome his disadvantages.

The wedding was fixed for 10 August and was to take place in St. Petersburg. Despite her disenchantment with France, Elizabeth decided to model it on the example the French had set when the Dauphin had married the Infanta of Spain—only to make it more magnificent.

Rastrelli was entrusted with the design of a whole series of statues and fountains; the greatest care was lavished on the design of each dress to be worn at every ceremony and function, and courtiers were paid a year's salary in advance to ensure they would create the due amount of glitter on the day. Orders flowed from her pen and money from her purse.

The wedding was preceded by a week of religious pilgrimage, and on the day itself Elizabeth was up at dawn, and having sent for her jewel boxes and spent some time smothering her ladies-in-waiting with diamonds, she called on Catherine and began to fuss over her. The bride's hair-style would not do, she suddenly decided, probably because it would not hold all the jewels she wanted to lavish on it. Catherine protested, and her valet threw up his arms in horror—at which Elizabeth stalked out of the room. It took her several moments to compose herself, but finally she returned to place the ducal crown on the bride's head, to tell her she might wear as many of the imperial jewels as she pleased, and to watch her being dressed and made up.

By three in the afternoon everyone was ready. The huge state coaches came lumbering up to the palace doors and the party set out for the Cathedral. They returned to a formal dinner in the public gallery of the Winter Palace, and a ball which was extremely formal and extremely short, for fear that the couple might become too exhausted to consummate the marriage. There was only one dance—a polonaise—and soon after nine Elizabeth was able to accompany the bride to her apartments. She supervised her undressing, yelled to the Grand Equerry to hurry up with the groom, and at last saw the two placed side by side in a vast new bed with a poppy-coloured canopy. She blessed them, shed a tear or two, and left.

There followed ten days of entertainments including a public masquerade, a long French comedy which lasted until three the following morning, a ball with fireworks, a formal supper, an Italian *pastorale*, Araja's opera *Scipio* with a ballet staged between each act, and a stiffly formal ball where a quadrille was danced by forty-eight selected couples, including bride and groom. There were four sets, dressed respectively in silver and rose, white and gold, pale blue and silver, and yellow and silver—so that each formed a distinct colour-pattern in its corner of the ball-room. It was all very symmetrical, extremely gaudy, and so far as young Catherine was concerned, rather dull. But this was the way the French court did things and Elizabeth was so delighted with the performance that she had it done all over again the following night.

Nor were the common people forgotten. A great feast was laid out in the streets for them. Only the waiting crowd became impatient. They broke through the protective line of soldiers and finished off every scrap of food before Elizabeth and her guests had had a chance to see them. By way of retaliation, the fountains of wine which had been prepared were not released and the crowd eventually dispersed home somewhat thirsty.

Otherwise everything passed off just as the Empress had hoped it would, and now that the wedding was over, she was free to get rid of Catherine's troublesome mother. Elizabeth had long believed that Joanna was a spy for King Frederick, the 'Nadir Shah of Berlin' as she referred to him these days, and relations with Prussia were now extremely strained. After Frederick's attack on Saxony in May 1745 Elizabeth had ordered sixty thousand troops into Courland, and let it be known that she did not intend to let Saxony go undefended. Privately, however, she was very disturbed at the prospect of war. She prayed fervently for the safety of her troops and took particular care to supply their commanders with 'good luck' charms to wear in battle. She need not have bothered. Her army was not to be engaged. Saxony was ravaged, and its King and his Austrian ally quickly sued for peace.

Prussia was obviously dangerous and so, by extension, was Joanna. She had been warned before about her intrigues, apparently to no effect, and if she were allowed to stay, she might gain a dangerous influence over Catherine and the heir apparent. Two months before the wedding the watch on Joanna had been intensified. All her letters, and those of her retainers, were intercepted, and evidence of various improprieties was duly brought to light. At their final interview Joanna threw herself at Elizabeth's feet and begged forgiveness for her 'unintentional' offences. But the Empress stood firm. Joanna was packed off out of Russia together with innumerable presents collected over the past months—including a parting gift of fifty thousand roubles from Elizabeth herself.

Elizabeth had been Empress for five years. She was the autocratic ruler of a sixth of the world's surface, and her word was law to millions. Yet though her influence on Russia's future was considerable, in the long run her conscious acts of policy were to have less effect than her totally thoughtless influence on those around her, particularly in encouraging them to spend more than they could afford.

Elizabeth's love of show and richness outstripped even that of her predecessors, and proved highly infectious. She spent lavishly, and those about her followed her example; she changed her dress several times a day, and those about her began to do the same; she loved glitter and her courtiers made themselves glitter to win her favour. Count Peter Sheremetev wore clothes weighed down with so much gold and silver decoration that eyes were dazzled just to look at him. Count Ivan Chernyshev ordered rich suits by the dozen, while Sergei Naryshkin had a uniform made so delicately embroidered with silver, gold and jewels that it became the talk of the town for weeks. Such men set the standards for high society.

'The wardrobe of some courtier or fop', wrote Prince Shcherbatov, 'was sometimes equal to the rest of his fortune', and clothes were not the only marks of eminence. Elizabeth built fabulous palaces and gardens, engaged the great Boucher to decorate her coach, ordered china from Dresden, silk from Lyons and furniture from London—and others emulated her. Grandees built palaces for themselves modelled upon hers, and felt they were failing to live up to their station in life if they did not wear diamonds and drink champagne.

Seeing the Empress's favour extended to those who lived lavishly, lesser folk often confused cause with effect. Elizabeth gave Cyril Razumovski a hundred thousand serfs so he could afford to live on a generous scale. Chancellor Bestuzhev could afford to live lavishly on the Empress's gifts and the perquisites of office, and Peter Sheremetev who 'lived with all possible magnificence, and always with the monarch's approval' owned a hundred and sixty thousand serfs.

Yet even the recipients of imperial largesse were beginning to spend beyond their means. By the end of his life Count Peter Shuvalov was making forty thousand roubles a year by manipulating the tobacco, fishing and timber monopolies Elizabeth had put at his disposal, and was probably getting a similar amount from bribes—yet he was to die in debt to the tune of a million roubles. It was hardly to be wondered at. His house was decorated in the finest style; his sideboard laden with everything that was most delicious and expensive, including an abundance of such exotic rarities as pineapples and bananas; and he was as famous for his wines, his horses, his diamonds and his many mistresses as he was for his exotic fruits.

Lesser noblemen were infected by the fashions sported by the great. No longer content with plain white-washed walls, they began to decorate their residences with expensive damask, and before long even the merest gentry were taking such luxuries as perfume, pocket mirrors and apricot jam for granted. Gone were the days when a nobleman was satisfied with vodka and Tokay—a dinner was not regarded as fit to offer guests in society now unless several fine wines were served. And if every gentleman could not afford to supply his guests with pineapple, at least he made oranges and lemons available—almost unheard-of luxuries in Peter the Great's time.

And as the fashions for opulent dress, large entourages, French wine and English horses seeped down the social scale to be adopted by the lesser breeds of the nobility, all sections of Russia's upper class were encouraged to overspend.

But as the gentry was the class on which Elizabeth's government depended, as more and more of its members fell into debt, the state stepped in to help them. In 1746 the gentry was given the exclusive right to the ownership of land and serfs; from 1747 they were allowed to sell their serfs as army recruits; various trading rights were soon added to their privileges and the state even funded a bank to lend them money to improve their estates and make them more profitable, though most of the loans seem to have been spent on consumer goods or on funding other debts rather than on improvements.

Still, there were other means a resourceful nobleman could use to force his income up. He could borrow the taxes he collected from his peasants on the government's behalf, claiming that the peasants were too poor to pay them (a device Elizabeth seems to have used herself when in financial difficulty under the Empress Anne). Or, more commonly, he could demand more cash, goods and services from his serfs, confident that if they objected, the government would send troops in to quell them and cart the troublemakers off to Siberia.

So, as high society in St. Petersburg and Moscow became ever more glittering and spendthrift, the background darkened in provincial Russia. As more and more gentlefolk acquired some veneer of 'culture' they began to speak the 'secret language', French, which the common people could not understand; as more and more landowners formed a taste for the high life they began to treat their serfs like cattle who existed only to be exploited. And the oppressed were beginning to react not merely by petitioning or by running away, but by burning down their masters' houses or slitting their masters' and mistresses' throats. The great families remained comparatively unaffected by this trend. They had bailiffs to run their estates and run the risks on their behalf while they indulged themselves in the comparative safety of St. Petersburg or Moscow. Indeed, their awareness of unrest and violence in the countryside, while it aroused some concern, also introduced a rather enjoyable element of piquancy into their lives.

The seeds of class hatred were germinating and later Romanovs would reap a bitter crop, but Elizabeth was quite oblivious of the long-term situation her indulgences were helping to create. Even if she had, political pressures and her own easy-going nature would have vitiated any attempt to remedy the situation, as they had when she revived her father's order that gentlemen should begin their army service in the ranks, for instance, and then allowed them to enlist as children and be 'trained' at home so that they could reach commissioned rank through a purely formal seniority by the time they actually joined a unit.

Ever easy-going, Elizabeth tolerated sexual indulgence too. Adultery not only became commonplace; it became respectable as in the rest of Europe. A leading socialite like Alexander Tatishchev could live quite openly with a serf girl, confident that an indulgent Empress would ennoble the offspring, and a whole series of Russian princely houses were to trace their descent to aristocratic bastards born in her reign.

Elizabeth was presiding over a slow break-down of the old Muscovite social values and their replacement by a new, corrupt set of values modelled on the French. It was all done without malice, without thought.

So, while the Russian peasant pursued his dreary, bitter and often hungry routine in the countryside, the court pursued its own routine—a routine which consisted principally of playing cards, back-biting and engaging in love affairs and intricate intrigues. Personal intrigue, like diplomacy, involved bribery and spying, dark passages and secret stairways. Indeed it was impossible to separate the two. A love affair could have international repercussions and everyone at court was the object of suspicion by one party

or another—none more so than the heir to the throne, the Grand
Duke Peter, and his wife Catherine.

The gawky Peter behaved very strangely. He gave public displays
of ill-manners on occasion and once went so far as to bore holes
through the doors of Elizabeth's apartment so as to be able to keep
a watch on her activities. The Empress was furious. Peter, she said,
was ingratitude personified. She remembered times, she said, when
an Empress imprisoned anyone who failed in courtesy towards her,
and when Peter interrupted she turned extremely red and silenced
him. Somehow, she warned, she would find a way to deal with him.

And if Elizabeth was worried about Peter, she was no less concerned about young Catherine. The girl's mother was safely out
of the way now. But in view of her birth and parentage, pro-Prussian
sympathies might come naturally to Catherine, and she must be
insulated from them at all costs. Even more seriously, Catherine
showed no sign of pregnancy, and rumour reached her that relations
between the Grand Duke Peter and his wife were not all they should
be. Countess Choglokov, Elizabeth's own cousin who had been
attached to Catherine's suite, was told to bring the Grand Duchess to
a sense of her responsibilities and in May 1746 Elizabeth had a word
with her herself, in private.

According to Catherine's account, the Empress seemed extremely
angry and not a little confused. She accused her of betraying her
for Frederick of Prussia, warned her that young girls who did not
love their husbands were always crying, said she had reason to
suspect that Catherine loved someone else, and blamed her for the
fact that no heir to the throne had yet been born. On hearing out
this curious assemblage of accusation and warnings Catherine
sensibly burst into tears and muttered an ingratiating *Pardon
maman*, at which Elizabeth, apparently satisfied with this show of
contrition, left; but relations between the two were to remain
strained for some time. Catherine later attributed the scene to the
enmity of Chancellor Bestuzhev, and her relations with the Empress
were certainly affected by the intrigues of rival groups of politicians
and diplomatists.

Elizabeth was well aware of this. Though trusting by nature,
bitter experience had taught her how easily confidences could be
betrayed—hence her attitude towards Catherine. Indeed, she was

much more careful than she used to be in all matters tinged with politics. She was slower than ever now to reach decisions and slower still to pledge her friendship, especially in the diplomatic sphere.

It had taken years for example to dispel her old antipathy to Austria, though relations were at last becoming warm again. The Austrian Ambassador was invited to a special party on the Gostilitsa estate where all the ladies were dressed as shepherdesses in huge pink skirts and floppy English hats; and Elizabeth also consented to act as godmother to Maria Theresa's new-born son. As for England Elizabeth had listened to Bestuzhev's arguments in favour of an alliance for two years now, and though she did not really understand all the subtleties of the business, claimed at last to have been persuaded that England's sea-power could prove invaluable if Russia, as seemed increasingly likely, had to face France and Prussia on the battlefield. Besides, England was prepared to pay good money for Russia's co-operation. So Elizabeth consented to keep thirty thousand troops on the Courland frontier and a further thirty thousand on the Rhine in return for a subsidy of £400,000. Ratifications were exchanged in January 1748, and next day the troops marched.

Fortunately, they did not have to fire a shot. Their mere presence persuaded the French to negotiate, and a general peace was soon concluded. Russia had proved herself to be a vital factor in the balance of power; her prestige in Europe stood higher than at any time before.

All this time money had continued to flow out of the imperial exchequer rather faster than it came in. The deficit in 1748 amounted to three million roubles. Yet Elizabeth's expenditure continued on its upward course and approached Promethean proportions as her clothes became increasingly lavish, her entertainments more extravagant, her residences ever larger and more ornate.

Yet with so many palaces disfigured by scaffolding and overrun by workmen, accommodation became scarcer and sometimes more squalid than ever. Courtiers had to share rooms and endure discomforts—and sometimes they risked danger too. In the spring of 1748 Elizabeth visited Tsarskoye. Because of the construction work in progress there Peter and Catherine were housed in a lodge built on a nearby hill. They had retired to bed in the early hours one morning when they were disturbed by a frantic chamberlain who rushed in to warn them that the building was collapsing. They were dragged out half asleep and had barely reached a place of safety when the ground trembled, there was a great rumbling sound, and the entire edifice slipped down the hill. A cloud of dust rose up around it. When it settled, three servants were found to have been killed outright, and sixteen others were buried in the rubble.

Alexei Razumovski, who was in charge of the arrangements, felt himself to be responsible. He beat his breast, wept with despair, even threatened suicide. Elizabeth managed to dissuade him. But though she tried to make light of the whole affair, she also ordered immediate surveys to be carried out of all her residences.

Unstable foundations were revealed, damp walls uncovered and rotting beams laid bare—all sorts of faults due to poor materials and faulty workmanship were diagnosed, the inevitable consequence of builders being pressed for quick and showy results by their impatient patrons. Plans for demolitions and rebuilding were put in hand at once, but the incident had produced a nervous mood at court which was to last for months. People started with fright every time a door was slammed, no one slept easily in a building, and Elizabeth decided always to sleep in tents in future.

The summer's hunting helped to dispel the trauma, however. The baying of hounds, the joyful sounds of the huntsmen's horns, the graceful sight of running animals, the sheer exhilaration of the chase had lost nothing of their charms for her. She knew every dog and ostler by name, and engaged the younger de Groot to decorate Monbijou, her new lodge at Tsarskoye, with delightful reminders of the hunt.

Another of her delights these days was cooking. At least one of her hunting lodges was equipped with a special kitchen in which, when the mood came upon her, she would prepare pancakes, salmon pie and pickled pork with onions for her intimates. And cooking seemed an appropriate occupation for a woman now approaching middle age.

Yet though Elizabeth had lost her figure and her beauty was under siege, she still kept up a desperate battle to compete in appearance with other women, and she used the weapons at her disposal with more ruthlessness than ever. Once, she dyed her hair black, but when she became tired of the experiment she found to her horror that the dye would not come out. As a result she had to shave her head—and since she had to, all the ladies of the court had to as well, and wear unflattering black wigs until it grew again. On another occasion she sent for the pretty wife of the new Master of the Hunt and tore off all the ribbons that adorned her lovely neck. She would cut the curls off her ladies in waiting, claiming that she did not like the way they had done their hair, and when Catherine appeared in a flattering white dress embroidered in large Spanish stitch, she was told to change at once.

Elizabeth was becoming increasingly dissatisfied with Catherine. The girl had still not produced the child she was supposed to produce, and yet she was taking lovers. And the Empress was becoming more and more suspicious of her involvements with diplomatists and politicians. Catherine was far too friendly with Lestocq and other members of the pro-Prussian clique; and by her own admission made years later in her memoirs, she was maintaining contact with her mother through the dubious channels of a court cellist and Joanna's agent, Sacrosomo. Catherine was clever, but she was playing with fire, and was soon to feel the heat of it.

One day in the autumn of 1748 she ran into Lestocq who was emerging from the Empress's apartments. Usually the very essence of good humour, on this occasion the doctor behaved very strangely. He seemed preoccupied and distressed, and when he saw Catherine approaching he motioned her away, whispering 'Don't come near me. I'm under suspicion.' Two days later he was arrested, accused of intriguing on behalf of France, accepting bribes from the Prussians and of poisoning a witness. His sudden fall came as a shock to almost everybody, and everyone waited to see whom the axe would fall on next. Catherine must have trembled, but for the moment nothing happened.

In February 1749 Elizabeth retired to bed with a fierce attack of colic. She proved to be a bad patient, insisting on getting up before the doctors thought her strong enough, and despite their protestations accepting an invitation to visit Count Apraxin's new house in Moscow. The feast provided was worthy of a man whose wardrobe contained hundreds of suits and who kept a different exquisite snuff-box for every day of the year. But that night the unfortunate host dropped dead. Rumour to the effect that he had smallpox which created something of a panic at the court proved groundless, but some weeks later while visiting Alexei's house at Perovo, Elizabeth suffered an attack of colic which was even sharper than the first, and bad enough for her to vow to make another pilgrimage if she recovered.

She did recover and she kept her vow, but found she could manage no more than a mile a day instead of her usual six, and on some days she lacked the strength to walk at all. The journey of thirty miles from Moscow to the monastery took her several weeks to complete. And even though her strength eventually returned, the illness seemed to rob her of her fire. Henceforth, despite all efforts and devices she was to look her age.

As she returned to health the palace ante-rooms, temporarily hushed, regained their former liveliness, and the merry clink of coins was heard again as innumerable gambled roubles passed once more from one hand to another. True, the courtiers had to endure another series of fasts ordered by the Empress—sometimes they had to subsist on fish, sometimes on mushrooms, sometimes on a curious diet of jam and *kvass*—but there were always those who, like the Grand Duke Peter, contrived to smuggle forbidden delicacies into their rooms, and Alexei Razumovski was of course exempt.

Now that he was gouty and Elizabeth's radiance had dimmed a little, their relationship was less fiery than it once had been, though they were still more than fond of one another. Elizabeth spoiled him, nursed him, cooked special meals for him, and he cosseted her as if she were a child, muffling her up in furs whenever they went out into the cold, and almost smothering her with his attentions.

But coddling alone did not satisfy Elizabeth. Though she sometimes talked of retiring to a nunnery one day, that day had not come yet. Her sexual appetite was still strong, and she meant to indulge it. So, in the autumn of 1749, just before celebrating her fortieth birthday, a new gentleman of the bedchamber, Ivan Shuvalov, moved into an adjoining apartment. Ivan was handsome, and almost half her age.

The appointment was seen to have political implications, and not surprisingly, for about the same time Ivan's cousin Peter, a retainer of Elizabeth's since her days as a princess, was promoted to the highest rank, given the farming of several profitable monopolies and increasing power in home affairs. Peter Shuvalov's air of *bonhomie* was said to mask a ruthless spirit and a grasping hand— but as much could be said of most Ministers of the time. He was also said by his enemies to bribe 'all the base and dissolute women' who surrounded the Empress—the ladies who sat up with her all night massaging her legs and tickling her feet—and cynics attributed his advancement to such unctuous contrivances as carrying a huge prayer-book around with him whenever Elizabeth seemed to be in a religious mood. But Peter Shuvalov was certainly a man of unusual ability and ideas. He was to found Russia's first savings bank, attempt a reform of the coinage, and give a powerful boost to the economy by abolishing internal tariffs. His interests ranged from land surveys to the preparation of a new code of laws and even as far as the invention of a howitzer. But his first concern was to consolidate his own position, and in this he was fortunate. His wife Mavra was a favourite of Elizabeth's; the secret police was put into the hands of his elder brother Alexander (who, thanks to a pronounced nervous tic on one side of his face, looked appropriately sinister in the role); and his cousin Ivan shared the imperial bed.

Ivan's influence on Elizabeth was altogether beneficial. He not only made her happy, but his enthusiasm for the theatre, for music and particularly for literature encouraged her to broaden her patronage of learning and the arts. Ivan's was the inspiration behind the new Academy of Fine Arts, and Russia's first university, soon to be established in Moscow, and though he encouraged Russian talents especially in the theatre, he had a particular passion for things French. French comedies were presented twice a week at court these days, but it was at a performance of Sumarokov's tragedy *Khorev*, a fabulous story set in the Ukraine, that Elizabeth fell in love with an unusually pretty boy who took the leading role. The lad, a cadet called Nikita Beketov, was promptly raised to the rank of Colonel and installed in the Palace.

As usual, there were sinister implications which Elizabeth did not suspect. Nikita was a pawn of Chancellor Bestuzhev's. The Chancellor did not like the Shuvalovs' influence extending to the imperial bedroom, and he had determined to put his own man there instead. It was he who had arranged for Nikita to be cast in the play, confident that he would appeal to Elizabeth. And just to make sure, he had had the boy smothered in diamonds, buckles, rings and lace.

The potion worked. But though Elizabeth took Nikita to her heart, Ivan was not turned out as the Chancellor had hoped. Indeed, not content with keeping these two lovers and maintaining her liaison with Alexei Razumovski, who took a complaisant attitude towards her other lovers, she soon took on a fourth—a chorister named Kachenevski. In sexual affairs at least, Elizabeth was her father's daughter.

The *ménage à cinq* was not to last for long, however. For almost a year the rival political cliques employed all manner of devices to remove their opponents' man and in the end it was the Shuvalovs who succeeded. By spreading rumours to the effect that Nikita indulged in unmentionable homosexual practices, and by persuading him to use a supposedly cosmetic ointment which induced a rash looking suspiciously like smallpox, they succeeded in procuring the poor boy's dismissal.

The new year of 1751, Elizabeth's tenth upon the throne, was saluted with 101 guns, a grand ball in the palace and a series of splendid masquerades. *Opera buffa* and German *Singspiele* were produced full of florid arias with amazing cadenzas and of love songs so touching that she wept to hear them. But the success of the season was a new theatrical company which Ivan Shuvalov had brought to town. It was run by Fedor Volkov, a merchant's son from Yaroslav whose productions of *Tamira and Selim* and of the *Sinner's Repentance*, a comedy with musical interludes, were received with much applause.

Even in summer, the season of trips to country palaces, the court was not deprived of theatrical spectacle, for Peterhof was now equipped with a theatre for the performance of 'night comedies'. And when winter came again there were productions of Molière's *Le Bourgeois Gentilhomme* and of Araja's *La Clemenza di Tito* in a Russian version, besides the usual balls for the court and for 'the public' marked as ever 'by tremendous splendour and studied elegance in fancy dress'.

Then Elizabeth decided to spend Christmas in Moscow. Cohorts of chamberlains and lackeys rushed ahead to see that the Kremlin was cleared of the rubbish and excrement which invariably accumulated when she was not in residence, and make the place generally fit for habitation. These peregrinations produced considerable inconveniences for her entourage. Princes and generals sometimes counted themselves lucky to find a space to doss down in some dingy post-house on the way; ladies would find themselves ankle-deep in water outside their tents, or have to dress by some stinking oven in a tavern. And the inconveniences did not end there.

The court was still poorly supplied with furniture, for instance, and beds, tables, chairs and chests had to follow the Empress wherever she chose to go. As a result, breakages were frequent and most of what remained intact was in such a dilapidated condition that the more fastidious courtiers found no other solution than to buy furniture of their own, for Elizabeth had taken it into her head to insist on signing all orders for replacement personally, and she was very dilatory when it came to paper work. Even important state papers lay on her dressing table for weeks and months sometimes awaiting signature. Some called her lazy on this account, though she always insisted that she was merely cautious.

Among the orders she did sign in December 1752 was one remitting two and a half million roubles' worth of poll-tax arrears. This was less a reflection of the Empire's increasing wealth, however, as was suggested in the preamble, than of the impossibility of collecting arrears dating back more than five years anyway. The growth in wealth was mainly due to an increase in population, and since landlords (whether the state, the church or individuals) took most of the increased surplus, most people were no better off, and some were worse off than they were before, particularly those peasants who had the misfortune to belong to monasteries. Complaints flooded in to her about the unfair burdens placed upon them, the bribes they had to pay, and the beatings they had to suffer. And as more members of the landowning classes, influenced by the luxurious standards set at court, began to live beyond their incomes, the condition of many privately-owned serfs became even worse. On some estates peasants were ordered to work not three, but four or even five days a week on their master's land rather than on their own. And the pressure on those serfs belonging to the state was also deteriorating. Nowhere else in Europe, not even in Austria, were there peasants who were quite so poor or ill-treated as in Elizabeth's domains.

She did nothing to alleviate the general suffering, and yet she was rarely less than generous to unfortunates of humble origins with whom she happened to come into contact. When a palace menial went insane she sent her own physician, Dr. Boerhave, to attend him; she had a mad monk who had attempted self-castration cared for; she saw to it that a minor functionary who imagined himself to be the Shah of Persia received appropriate treatment and attended his exorcism in person. But she could find no remedy for the condition of her people as a whole, and not even the more violent symptoms of their distress, such as fire-raising and armed banditry, were allowed to disturb the serenity of court life or restrict her personal expenditure.

Rastrelli showed her the plans he had drawn up for the reconstruction of Tsarskoye Selo. There was to be an immense forecourt entered by three vast gates; a sweeping curve of outhouses and servants' quarters and, opposite, a palace to cast Versailles itself into the shade—a long flow of columns and caryatids, windows, pediments and balustrades. There would be a classical cupola, a chapel surmounted by onion-shaped domes, gilding, statues, urns, and an intricate mass of plaster-work and carving. And the palace would back onto a magnificent park complete with water-gardens and numerous pavilions.

The project was approved, and artists called in to advise on decorations. Notable among these was Giuseppe Valeriani the master of 'perspective and Theatrical Engineering' and a favourite set-designer for the court theatricals and operatics. Others to be involved included the painters Pietro and Francesco Gradizzi, newly arrived from Verona, Georg de Groot the portrait painter, and Johann de Groot who was commissioned to buy a hundred and fifty fine canvasses in Prague to form the basis of a new picture gallery at the palace. Then a Russian artist called Makhayev completed a folio of drawings depicting every worthwhile scene in St. Petersburg together with a plan-map of the city on which the Empress was depicted standing on a pedestal attended by angels bearing flags and laurels. It was such a fine advertisement that engravings were made and copies of the set dispatched to every royal library and Russian embassy abroad.

Yet most of her palaces were still made of wood, and were extremely vulnerable to fire. Towards the end of 1753 her favourite palace in Moscow was burned down. She showed no sign of distress at the loss of four thousand dresses in the blaze, but the loss of the palace itself did present an inconvenience, so hundreds of carpenters were immediately rounded up and worked day and night to build a fine new residence with sixty rooms within six weeks. Then the very same month fire broke out in the Lefort Palace in Moscow where Peter and Catherine were staying. Elizabeth who was attending a performance of a French comedy at the time rushed to the scene of the blaze in time to see people jumping out of the upper windows and hordes of rats scurrying out to safety down below. But Peter and Catherine were, fortunately, safe, and even news of another serious fire at Krasnoye and rumours that these conflagrations were occurring with such abnormal frequency that, as an Amsterdam paper reported, they must be the result of 'a plot . . . to destroy this extensive Empire by fire', did not seem to dampen the Empress's spirits. Indeed, at the New Year celebrations which took place shortly afterwards Elizabeth was unusually gay and loquacious. She ate with appetite, danced energetically, and sweated profusely in the overheated ballrooms—and though her exertions soon left her flushed and out of breath, she seemed ready to burst out laughing at the slightest joke. She was still in good humour when, in the spring of 1754, she returned to St. Petersburg.

All this while the political jockeying among her Ministers had continued unabated. Vice-Chancellor Vorontsov in particular had been striving valiantly to undermine the Chancellor. In an effort to destroy her confidence in Bestuzhev, he reported that there was evidence of the Chancellor's having taken bribes from the English. This Elizabeth could not ignore. But Bestuzhev had taken good care to cover himself. He was quite frank about his need for money. His salary, he explained, was not sufficient to entertain on the scale expected of him, and though the Empress had given him a splendid house, he had lacked the means to furnish it. He had therefore been 'forced' to take fifty thousand roubles offered by the British Government. But it was not a bribe. He had contracted to repay the loan;

he had even found fifty Russian notables to guarantee it. Elizabeth found it all very difficult to understand, and very trying, but she allowed him to convince her. So the Chancellor's enemies had to rack their brains for some other device with which to bring him down.

Peter Shuvalov, however, was already firmly entrenched as the major influence in home affairs, and was very active in more important matters. He was particularly concerned with the rising tide of lawlessness. Harsher penalties were prescribed for monetary offences and the harbouring of runaways—so harsh that when Elizabeth saw the proposals she is said to have remarked that they were 'written in blood, not ink'. And when the restoration of the death penalty was mooted she put her foot down. She had vowed never to do it. But Shuvalov was insistent, and she found the pressures put upon her very difficult to resist. At last the Church, which was increasingly concerned with the problems of keeping its own serfs in order, begged her to renounce her vow as well, and Elizabeth allowed her sense of duty to the Church to triumph over conscience. She signed the order, though not, it was said, without shedding tears.

Another of Shuvalov's preoccupations was finance, and here he was even more successful. His increases in important duties protected Russian industries and his imposition of new indirect taxes, especially on vodka, while universally detested, especially by the gentry who expected only serfs to pay taxes, was to bring money flowing into the exchequer. Considerations of economy did not weigh with Elizabeth however. In the summer of 1754 the court moved into temporary wooden accommodation near the Admiralty while the old Winter Palace was torn down and foundations sunk for a new one. The last of all the Winter Palaces, it had been four years in the planning: it was to be built of stone, and was to be more opulent than any of its predecessors—a vast construction containing 1,500 rooms, with Corinthian columns, caryatids and silver ornaments—the summation of the style of rococo. The whole confection would be finished in Elizabeth's favourite colour, turquoise, with details picked out in white and silver. And as the great Winter Palace was begun, construction at Tsarskoye Selo was finished.

On 7 September Elizabeth invited the diplomatic corps to see it.

They were shown the plans first, then guided up the grand staircase and through the state apartments. They saw the chapel, the gardens, the grottos, the Hermitage with its new picture gallery, and the Empress's private zoo. Then they were wined and dined, and when their eyes had been dazzled, their stomachs filled, their tongues made weary expressing admiration, their ears were deafened by a 71-gun salute, and they were allowed to depart on the fifteen-mile journey back to St. Petersburg.

Elizabeth's pride in her new property was only exceeded by her joy at the birth of a grand-nephew. For five years now she had fretted over Catherine, who seemed unable to produce a child and now, at last, a healthy male child had been born, assuring the future of her father's dynasty. She attended the lying-in, and as soon as the baby was delivered she had it gathered up and brought to her apartments, just as the Empress Anne had done when poor Ivan was born. While a firework display lit up the town outside in celebration of the great event, the baby was swaddled in flannel in the Russian style, wrapped in furs and satin, placed in an excessively overheated room, and subjected to the ministrations of a dozen matrons whom she considered to be expert in child health. The baby was christened Paul after Elizabeth's brother who had died in infancy, and as a reward for having done her duty, Elizabeth presented Catherine with a draft for a hundred thousand roubles, though, in a sudden seizure of economy, she borrowed it back again almost immediately.

In November 1754 the Empress suffered another painful attack of colic. The attacks were occurring with increasing frequency and, always superstitious, she had come to believe that they could only be caused by spells which evil spirits had cast on her. Evidence to support this hypothesis soon came to light in the form of a piece of root tangled in a lock of hair found under her mattress. At once Elizabeth raised the cry of sorcery. The witch-hunt which followed uncovered a maid-in-waiting and a valet. They were arrested. The woman, having been persuaded to admit her guilt, was exiled, the valet cut his throat.

Despite this remedy, she was taken repeatedly ill the following winter. The exact nature of the trouble is uncertain, but there was talk of hysteria, of fainting fits, convulsions, and the menopause.

She would lie in bed for hours gazing up at the ceiling where cupids, those symbols of perpetual youth, only seemed to mock her. And whenever the pain returned, neither her doctors' assurances, nor all her fervent prayers could overcome her fear of death, a fear which became so obsessive that coffins were never allowed to be taken within view of the Palace, and anyone who fell seriously ill had to be smuggled out just in case he should happen to die there. Elizabeth seemed to resent the fact that she was not immortal.

And not only did she try to protect herself from any association with death, she was vain enough to try to insulate herself from any sight of ugliness or poverty as well. Whereas her mother had created a park in St. Petersburg 'for the pleasure of all classes of people', in 1756 when the gardens of the Summer Palace were opened to the public twice a week, Elizabeth insisted that 'base people' such as sailors, serfs and servants, or anyone with unkempt hair or wearing boots, beards or traditional Russian dress, was 'on no account to be admitted'. She was coming to see people as furniture to set off the grandeur of her buildings and the beauty of her parks.

Yet while she was insulated from the ugliness of the outside world, the outside world was spared knowledge of her frailties. Clouds of propaganda hid her every weakness. According to a panegyric of the time she was 'laurelled ELIZABETH'—the peaceful arbiter of Europe, the guardian of the Russian heritage, a paragon, a goddess embodying Promethean strength and all the virtues. 'Gold and silver flowed out from the entrails of the earth' for her; thanks to her, her subjects did not have to pay heavier taxes than they did; and magnificent buildings, scientific progress, even the increase in population, were all attributed to her.

But, like Olympus or Valhalla, Elizabeth's court was permeated by jealousy, intrigue, hatred and distrust. Peter Shuvalov hated Bestuzhev; Bestuzhev hated Vorontsov; Vorontsov mistrusted Catherine (who was having an affair with Stanislaus Poniatowski, the British Ambassador's Polish Secretary), and Catherine loathed her husband Peter. But even Elizabeth was finding him very difficult to love. Not only was he ugly, ill-mannered and obtuse, but he had an obvious admiration for all things Prussian, especially for King Frederick who was far from popular with Elizabeth at the moment.

And now, in addition to her troubles first with Peter, then with his unfaithful, devious, ambitious little wife and on top of that with the problem of keeping Peter Shuvalov and Bestuzhev apart, there was the problem of a new military alliance with England that was being pressed upon her. Typically for such a commercial nation, England was again to supply the money, and Russia the men. The alliance was directed against Prussia, but though she signed the Treaty in November 1755, Elizabeth began to hesitate when ratification became due. Should war be risked? Should Russian blood be shed in England's interests? In the end only Bestuzhev's insistence pushed it through. But while she hesitated, the participants in the stately quadrille of European diplomacy had suddenly changed partners. Without consulting her the perfidious English concluded an alliance with Frederick of Prussia.

Elizabeth was mortified and Bestuzhev was appalled. His policy in ruins, his credibility lost, he prepared to face the worst. But for the moment Elizabeth allowed him to continue in office. Russia's foreign policy, made now by a consortium of Ministers rather than by a single man, was predictable in the circumstances. The British Treaty was abrogated, the army reinforced, and since for the moment Russia had no active ally, feelers were extended towards Austria and France, and from here on events moved fast.

In the spring of 1756 France and Austria concluded an alliance; in August of that year the Prussians marched against Austria. Maria Theresa's army was defeated; King Frederick occupied Dresden. The Seven Years' War had begun.

Hanbury-Williams, the British Ambassador in St. Petersburg, used all his guile to stop Elizabeth joining in on Austria's side. He exploited the vestiges of Bestuzhev's goodwill, which still had value since he still held office, the pro-Prussian sentiments of the Grand Duke Peter, and his own secretary's liaison with Catherine. Elizabeth, however, remained obstinately anti-Prussian. So long as she was Empress he realized there could be no hope, and her secret service was too active and her army too passionately loyal for any rebellion to succeed against her. If she were to die, however, Russia could be held at bay, and Elizabeth seemed to be a very sick woman at times these days. . . .

Throughout 1756 she hardly ever left her apartments—except to go to chapel or to visit her country residences. Ministers called in for frequent consultations, and every day crowds of uncertain courtiers assembled in her ante-chamber; what was the true state of her health? Would Russia go to war, and if so on what terms? The tension lasted all that summer and it was autumn before the answer came: Elizabeth the Empress of peace was preparing to do battle.

Frederick threatened to restore Ivan VI to the throne if she dared to take up arms against him, but that only made her more determined. If Frederick tried to do anything of the kind, she said, she would 'have Ivan's head cut off'. If necessary she would lead her troops personally against Prussia. Her blood was really up now that her own pride, the pride of Russia, was at stake. Frederick's portrait was turned face to the wall; her armies made ready to march.

She watched them pass by her window—the slow-stepping infantry behind their regimental bands, the golden breastplates of the Cuirassiers, the glittering swords and green coats of the Guards, the mounted grenadiers, the hussars with flowing side-curls, the cool-looking artillerymen in tricorn hats. They made an inspiring show. They were patriots like her, prepared for sacrifices, and how they hated Germans!

But for once the army was going to war without expert foreign leaders. Marshal Lacy had died years before; General Keith had left the Russian service despite all Elizabeth's attempts to keep him; most of the senior German mercenaries had been dismissed, and the new men were untried. Despite his protestations that he would not make 'a decent captain', Alexei Razumovski had been made a Field Marshal, and though Elizabeth promoted him for honour rather than command, the other generals were not much more experienced. But at least they were Russians. Hers was the only army in Europe not staffed by mercenaries.

Their commander, Marshal Apraxin, however, was by no means confident. He complained that the troops were in poor condition and blamed Peter Shuvalov who had overall charge of the war machine for the fact. Shuvalov hotly denied the charge and blamed Apraxin for any shortcomings. Not even war, it seemed, could put an end to the intrigues and hatreds of her underlings.

That autumn Elizabeth sat for the celebrated portrait-painter Jean-Louis Tocqué—after all, the French and all things French were fashionable now that an alliance with France was looming near. Bestuzhev was very upset about it all. He went about cursing Ivan Shuvalov who was always encouraging the Empress to read French books and whom he blamed for Elizabeth's hatred of Frederick getting out of hand. But on 20 December 1756 Elizabeth officially acceded to the Treaty of Versailles. Madame de Pompadour, who was said to pull the strings that manipulated Louis of France, Maria Theresa of Austria and Elizabeth of Russia were now united. The stage was set; the performance was about to begin.

In May 1757 Marshal Apraxin led his army towards Königsberg. He believed in comfort; five hundred horses were needed to carry all the luxuries of toilet and table he required for the campaign. Wits dubbed him 'the peaceful Field Marshal' because he marched so slowly, but when Elizabeth became impatient with him, the Marshal was always ready with an excellent excuse—the heat, the rain, the roads, the enemy's movements, the need to preserve the health of his men.

Meanwhile, Elizabeth had been contributing to the war effort by charming the new French Ambassador, the Marquis de l'Hopital. She turned the great house that had once been the British Embassy over to him and gave a most splendid banquet in his honour at Tsarskoye Selo.

There were four hundred guests and the menu listed 'the ragouts of all the nations', though whether because of the celebrated skills of Elizabeth's new chef, a Frenchman called Vatel, or for diplomatic reasons, almost everyone chose the French alternative. And Elizabeth paid her own special compliment to the Ambassador and his suite by preparing dishes of strawberries and cream for them with her own hands. There followed a ball at which she appeared in a jewelled diadem and great hooped petticoats under a most 'expensive and impressive' costume. She smiled, went graciously from group to group, and spoke to the Ambassador in French. She would have been satisfied, but not in the least surprised, had she read his reports to Versailles that her carriage had 'nobility', that her

features had a 'natural charm' and that her 'air of affable bene-
volence' reflected the 'very foundation of her character'.

The following August her hard-kept patience with the slothful
Apraxin was rewarded at last. Somehow, he had managed to defeat
General Lehwalt's troops at a place called Grossjägersdorf. Frede-
rick, hitherto contemptuous of the Russians, was quite amazed.
And even though they sustained more casualties than the enemy,
and only an attack by the reserve, made, apparently, without
Apraxin's orders, turned impending defeat into startling victory,
Elizabeth was beside herself with gratification.

The news was greeted at St. Petersburg at seven o'clock in the
morning by a salute of 101 guns. But Apraxin's next report received
a fortnight later disappointed all the Empress's expectations. He
wrote to explain that he had retired to Tilsit because his troops were
short of forage. Then he moved still further back—because of bad
weather, bad roads, and sickness in the ranks. A victorious army was
retreating, and Elizabeth was enraged. She ordered him to advance
again, but Apraxin was a cautious, not to say a devious, man. The
Empress's health had not been sound since her bout of colic the
previous autumn. She was said to have violent convulsions every
month which left her powerless and unable to discuss anything for
days at a time. Moreover the Grand Duke was known to be pro-
Prussian, and it might not do to be too near Prussia or too far from
St. Petersburg if the Empress should die suddenly. This, at least,
was the way his enemies interpreted his actions, and when he disobeyed the order to advance, Elizabeth dismissed him from command and ordered his arrest.

But the war continued and the Empress's health remained uncertain—a combination of circumstances which served to keep the
political situation tense. On 8 September she was attending a service
at the parish church at Tsarskoye when she complained of feeling
unwell. She started back for the palace but collapsed on the way.
Members of her entourage rushed from the church, sent for
Fousadier, the court surgeon, and covered her with a cloth to hide
her from the crowd of curious rustics that had gathered round.
Some time later Fousadier arrived, and then the court physician, a
Greek called Condoidis. Screens were laid around her, she was
purged, then carried to the palace on a sofa. After two hours she

began to revive, glanced hazily around her, asked where she was, but appeared to recognize no one. She lay virtually speechless for several days afterwards, and when she spoke, what she said was mostly unintelligible.

The news of her impending death caused consternation. A halt was called to all building projects she had ordered, and the Court buzzed loudly with intrigue. The Shuvalovs accused Bestuzhev quite openly of conniving at Apraxin's withdrawal, and when Elizabeth began to recover they began to feed her with their suspicions not only about him, but about Catherine as well.

But neither her latest illness nor the political situation induced her to adopt a healthier mode of life. As soon as she felt at all better she began eating and drinking far more than was good for her; she continued to keep irregular hours; and she did not spare her entertainments either.

Indeed, an innocent observer viewing St. Petersburg society at this moment would not have suspected that Russia was at war at all. Fedor Volkov's productions of *Amphytrion*, *Tartuffe* and various Russian comedies were well attended, and the latest rage was Giovanni Locatelli who arrived in the autumn of 1757 with a whole 'caravan of new musicians' and *opera buffa* talents. Experienced diplomatists averred that there was nothing finer to be seen in all of Europe, and Elizabeth immediately booked the first three rows of loggias for the season at a cost of a thousand roubles.

She saw the company's performance of *La Retraite des Dieux*, Madame Beluzzi in *The Rape of Proserpine*, and Madame Sacchi in *Amor and Psyche*. Among other successes were *Cleopatra's Feast*, *The Ladies of the Harem*, and *The Fair of London, or Vauxhall*. And London provided another talking-point that year when an enterprising shipper imported a marvellous contraption manufactured there—a cabinet which not only showed the time and date and produced the sounds of the viol d'amore and of harps, but contained an automatic clavichord which played music by Corelli, Albinoni and that 'celebrated English Doctor of Music, Handel'. The price asked was a mere fifteen thousand roubles, but no buyer was found and it was eventually shipped off back to England.

Devices of quite another kind were employed when on 18 January Alexei Shuvalov, head of the Office of Secret Investigatory Affairs, began the interrogation of Marshal Apraxin. Apraxin denied that he had been disloyal, of course, and claimed that his decision to retreat had been fully supported by a council-of-war. But the odds were against him from the start. Even his old friend Bestuzhev attacked him, hoping to avoid being implicated himself. But he was still in danger.

A new British envoy, Robert Keith, was due to arrive, and Russia's French and Austrian allies were disturbed that Bestuzhev with his pro-English record should still be in charge, albeit nominally, of Russia's foreign affairs. Vice-Chancellor Vorontsov and Peter Shuvalov carried the message to Elizabeth. Bestuzhev, they explained, could have a deleterious effect on Russian interests abroad; moreover his loyalty was in question. True, evidence of his involvement in Apraxin's treachery had not yet come to light, but then how could it until his correspondence was seized? And how could that be done until he was arrested? Elizabeth sighed, and signified assent.

On the evening of 10 February she called a conference of Ministers. Bestuzhev, ever sensitive to the political climate, sent a message saying he was ill. He was then commanded to appear. He took a large dose of his nerve tonic, and obeyed. When he arrived, the Order of St. Andrew was torn off his breast, and the Captain of the Guard took him into custody. Next morning, Catherine heard from her lover, Poniatowski, that Bernardi, the jeweller who ran errands for her, her ex-tutor Adadurov, and Poniatowski's friend Yelyagin were under arrest too. Somehow, she knew not how, she managed to smile gaily at the court balls and receptions in the days that followed.

No incriminating evidence was found among Chancellor Bestuzhev's possessions—no evidence of plotting with Apraxin, no evidence of correspondence with Catherine, no evidence of preparing a *coup d'état* in case Elizabeth should die. Bestuzhev had burnt all the papers that might have incriminated him before he was arrested. He had also advised Catherine to do the same, and she had taken his advice.

Bestuzhev's trial lasted several months. He, too, denied everything, but they found him guilty of sedition just the same. He had done nothing, after all, to *prevent* Apraxin's retreat. The death sentence was recommended; but Elizabeth had pity and merely exiled him to his own estates. Apraxin had died before his formal trial began, so only Catherine's fate had yet to be resolved.

No formal charge had yet been laid against her but she was clearly under an official cloud. For weeks she had been denied access to her baby, Paul, and, much more seriously, the Empress was ignoring her. With the whole court aware that Elizabeth and she were estranged, Catherine at last decided to take the initiative. On 18 May she wrote to Elizabeth begging for an interview. Her eyes filled with tears, she said, whenever she thought of Elizabeth's kindness to her. She would always be obedient, loving, and sincere, if only she could gaze on her Majesty's face for a moment. There was no reply, so Catherine wrote another letter. She was ill, she claimed. She wanted permission to go abroad to join her mother. She got her interview.

It was half-past one in the morning and Elizabeth was pacing up and down her bedroom. The Grand Duke Peter was there; so was Alexei Shuvalov, his face twitching. Ivan Shuvalov may have been eavesdropping behind a screen. Catherine entered and flung herself at the Empress's feet. After a great deal of difficulty she was eventually persuaded to stand up.

Elizabeth opened the proceedings: how could Catherine think of abandoning her children? The Empress would see to it that they were well cared for, replied Catherine. 'But how could I explain such a thing?' asked Elizabeth. 'By listing the reasons that have brought me into disfavour', replied Catherine. 'And how would you support yourself living with your parents?' asked Elizabeth. 'As I did before.' 'But your mother', Elizabeth insisted, 'has gone to Paris.' 'I know', said Catherine. 'They suspected her of being too pro-Russian. The King of Prussia persecuted her.'

This irritated Elizabeth. Her information was that Joanna was in Paris as Frederick's agent. And her irritation showed. Examples of Catherine's faulty behaviour months and even years before flooded into her mind. 'You think you're very superior', she said. 'Remember that time at the Summer Palace when you hardly bowed to me, and I asked you if your neck was hurting? You were too proud to do more than nod.' Catherine protested. 'If I ever thought so', replied Catherine smoothly, 'nothing would be more likely to correct me than this conversation. After all, I misunderstood what you did me the honour of telling me four years ago at the Summer Palace.' The girl was quick—too quick to be believed.

Elizabeth moved away from her and her nephew Peter began to speak. She had heard his list of whining complaints about his wife's cruelty to him several times before, but though he talked in what for him was an undertone Catherine must have overheard him. 'I'll be happy to admit my cruelty'—her voice came shrilly from across the room—'to people who advise you to commit injustices.' Elizabeth pretended not to hear her, and Peter ranted on at even higher pitch about her 'wickedness', her transactions with Bestuzhev, her involvement in plots. It was time to take things in hand. Elizabeth walked over to her. 'What excuse can you offer for communicating with a prisoner?' Catherine did not answer. 'How dare you send instructions to Apraxin?' she demanded. 'Me? Send instructions?' protested Catherine. 'How can you deny it when I've got your letters over there?' And there, lying on the dressing table were three letters.

As it turned out, they were not very incriminating; Elizabeth was bluffing. Catherine thought quickly. 'It's true I disobeyed. I beg Your Majesty's forgiveness. But if those letters are mine, they'll show that I never sent him any instructions. In one of them I told him what was being said about him. . . .' 'Why?' enquired Elizabeth. 'Because I took an interest in him, because I liked him. I begged him to obey your orders. As for the others, one congratulates him on the birth of his son; the other's a New Year's greeting.'

'Bestuzhev says that there were others.' 'Then he's a liar.' 'Well, if he's telling lies we'll have to put him on the rack.' But Catherine would not be moved by threats of torture. Elizabeth began to pace up and down the room again, though more thoughtful now than angry. Perhaps the rumours about Catherine's intrigues and her inordinate ambition were untrue. Perhaps the girl was innocent. 'I've a lot more to say', she said at last, 'but now is not the time.' She glanced towards Peter. 'I don't want to make things worse between you than they are already.'

A few days later she saw Catherine again. No one else was present and there is no account of what was said apart from a few inconclusive lines from Catherine's own pen. Perhaps Catherine convinced her of her political innocence. Perhaps she admitted that she was taking lovers. If so, Elizabeth already knew. But from that time on, relations between them seemed to improve, and Catherine was even allowed to visit her son Paul once a week.

Meanwhile the campaign in Prussia had been going well. Apraxin's successor, General Fermor, had taken Königsberg and marched into Brandenburg where, on 14 August, he had stumbled across Frederick's army at Zorndorff. The fighting was fierce and the casualties heavy. Both sides retired from the field; both sides claimed the victory.

Elizabeth was more than satisfied—until she saw the casualty lists. There were too many familiar names on it. She came to distrust Fermor and his ambiguous despatches. And she became increasingly impatient with his constant recourse to expressions like 'if time, circumstances and the enemy's movements permit'. 'Such decisions', she wrote, 'amount to mere indecision. A general's skill lies in his taking actions which are independent of "time, circumstances and the enemy's movements".' Fermor bungled on without doing very much damage to his own men or the enemy until mid-autumn when the time came to retire to winter quarters.

To the day-to-day observer, Elizabeth seemed to be immersed in trivia. Sometimes she would sit up all night playing cards or listening to gossip—though subjects for conversation had become even more limited of late, mention of Voltaire being forbidden now, along with the King of Prussia, illness, death, beautiful women and scientific matters. Tocqué's portrait of her, which she held in high esteem, showed her to be comely still, with large, soft eyes, a pretty nose and cupid lips. But her double chins and her immense bosom betrayed her continuing overindulgence in pâtés de Perigord, pâtés de Versailles and pâtés aux perdrix rouge with truffles. She was running blatantly to fat, but though her French physician Dr. Boissonier warned her of the dangers, she took no notice. She defied death as she defied age.

'Wisdom Triumphs over Voluptuousness' was the subject of a painting being done at Tsarskoye. In her case the reverse was true. She spent hours beautifying herself before every public engagement. Rouge, rosewater and camphor were all used in quantity. Ice was applied to her eyes each morning to keep them fresh; her hair, her eyebrows—even her eyelashes—were dyed beguiling colours, and her maids worked their fingers to the bone massaging her wrinkled face, easing her tired joints, and working in the creams and lotions. Thanks to them there were still those who thought she looked miraculous for her age (though those who said so were diplomatists). And lest their employers should labour under any doubt about it, suitable portraits of herself done in earlier years and for which artists had been paid up to 1,200 roubles a dozen, were sent abroad.

Count Pietro Rotari from Verona caught the spirit of her fleshy paradise in his informal, dream-like portrait of her, of her lover Ivan Shuvalov, and of 328 young women of the court, all charm and smiles. And the setting of her paradise was almost, but not quite complete. The structure of the Winter Palace was virtually finished now, and Jean Baptiste le Prince was busy with the decorations. The Director of the new Academy of Fine Arts, Louis Joseph de Lorraine, and his assistant Jean Moreau were also hard at work. Their bills, the bills of colleagues and assistants, the bills for materials and labour; bills genuine and bills invented, bills modest and extortionate, piled high—the cost of completing the perfect setting for Elizabeth.

And the cost of the war had been mounting even higher. A million ducats had had to be borrowed from foreign bankers, half a million roubles from the Church, and as the country was squeezed for yet more money, some Ministers began to question the wisdom of it all. But in the spring of 1759 the army was sent out on a new campaign.

In June General Fermor was replaced. His successor Peter Saltykov was a small, elderly, wizened man with no military reputation. He began briskly enough—took Frankfurt and made contact with the Austrians. But the same month Frederick beat the French at Minden and now he was bearing down upon them, confident of success.

At tea-time on the afternoon of the battle of Künersdorf, Saltykov took to his knees in prayer. The Russian army seemed lost and Frederick, having signalled victory, was pressing forward to deliver the *coup de grâce*. But to everyone's surprise the Russians stood firm. Time and again the Prussians were thrown back, and when, at last, the Russians counter-attacked, the enemy broke completely, scattering in all directions. Frederick escaped with only three thousand men. It was a crushing defeat.

Elizabeth was at Tsarskoye when the news came through. She left immediately for St. Petersburg to attend a thanksgiving service. Guns fired a proud salute, church bells rang out, and rewards were distributed. Saltykov received promotion to Field Marshal, a jewelled snuff-box, a diamond ring, and five thousand ducats from Maria Theresa.

Frederick sued for peace with Russia, but Elizabeth stuck loyally by her allies, even though she had long suspected that France and Austria were content to see the Russians do most of the fighting, while arranging to take the lion's share of Prussian territory when the time came to divide the spoils of victory. She still meant to crush Frederick.

Nevertheless, when Austria proposed that her army undertake a winter campaign in Silesia she refused. The Austrians then hinted that she might be unduly influenced by England. Elizabeth retorted that she found the suggestion 'offensive . . . We have never given the least cause to be reproached for double-dealing. . . . We would never allow the glory won by the precious blood of our subjects to be besmirched by the least suspicion of bad faith.' She meant it too. Maria Theresa made haste to reassure her.

Competition on the home front, and especially in theatrical St. Petersburg, had been almost as keen as on the battlefield. Araja's opera *Cephalus and Procris* was performed and Ivan Narylov, once a pupil of Garrick's, had graduated from female parts in Volkov's company to play Richard III at the Winter Palace. Hilferding, the Viennese ballet-master, was introducing the *pirouette* and the *entrechat-quatre* into the ballet, Joseph Starzer was the new musical director of the Court; Raupach was staging gaudy celebrations of the allied victories and the Venetian Brigonzi devising all manner of ingenious theatrical machines. Niodini, the great new *prima ballerina*, and the castrato Guiseppe Millico (the finest ever according to the composer Glück) had been brought to St. Petersburg, and for the anniversary of the coronation in April 1759 there was a performance by native Russians of a *ballet pastorale* complete with river scene, mountains, 'fishermen', 'Tyrolean girls', 'pilgrims' and a wedding scene.

But the lavish patronage of the arts and the undiminished luxury of life at court, combined with the continuation of an expensive war, was beginning to strain the peasant population to breaking point. Even before the war there had been rebellions on some estates serious enough to require whole companies of troops with artillery support to quell them, and the war had brought increased taxes, and compulsory recruitment, which peasants saw as an additional tax—in blood. The flight of serfs from their masters' estates to the poorly policed borderlands had now reached unmanageable proportions, and sufficient troops could not be spared to police the countryside. For once, the government tried measures other than repression. In 1759 a special commission was formed to review peasant petitions; preparations went forward to secularize the unhappy church estates, and in November an amnesty was proclaimed for deserters and peasants who had fled abroad. But none of it seemed to be of much effect. The cost of the war was mounting to almost insupportable proportions. Yet when on New Year's Day 1760 the Austrian Ambassador, Prince Esterhazy, expressed the hope that Elizabeth would continue with it, her reply was forceful. 'I intend to continue with this war . . . even if I have to sell half my clothes and all my diamonds.' All she wanted once the war was won was East Prussia, which her troops had already occupied, but both France and Austria, who had already secretly agreed to support each other's claims, refused. Then Maria Theresa offered Elizabeth a secret guarantee, provided that the news should not reach France.

Saltykov's ideas for the campaign of 1760 were much like the Grand Old Duke of York's. Battle must be avoided at all costs, so that 'the glory of Her Majesty's arms might not be tarnished'. Elizabeth, however, had other ideas. She knew by instinct that the first purpose in war must be to destroy the enemy's armies. Saltykov's proposals were rejected tactfully on 'political' grounds. Orders and exhortations couched in vigorous terms streamed from her pen and in October she was rewarded by the news that a raiding party of her Cossacks and Kalmyks had pierced the defences of Berlin and sacked it. Yet King Frederick kept on fighting.

Russia needed peace now almost as much as he did. Taxes and prices were rising fast; recruitment was denuding villages of young men; there were peasant riots in several provinces, and now the

Bashkir warriors beyond the Volga were treading the war-path once again. Ministers threw up their hands in horror at the cost. France and Austria suggested peace talks, but Elizabeth was adamant. Frederick would not give up and nor would she. Final victory, it seemed, was only one tantalizing step away.

She made personal sacrifices to mount one last campaign. A sum of 380,000 roubles was still needed to complete her apartments at the new Winter Palace, but with the Treasury short of funds she called work to a halt for the duration of the war. The allies put a quarter of a million men into the field and Frederick could raise barely a third of that number.

The Russian commander of the season was General Buturlin, a veteran of her father's army and a personal friend. But when he failed to capture Breslau she was almost beside herself with fury. 'Determination and courage' were needed, 'not councils of war', she told him, and added almost desperately: 'If some important success is not achieved in this campaign, it will be difficult to find enough money for another.' Buturlin summoned up enough energy to capture Liegnitz, then made another tactical withdrawal. 'The news of your retreat', fulminated Elizabeth, 'has caused Us more sorrow than a lost battle would have done. . . . We command you without further wastage of words to move directly on Berlin and occupy it. . . . The very term "Council of War" has become abominable to Us. Henceforth if anyone should say that Our army is not fit to storm fortresses, he is to be arrested at once and brought here in chains.'

Buturlin did not take Berlin, but he did capture the strongest Prussian fortress in Silesia. It was enough to drive Frederick to despair. His army was a fraction of the size it had been; his best officers had been lost; he was bankrupt. The only honourable way out, he decided, was to die in glory on the battlefield. But he did not have to. Two weeks later news reached him that Prussia was saved. '*Morta la bestia*', he wrote triumphantly, '*morto il veneno!*' Elizabeth was dead.

In her last few months Elizabeth hardly ever left the Palace. When she returned from Peterhof that autumn she was very weak. With the delights of youth behind her she had gorged herself, as if by way of consolation, on the richest, most unhealthy foods. Now she was paying the price. Her legs were so swollen that she needed help to hobble about her room, and when she felt the need to visit Ivan Shuvalov in the next apartment she had to be carried to him on a litter. She still had friends to supper and Ministers still called, but mostly the court diarist noted: 'Nothing particular happened today.'

Occasionally she would go through the tedious operation of dressing for a ball, but then look at herself in a mirror and decide not to go. The loss of her beauty depressed her and she felt drained of energy. Ivan Shuvalov and her old friend Alexei Razumovski provided comfort; the infant Paul was always kept close by, and in cuddling him she could forget her troubles. But otherwise she took little pleasure in life, and the spectre of 'the prisoner without a name', the infant Emperor Ivan whom she had locked away some twenty years ago and who had lost his sanity in prison, must have haunted her at times.

She thought more now, and doubted more than she had ever done before. What would she leave behind but fifteen thousand gowns, two chestfuls of silk stockings and a mass of unpaid bills—the symbols of her vanity and of her wastefulness? What would she be remembered for?—beautiful palaces, a victorious army, a Russia at last respected and feared by the world? Or would they remember her for encouraging the arrogance of the nobility, for neglecting the serfs, for allowing the Empire to be administered as laxly and corruptly as it had ever been? In December 1761 she told the Secretary to her Cabinet to draft a fierce note to the Senate, rebuking it for allowing urgent public affairs to slide. It was one of her last displays of spirit.

On 12 December 1761 she fell into a fever and vomited some blood. Her doctors became seriously alarmed. After a day or two, however, she began to feel better. Hearing that her jeweller had fallen ill, she sent her doctors away to attend to him, and by the 17th she was well enough to sign an order reducing the salt tax and proclaiming amnesties for tax offenders. But at ten o'clock on the evening of the 22nd she had a relapse. Next day the priests were sent for. Twice that night she said the prayers for the dying, repeating each phrase after the priest with great emphasis and feeling.

Peter and Catherine arrived at her bedside. She talked quietly to them—assured Peter that he would succeed, and begged him to care for little Paul and for her favourites. Alexei Razumovski also came, and Ivan Shuvalov and other of her friends. By now the Palace was thronged with people. Many of them were on their knees, and some were red-eyed from hours of weeping. Others, however, were making dispositions for the future; and Peter and Alexei Shuvalov in particular were busy ingratiating themselves with the Grand Duke Peter.

Elizabeth's agony lasted until noon on Christmas Day. Then, shortly after three o'clock Prince Nikita Trubestskoi emerged from her room: 'Her Imperial Majesty', he announced, 'has fallen asleep in God. God save Our Most Gracious Sovereign the Emperor Peter III!' That night, while Alexei Razumovski, sick with grief, shut himself up in his rooms, the Emperor Peter gave a grand supper party in the hall adjoining the chamber in which the body lay.

Elizabeth was laid out in state with silver robes and a golden crown upon her head. And in the days that followed thousands clamoured for admission to pay their last respects. Some simply bowed and kissed her hands; others showed grief in the old style, prostrating themselves and howling as they banged their heads upon the floor. For all her faults, Elizabeth had been generous, patriotic and sincere, and people mourned her passing with sincere affection.

The funeral took place on 25 January. The cortège was huge and magnificent, but according to Catherine, Peter chose the occasion to amuse himself. He would loiter behind the hearse, then run full pelt to catch it up again, so that the procession behind him strung out and concertinaed up again in turn. At last the ancient courtiers carrying his train lost hold of it. The wind caught it up, and as the diminishing figure of the Emperor stumbled on into the distance, his huge cloak billowed out behind him like a mad black sail against the tranquil sea of snow.

Elizabeth the charming, Elizabeth mother of all Russians, had gone to her Maker. Her nephew Peter would not survive her long. The future, with all its brittle glories, belonged to Catherine.

Bibliography

ALEFIRENKO P. K. *The Peasant Movement and the Peasant Question in Russia (1730–1760)*, Moscow 1958 (Russian)

ANDREYEV V. V. *Representatives of power in Russia after Peter I*, 1870 (Russian)

— *Catherine the First*, 1869 (Russian)

BAIN, NISBET R. *The Daughter of Peter the Great*, London 1899

— *Peter III: Emperor of Russia*, London 1902

— *The Pupils of Peter the Great*, London 1897

BARANOVICH, A. I. (ed.) *Russia in the Second Quarter of the 18th Century* (Outlines of USSR History: Period of Feudalism), Moscow 1957 (Russian)

BARTENEV, P. I. *The Eighteenth Century*, 4 vols., Moscow 1868–9 (Russian)

BARTHOLD, F. W. *Anna Ivanovna: Cabinet, Court, Customs & Social Refinement in Moscow and St. Petersburg*, Leipzig 1836 (German)

BELL, JOHN. *Travels from St. Petersburg*, 2 vols, Glasgow 1763

BERGHOLZ, F. *Diary 1721–1725* (trans Ammon; ed. Bartenev), 1902–3 (Russian)

BILLINGTON, J. H. *The Icon and the Axe*, London 1966

(BIRON) *The Remarkable Life of Ernest Johann Biron*, Bremen 1742 (German)

BLOMBERG, C. VON. *An account of Livonia*, London 1701

BRUCE, P. H. *Memoirs*, London 1782

BRÜCKNER, A. G. *Peter the Great's Correspondence with Catherine*, 1880 (German)

(CATHERINE I) *The Testimony of Her Imperial Majesty*, May 1727 (German)

CATHERINE II *Memoirs* (ed. Maroger), London 1955

Ceremonial Journal for 1727–1739, 3 vols., 1854 (Russian)

Commentaries of the Imperial Academy of Sciences

Description of Anna Ivanovna's Coronation, Moscow 1730 (Russian)

Detailed Description of Elizabeth Petrovna's Coronation St. Petersburg 1744 (Russian)

DIRIN *Grand Duchess Catherine (1729–61)*

DOLGORUKI, P. V. *Count A. I. Ostermann*, 1841 (Russian)

ELIZABETH *Letters and Notes 1741–61*, Moscow 1867 (Russian)

FILIPPOV, A. N. *Papers of the Empress Anne's Cabinet 1731–40*, 1898 (Russian)

FIRSOV, N. N. *The Accession of Elizabeth*, 1887 (Russian)

FONTENELLE *Eulogy of Peter the Great*, 1728 (French)

— and ROUSSETT, Jean *The Northern Worthies*, 1730

GRAY, IAN *Peter the Great*, London 1962

GROT, YA. K. *Bibliographical and Historical Notes on the Origins of Catherine I*, 1877 (Russian)

HAIGOLD, M. J. *Haygold's Supplements*, Riga and Leipzig 1770 (German)

HAMILTON, G. H. *The Art and Architecture of Russia*, Harmondsworth 1954

HANWAY, JONAS *An Historical Account of the British Trade over the Caspian*

HAUMANT, E. *French Culture in Russia 1700–1900*, Paris 1910 (French)

HERRMANN, E. *The Russian Court under the Empress Elizabeth*, 1882 (German)

Historical Monographs, St. Petersburg 1901–. (Russian)

Journals of the Court Chamberlains, 60 vols., 1853–4 (Russian)

JUSTICE, E. *A Voyage to Russia*, London 1746

KAHAN, A. 'The Costs of Westernization in Russia', *Slavic Review*, 1966

KLYUCHEVSKI, V. *Peter the Great* (trans. Archibald), London 1965

KOMELOVA, G. *Views of Petersburg* (Makhayev), Leningrad 1968 (Russian)

KORSAKOV, D. A. *The Empress Anne's Accession to the Throne*, Kazan 1891

KOSTOMAROV, N. *Catherine Alexeyevna: the First Russian Empress*, 1877 (Russian)

KRAFFT, G. W. *A True and Detailed Description of the Amazing Palace of Ice*, St. Petersburg 1741 (German)

KUDRYAVTSEV *Notebook of letters and orders of Anne and Elizabeth to S. A. Saltykov 1732–1742*, Moscow 1878 (Russian)

KURAKIN, A. B. *Ceremonials of the Sovereign Empress Elizabeth* (Russian)

The Large Soviet Encyclopaedia (Russian)

LOMONOSOV, M. *Panegyric to the Memory of Peter the Great*, 1755 (Russian)

Manifesto concerning Counts Ostermann, Münnich, Golovkin, St. Petersburg 1742 (German)

MANSTEIN *Memoirs of Russia*, 1856

MARSDEN, C. *Palmyra of the North*, London 1942

MAVRODIN, V. *Class War* (Russian)

MISSY, J. DE *Memoirs of the Reign of Catherine*, 1728 (French)

Morals and Explanation of the Firework of Dec. 18 1741 (German)

MOTRAYE, A. DE LA *Voyages and Travels*, 3 vols., London 1732

MOTTLEY, J. *History of the Life and Reign of the Empress Catherine*, 1744

— *History of the Life of Peter I and the Birth & Rise of the Empress Catherine*, 1739

— *The History of the Russian Empire to the death of the Empress Catherine*, 2 vols., London 1757

The Northern Heroine being Authentick Memoirs of the late Czarina, 1727

PARAMONOV. A. S. *On the Legislation of Anna Ivanovna,* 1904 (Russian)

(PETER I), *The Letters and Papers of the Emperor Peter,* 1887–1952 (Russian)

POLOVTSEV, A. *The Russian Dictionary of Biography,* 25 vols., 1896–1918 (Russian)

Proceedings of the Imperial Historical Society (Collection and Readings), (Russian)

PROZOROVSKAYA, B. D. *A. D. Menshikov,* St. Petersburg 1895 (Russian)

Public Records Office, file series SP 91

PUTNAM, P. (ed.) *Seven Britons in Imperial Russia 1698–1812,* Princeton 1952

PYPIN, A. *A History of Russian Culture,* 3 vols. (Russian)

RAEFF, M. *Origins of the Russian Intelligentsia,* New York 1966

RÉAU, L. *Russian Art* 1947 (French)

— *St. Petersburg,* Paris 1913 (French)

A Representation of the Firework and Illumination of New Year's Day 1736, St. Petersburg 1736 (German and Russian)

The Russian Book of Genealogies, 4 parts, St. Petersburg 1854–7 (Russian)

SCHMIDT-PHISELDECK, *Materials on Russian History Since the Death of Peter the Great,* 2 parts, Riga 1777–84 (German)

SCHUYLER, E. *Peter the Great,* 2 vols., London 1884

SEMEVSKI, M. I. *The Tsarina Catherine, Anna and William Mons,* 1884 (Russian)

— *The Tsarina Praskovya 1664–1723,* St. Petersburg 1883 (Russian)

A Short Explanation of the Firework of 28.1.1737, St. Petersburg 1737 (Russian)

SHCHERBATOV, M. *On the Corruption of Morals in Russia* (Trans and ed. Lentin), Cambridge 1969

SHCHERBATSKI, P. K. *The Accession of the Empress Anne,* 1859 (Russian)

SHUBINSKI, S. N. *Court and Domestic Life of The Empress Anne,* St. Petersburg 1893 (Russian)

— *Court Jesters and their Weddings*

SOLOVEV, *A History of Russia,* Moscow 1857–79, vols., 19–22 (Russian)

— *Soviet Historical Encyclopaedia* (Russian)

STAEHLIN, K. *The History of Russia,* Stuttgart 1923–39, Vol. II. (German)

STEPANOV, A. V. *Elizabeth Petrovna, her origins, intimate Life and Reign* 1903 (Russian)

STROYEV, V. *Biron's period of Power and the Cabinet of Ministers,* 2 parts Moscow–St. Petersburg 1909–10 (Russian)

RICE, T. TALBOT *Elizabeth, Empress of Russia,* London 1970

Travelling Journals of Peter I (1706–1725), 1853

VANDAL, A. *Louis XV and Elizabeth of Russia,* 1882 (French)

VASILCHIKOV, *The Razumovski Family*, Moscow 1868–95 (Russian)

VEIDEMEIER, A. *Review of Main Events in Russia* (1725–41), 3 parts, St. Petersburg 1848 (Russian)

— *The Court and Notables in Russia in the second half of the 18th century*, 2 parts, St. Petersburg 1846 (Russian)

VERETEV, N. *Anna Ivanovna, her character, intimate life and reign*, 1912 (Russian)

VIGOR, MRS. W. (Jane Rondeau) *Letters from a Lady who resided some years in Russia*, 1775 (and additional letters)

VORONTSOV, M. L. *The Papers of Count Vorontsov* (Ed. Bartenev), 1870–, Vols. I–V (Russian)

WHITWORTH, LORD CHARLES, *An Account of Russia as it was in the Year 1710*, Strawberry Hill 1758

ZIEGLER (ed.) *The First Catherine: Notes and Anecdotes*, 1956 (French)

Index

Baltic territories 21, 69, 93
Baskhirs 15, 137, 145, 227
Bauer, Brigadier 5
Bazancourt, Phillippe 119
Beketov, Nikita 207–8
Beluzzi, Madame 219
Bering, Vitus Jonassen 66
Berlin 226, 227
Bernardi (jeweller) 220
Bestuzhev, Alexei 149, 175, 182, 184, 185,
  186, 188, 189, 199, 202, 203, 207, 211,
  214, 215, 217, 219, 220, 222
Bestuzhev, Anna 184
Bestuzhev, Peter 85, 87, 88, 95
Bidlo, Dr 56
Biren (later Biron), Ernest Johann 87, 90,
  92, 95, 99, 102, 103, 105, 107, 108, 110,
  111, 112, 117, 119, 120, 121, 123, 126,
  128, 129, 130, 136, 139, 141, 145, 146,
  147, 148, 149, 150, 151, 161, 163, 166,
  175, 176; character 87–8; appointed
  Anne's chamberlain 95; compared
  with Menshikov 105; love of good
  living 114; becomes Duke of Courland
  131, 138; wealth and estates 132–3;
  arrogance 131–2; unpleasant children
  132; protégés in the arts 135; enmity
  for Volynski 146, 147; nominated
  Regent by Anne 150; as Regent 152,
  165, 176; sent to Siberia 152, 165;
  efforts to make Elizabeth an ally 165
Biron, Karl 132, 137
Biron, Peter 132, 137, 139, 140, 142
Black Sea 18, 127
Blessing of the Waters ceremony 74
Boerhave, Dr. 210
Bohemia 189
Boissonier, Dr. 223
Bon, Girolamo 125, 179, 195
Bon, Rosina 125, 180
Botta, Marquis de 140, 177, 185
Boucher, François 199
Bourbon, Duc de 157
Bourgeois, Nicholas 33, 39, 44
Brandenburg 223
Brandt, Christopher 32
Breslau 227
Brigonzi 225
Bruce, Count 54
Brunswick-Bevern, Anton-Ulrich, Prince
  of 116, 117, 139, 140, 146, 151, 152,
  165, 168, 173, 175
Brunswick-Wolfenbüttel, Ludwig, Prince
  of 167
Bulfinger, Professor 72
Butter Week festivities 50, 135, 162
Buturlin, General 61, 72, 74, 75, 76, 182,
  227

Cadet Corps 109, 110, 135, 192, 195
Caravaque 125, 195

Carlsbad 24
Caspian Sea 48
Catherine I, Empress (born Martha
  Skavronska) 82, 109, 155, 158; early
  life 3–4; appearance as a girl 4, 5;
  marriage to Raabe 4–5; taken prisoner
  by Russians 5; in Sheremetev's household 6; in Menshikov's household 6;
  first meetings with Tsar Peter 8, 9;
  leaves for Moscow 9–10; adjusting to
  new life 10; instruction in Orthodox
  religion 11; gives birth to a son 11;
  christened Catherine 12; sets out to be
  perfect courtesan 12; understanding of
  Peter's needs 12–13; birth of second
  son 13; with Peter to Finnish gulf 13–
  14; emotional dependence on Peter 14;
  gives birth to daughter, Catherine 15;
  death of two sons 15; birth of second
  daughter, Anne 15; joins Peter in St.
  Petersburg 16; death of daughter
  Catherine 16; visits Peter at front 17;
  reconciles Peter with Tsarevich 17;
  tours southern Russia 17–18; birth of
  daughter, Elizabeth 19; security and
  recognition 19; intercedes for Menshikov 20; acknowledged as Tsarina
  21–2; goes on Turkish campaign with
  Peter 22–4; formal ceremony of
  marriage to Peter 24–6; feels neglected
  by Peter 27; birth of sixth child 27;
  birth of seventh child 28; given Order
  of St. Catherine the Martyr 28; death
  of two daughters 29; gives birth to a
  son, Peter 29; grand tour of Europe
  30–4; gives birth to a son 32; fear of
  Tsarevich Alexei 34; suspected of
  poisoning Alexei 35; gives birth to a
  daughter, Natalia 35–6; son Peter's
  death 39, 41; life at St. Petersburg
  40–1; resentment of Alexei's son 42;
  visited by brother and sister 42, 43;
  pride in daughters' education 43; in
  Moscow 47; goes with Peter to Asia
  47–9; Peter's increased dependence on
  50; love of food 51; coronation as
  Empress 52–6; collapses from exhaustion 56; scandal over William
  Mons 57–9; vulnerability of position on
  Peter's death 60–1; succeeds Peter 62;
  seeks affection of her soldiers 62, 67;
  first public act 62; dependence on
  Menshikov 63; in mourning 64; drawn
  into politics 65; need for guidance 66;
  concern for family 66–7; promotes
  daughters' interests 67; sensitive about
  appearance in middle age 67; becomes
  vain, self-indulgent 69, 70; more
  frequent public appearances 69; keeps
  erratic hours 70, 71, 73; heavy drinking
  70, 71; heads for self-destruction 71;